A Pocket Guide to Correct Spelling

by

Francis Griffith

Emeritus Professor of Education
Hofstra University

BARRON'S

BARRON'S EDUCATIONAL SERIES, INC.
New York • London • Toronto • Sydney

All inquiries should be addressed to:
Barron's Educational Series, Inc.
250 Wireless Boulevard
Hauppauge, New York 11788

International Standard Book No. 0-8120-2620-9

Library of Congress Cataloging in Publication Data

Griffith, Francis J.
    A pocket guide to correct spelling.
    1. Spellers. I. Title
PE 1145. 2. G 7   1982   423'. 1   82 - 13725
ISBN 0-8120-2620-9

PRINTED IN THE UNITED STATES OF AMERICA
789   550   987

INTRODUCTION

This book is intended to be used by secretaries, business executives, authors, proofreaders, and others who want a quick guide to correct spelling and syllabication.

Its handy size is an important advantage. It does not concern itself with etymologies, definitions, antonyms, synonyms, secondary accents, and all the other information which makes a dictionary so valuable—and so bulky. It is not a substitute for a dictionary. It is a valuable supplement.

The 25,000 word spelling list includes words commonly used in formal and informal correspondence. In addition, it includes thousands which, while not orally popular, appear frequently in print and writing. It includes widely known technical terms and proper nouns. It lists not only root words but gives their derivatives, especially those forms which are troublesome to spell, e.g., *picnic, picnicked,* and *picnicking.* It excludes one-syllable words except those which may give spelling difficulties.

By means of centered dots, it shows word divisions for hyphenating at the end of a line of type or print.

Besides the 25,000 word spelling list there is a section on spelling rules. This feature helps make it a useful and ready reference guide.

*Section on spelling rules begins with page 214.

25,000 Word
Ready Reference
Spelling List

A

aback
aba·cus
abaft
aban·don·ment
abase
abase·ment
abas·ing
abash
abate
abate·ment
ab·at·toir
ab·bé
ab·bess
ab·bey
ab·bot
ab·bre·vi·ate
ab·bre·vi·a·tion
ab·di·cate
ab·di·ca·tion
ab·do·men
ab·duct
ab·duc·tion
abeam
ab·er·rant
ab·er·ra·tion
abet
abet·ted
abet·tor
abey·ance
ab·hor
ab·hor·rence
ab·hor·rent
abid·ance
abide
abil·i·ty
ab·ject
ab·ju·ra·tion

ab·jure
ab·la·tive
ablaze
able-bod·ied
abloom
ab·lu·tion
ab·ne·gate
ab·ne·ga·tion
ab·nor·mal
ab·nor·mal·i·ty
aboard
abode
aboil
abol·ish
abol·ish·ment
ab·o·li·tion
A-bomb
abom·i·na·ble
abom·i·nate
abom·i·na·tion
ab·orig·i·nal
ab·orig·i·ne
aborn·ing
abort
abor·ti·fa·cient
abor·tion
abor·tion·ist
abor·tive
abound
about
about-face
above·board
above·ground
ab·ra·ca·dab·ra
abrade
abra·sion
abra·sive
abreast
abridge
abridg·ment

abroad
ab·ro·gate
abrupt
ab·scess
ab·scis·sa
ab·scis·sion
ab·scond
ab·scond·er
ab·sence
ab·sen·tee
ab·sen·tee·ism
ab·sent·mind·ed
ab·sinthe
ab·so·lute
ab·so·lu·tion
ab·solve
ab·sorb
ab·sor·bance
ab·sor·ben·cy
ab·sor·bent
ab·sorp·tion
ab·stain
ab·ste·mi·ous
ab·sten·tion
ab·sti·nence
ab·strac·tion
ab·strac·tion·ism
ab·stract·ly
ab·struse
ab·struse·ness
ab·surd
ab·sur·di·ty
abun·dance
abun·dant
abuse
abus·er
abu·sive
abut
abut·ment
abut·ting

1

abysm
abys·mal
abyss
ac·a·deme
ac·a·dem·ic
ac·a·dem·i·cal·ly
ac·a·de·mi·cian
acad·e·my
a cap·pel·la
ac·cede
ac·ced·ed
ac·ced·ing
ac·cel·er·ate
ac·cel·er·a·tion
ac·cel·er·a·tor
ac·cent
ac·cen·tu·ate
ac·cept
ac·cept·able
ac·cept·ably
ac·cep·tance
ac·cept·ed
ac·cept·er
ac·cess
ac·ces·si·ble
ac·ces·sion
ac·ces·so·ry
ac·ci·dent
ac·ci·den·tal
ac·ci·den·tal·ly
ac·ci·dent-prone
ac·claim
ac·cla·ma·tion
ac·cli·mate
ac·cli·ma·ti·za·
   tion
ac·cli·ma·tize
ac·co·lade
ac·com·mo·date

ac·com·mo·dat·
   ing
ac·com·mo·da·
   tion
ac·com·mo·da·tor
ac·com·pa·ni·
   ment
ac·com·pa·nist
ac·com·pa·ny
ac·com·plice
ac·com·plish
ac·com·plish·
   ment
ac·cord
ac·cor·dance
ac·cor·di·on
ac·cost
ac·couche·ment
ac·count·able
ac·coun·tan·cy
ac·coun·tant
ac·count·ing
ac·cred·it
ac·cre·tion
ac·cru·al
ac·crue
ac·cul·tur·a·tion
ac·cu·mu·late
ac·cu·mu·la·tion
ac·cu·mu·la·tive
ac·cu·ra·cy
ac·cu·rate
ac·cursed
ac·cu·sa·tion
ac·cu·sa·tive
ac·cu·sa·to·ry
ac·cused
ac·cus·tomed
ac·er·bate

acer·bi·ty
ac·e·tate
ace·tic
ache
achiev·able
achieve
achieve·ment
achy
acid
acid·i·fy
acid·i·ty
ac·i·doph·i·lus
   milk
acid·u·lous
ac·knowl·edge
ac·knowl·edge·
   able
ac·knowl·edg·
   ment
ac·ne
ac·o·lyte
acorn
acous·tic
ac·ous·ti·cian
acous·tics
ac·quain·tance
ac·qui·esce
ac·qui·es·cence
ac·quire
ac·qui·si·tion
ac·quis·i·tive
ac·quit
ac·quit·tal
ac·quit·tance
acre
acre·age
ac·rid
ac·ri·mo·ni·ous
ac·ri·mo·ny

ac·ro·bat
ac·ro·bat·ics
ac·ro·nym
ac·ro·nym·ic
acrop·o·lis
across
acros·tic
acryl·ic
act
ac·tion·able
ac·ti·vate
ac·tiv·ism
ac·tiv·i·ty
ac·tor
ac·tu·al·i·ty
ac·tu·al·ize
ac·tu·al·iza·tion
ac·tu·al·ly
ac·tu·ar·i·al
ac·tu·ar·i·al·ly
ac·tu·ary
ac·tu·ate
acu·ity
acu·men
acu·punc·ture
acute
ad·age
ada·gio
ad·a·mant
ad·a·man·tine
adapt
adapt·able
ad·ap·ta·tion
adapt·er
adap·tive
ad·den·dum
ad·der
ad·dict
ad·dic·tion

ad·di·tion
ad·di·tion·al
ad·di·tive
ad·dle
ad·dle·pat·ed
ad·dress
ad·dress·able
ad·dress·ee
ad·duce
ad·e·noid
ad·e·noi·dal
ad·ept
ad·e·qua·cy
ad·e·quate
ad·here
ad·her·ence
ad·her·ent
ad·he·sion
ad·he·sive
ad hoc
ad ho·mi·nem
adieu
ad in·fi·ni·tum
adi·os
ad·i·pose
ad·ja·cent
ad·jec·ti·val
ad·jec·tive
ad·join
ad·join·ing
ad·journ
ad·journ·ment
ad·judge
ad·ju·di·cate
ad·junct
ad·ju·ra·tion
ad·jure
ad·just
ad·just·er

ad·just·ment
ad·ju·tant
ad-lib
ad·min·is·ter
ad·min·is·trate
ad·min·is·tra·tion
ad·min·is·tra·tive
ad·min·is·tra·tor
ad·min·is·tra·trix
ad·mi·ra·ble
ad·mi·ral
ad·mi·ral·ty
ad·mi·ra·tion
ad·mire
ad·mir·ing
ad·mis·si·ble
ad·mis·sion
ad·mit
ad·mit·tance
ad·mix·ture
ad·mon·ish
ad·mo·ni·tion
ad·mon·i·to·ry
ad·nau·se·am
ado
ado·be
ad·o·les·cence
adopt
adopt·ee
adop·tion
adop·tive
ador·able
ad·o·ra·tion
adorn
adorn·ment
ad rem
ad·re·nal

adrift
adroit
ad·sor·bent
ad·sorp·tion
ad·u·late
ad·u·la·tion
adult
adul·ter·ant
adul·ter·ate
adul·ter·a·tion
adul·ter·er
adul·ter·ess
ad·um·brate
ad va·lo·rem
ad·vance
ad·vance·ment
ad·van·tage
ad·van·ta·geous
ad·ven·ti·tious
ad·ven·ture
ad·ven·tur·er
ad·ven·ture·some
ad·ven·tur·ess
ad·ven·tur·ous
ad·ver·bi·al
ad·ver·sary
ad·verse
ad·verse·ly
ad·ver·si·ty
ad·vert
ad·ver·tence
ad·ver·ten·cy
ad·ver·tise
ad·ver·tise·ment
ad·ver·tis·ing
ad·vice
ad·vis·abil·i·ty
ad·vis·able
ad·vise
ad·vis·ed·ly

ad·vis·er
ad·vis·ing
ad·vi·so·ry
ad·vo·ca·cy
ad·vo·cate
ad·vo·ca·tor
adz
ae·gis
ae·on
aer·ate
aer·a·tor
ae·ri·al
ae·ri·al·ist
aero·dy·nam·ics
aero·naut
aero·nau·tics
aero·sol
aes·thete
aes·thet·ic
aes·thet·i·cal·ly
aes·thet·i·cism
aes·thet·ics
aes·ti·vate
af·fa·ble
af·fair
af·fect
af·fec·ta·tion
af·fect·ed
af·fec·tion
af·fec·tion·ate
af·fec·tive
af·fer·ent
af·fi·ance
af·fi·cio·na·do
af·fi·da·vit
af·fil·i·ate
af·fin·i·ty
af·firm
af·firm·able
af·fir·ma·tion

af·fir·ma·tive
af·fix
af·fla·tus
af·flict
af·flic·tion
af·flu·ence
af·flu·ent
af·ford
af·for·es·ta·tion
af·fray
af·fright
af·front
afi·cio·na·do
afield
afire
aflame
afloat
aflut·ter
afoot
afore·men·tioned
afore·said
afore·thought
afraid
afresh
Af·ro
af·ter all
af·ter·care
af·ter·glow
af·ter-hours
af·ter·math
af·ter·noon
af·ter-shave
af·ter·taste
af·ter·thought
af·ter·ward
against
agape
ag·ate
aged
age·less

agen·cy
agen·da
agen·dum
agent
ag·gior·na·men·
  to
ag·glom·er·a·tion
ag·glu·ti·nate
ag·glu·ti·na·tion
ag·glu·ti·na·tive
ag·gran·dize
ag·gran·dize·
  ment
ag·gra·vate
ag·gra·va·tion
ag·gre·gate
ag·gre·ga·tion
ag·gres·sion
ag·gres·sor
ag·grieved
aghast
ag·ile
agil·i·ty
agin·ner
ag·i·tate
ag·i·ta·tor
aglare
aglit·ter
aglow
ag·nos·tic
agog
ag·o·nize
ag·o·ny
ag·o·ra·pho·bia
agrar·i·an
agree·able
agree·ably
agree·ment
ag·ri·cul·ture
agron·o·my

aground
ague
ahead
ahoy
aide
aide-de-camp
aide-mé·moire
ai·le·ron
ai·lu·ro·phile
ai·lu·ro·phobe
air-con·di·tion
air·craft
air·field
air force
air·freight
air·ing
air·lift
air·line
air·lin·er
air·mail
air·man
air·plane
air·port
air raid
air·ship
air·space
air·speed
air·strip
air·tight
air·way
airy
aisle
ajar
akim·bo
akin
al·a·bas·ter
a la carte
alac·ri·ty
a la mode
alarm

alas
al·ba·tross
al·be·it
al·bi·no
al·bum
al·bu·men
al·che·my
al·co·hol
al·co·hol·ic
al·co·hol·ism
al·cove
al·der·man
al·der·man·ic
ale·a·to·ry
alem·bic
alert
al·fal·fa
al·fres·co
al·ge·bra
al·ge·bra·ic
al·go·rithm
alias
al·i·bi
alien
alien·ate
alien·ation
alien·ist
alight
align·ment
alike
al·i·ment
al·i·men·ta·ry
al·i·mo·ny
alive
al·ka·li
al·ka·line
al·ka·loid
all-around
al·lay
al·le·ga·tion

al·lege
al·leg·ed·ly
al·le·giance
al·le·gor·i·cal
al·le·go·ry
al·le·gro
al·le·lu·ia
all-em·brac·ing
al·ler·gic
al·ler·gy
al·le·vi·ate
al·ley
al·ley·way
al·li·ance
al·lied
al·li·ga·tor
al·lit·er·a·tion
al·lit·er·a·tive
all-night
al·lo·cate
al·lo·ca·tion
al·lo·cu·tion
al·lo·path
al·lop·a·thy
all-or-noth·ing
al·lot
al·lot·ment
all-out
al·low
al·low·able
al·low·ably
al·low·ance
al·loy
all-pow·er·ful
all-pur·pose
all right
all-star
al·lude
al·lure
al·lure·ment

al·lur·ing
al·lu·sion
al·lu·sive
al·lu·sive·ly
al·lu·vi·al
al·ly
al·ma ma·ter
al·ma·nac
al·mighty
al·mond
al·most
alms
alo·ha
alone
along·side
aloof
aloud
al·paca
al·pha
al·pha·bet
al·pha·bet·ic
al·pha·bet·i·cal·
   ly
al·pha·bet·iza·
   tion
al·pha·bet·ize
al·pine
al·ready
al·so-ran
al·tar
al·ter
al·ter·ation
al·ter·cate
al·ter·ca·tion
al·ter ego
al·ter·nate
al·ter·nate·ly
al·ter·na·tor
al·though
al·tim·e·ter

al·ti·tude
al·ti·tu·di·nous
al·to
al·to·geth·er
al·tru·ism
alu·mi·num
alum·na
alum·nus
al·ways
amal·gam
amal·gam·ate
amal·gam·ation
aman·u·en·sis
amass
amass·ment
am·a·teur
am·a·to·ry
amaze
amaze·ment
am·a·zon
am·bas·sa·dor
am·bas·sa·do·ri·
   al
am·ber
am·ber·gris
am·bi·dex·ter·i·
   ty
am·bi·dex·trous
am·bi·ence
am·bi·ent
am·bi·gu·ity
am·big·u·ous
am·bi·tion
am·bi·tious
am·biv·a·lence
am·biv·a·lent
am·ble
am·bro·sia
am·bro·sial
am·bu·lance

am·bu·lant
am·bu·la·to·ry
am·bush
ame·ba
ame·lio·rate
ame·na·ble
ame·na·bly
amend
amen·da·to·ry
amend·ment
amends
ame·ni·ty
Amer·i·ca·na
Amer·i·can·iza·tion
Amer·i·can·ize
am·e·thyst
ami·a·ble
ami·a·ble·ness
ami·a·bly
am·i·ca·ble
ami·cus cu·ri·ae
amid
amid·ships
ami·go
amiss
am·i·ty
am·me·ter
am·mo·nia
am·mu·ni·tion
am·ne·sia
am·nes·ty
amoe·ba
amok
among
amor·al
amo·ral·i·ty
am·o·rous
am·o·rous·ness
amor·phous

am·or·ti·za·tion
am·or·tize
amount
amour
am·per·age
am·pere
am·per·sand
am·phet·amine
am·phib·i·an
am·phib·i·ous
am·phi·the·ater
am·pho·ra
am·ple
am·pli·fi·ca·tion
am·pli·fi·er
am·pli·fy
am·pli·tude
am·pu·tate
am·pu·ta·tion
am·pu·tee
am·u·let
amuse
amuse·ment
amus·ing
anach·ro·nism
anach·ro·nis·tic
ana·gram
anal
an·al·ge·sic
anal·o·gous
an·a·logue
anal·o·gy
anal·y·sis
an·a·lyst
an·a·lyt·ic
an·a·lyt·i·cal
an·a·lyze
an·a·pest
an·ar·chic
an·ar·chism

an·ar·chist
an·ar·chis·tic
an·ar·chy
anath·e·ma
anath·e·ma·tize
an·a·tom·i·cal
anat·o·mist
anat·o·my
an·ces·tor
an·ces·tral
an·ces·try
an·chor
an·chor·age
an·cho·rite
an·cho·vy
an·cient
an·cil·lary
an·dan·te
and·iron
an·ec·dot·al
an·ec·dote
ane·mia
anem·o·ne
an·es·the·sia
an·es·the·si·ol·o·gist
an·es·the·si·ol·o·gy
an·es·thet·ic
anes·the·tist
anes·the·tize
an·eu·rysm
anew
an·gel
an·gel·ic
an·ger
an·gi·na pec·to·ris
an·gle
an·gled
an·gler

An·gli·can
an·gli·cism
an·gli·cize
an·gling
an·glo·phile
an·glo·phobe
An·glo-Sax·on
an·go·ra
an·gri·ly
an·gry
angst
an·guish
an·gu·lar
an·gu·lar·i·ty
an·hy·drous
an·i·mad·ver·sion
an·i·mad·vert
an·i·mal
an·i·mal·cule
an·i·mal·ism
an·i·mate
an·i·ma·tion
an·i·mos·i·ty
an·i·mus
an·ise
an·is·ette
an·kle
an·klet
an·nals
an·neal
an·nex
an·ni·hi·late
an·ni·ver·sa·ry
an·no·tate
an·no·ta·tion
an·nounce
an·nounce·ment
an·nounc·er
an·noy

an·noy·ance
an·nu·al
an·nu·itant
an·nu·ity
an·nul
an·nu·lar
an·nul·ment
an·nun·ci·a·tion
an·od·ize
an·o·dyne
anoint
anom·a·lous
anom·a·ly
an·o·mie
an·o·nym·i·ty
anon·y·mous
anoph·e·les
an·oth·er
an·swer
an·swer·able
ant·ac·id
an·tag·o·nism
an·tag·o·nist
an·tag·o·nis·tic
an·tag·o·nize
ant·arc·tic
an·te·bel·lum
an·te·ced·ent
an·te·cham·ber
an·te·date
an·te·di·lu·vi·an
an·te·lope
an·te me·ri·di·em
an·ten·na
an·te·pe·nult
an·te·pen·ul·ti·mate
an·te·ri·or
an·te·room
an·them

an·thol·o·gy
an·thra·cite
an·thrax
an·throp·ic
an·thro·po·cen·tric
an·thro·poid
an·thro·pol·o·gy
an·thro·po·mor·phic
an·ti·bi·ot·ic
an·ti·body
an·tic·i·pate
an·tic·i·pa·tion
an·tic·i·pa·tive
an·tic·i·pa·to·ry
an·ti·cler·i·cal
an·ti·cli·mac·tic
an·ti·cli·max
an·ti·dote
an·ti·es·tab·lish·ment
an·ti·freeze
an·ti·his·ta·mine
an·ti·ma·cas·sar
an·ti·mo·ny
an·ti·nov·el
an·ti·pas·to
an·tip·a·thy
an·ti·phon
an·tiph·o·nal
an·tiph·o·ny
an·ti·pode
an·ti·pov·er·ty
an·ti·quar·i·an
an·ti·quary
an·ti·quat·ed
an·tique
an·tiq·ui·ty
an·ti-Se·mit·ic

an·ti-Sem·i·tism
an·ti·sep·tic
an·ti·so·cial
an·tith·e·sis
an·ti·thet·i·cal
an·ti·tox·in
ant·ler
ant·lered
ant·onym
anus
an·vil
anx·i·ety
anx·ious
anx·ious·ly
any·where
aor·ta
apace
apart
apart·heid
apart·ment
ap·a·thet·ic
ap·a·thy
aper·çu
aper·i·tif
ap·er·ture
apex
apha·sia
aphid
aph·o·rism
aph·ro·dis·i·ac
api·a·rist
api·ary
apiece
ap·ish
aplen·ty
aplomb
apoc·a·lypse
apoc·a·lyp·tic
apoc·ry·pha
apoc·ry·phal

apo·gee
apol·o·get·ic
apol·o·get·ics
ap·o·lo·gia
apol·o·gist
apol·o·gize
apol·o·gy
ap·o·plec·tic
ap·o·plexy
apos·ta·sy
apos·tate
apos·ta·tize
apos·tle
ap·os·tol·ic
apos·tro·phe
apoth·e·cary
ap·o·thegm
apo·the·o·sis
ap·pall
ap·pall·ing
ap·pa·nage
ap·pa·ra·tus
ap·par·el
ap·par·ent
ap·pa·ri·tion
ap·peal
ap·peal·able
ap·peal·ing
ap·pear·ance
ap·pease
ap·pel·lant
ap·pel·late
ap·pel·la·tion
ap·pend
ap·pend·age
ap·pen·dec·to·my
ap·pen·di·ci·tis
ap·pen·dix
ap·per·cep·tion
ap·per·tain

ap·pe·tite
ap·pe·tiz·er
ap·pe·tiz·ing
ap·plaud
ap·plause
ap·pli·ance
ap·pli·ca·ble
ap·pli·cant
ap·pli·ca·tion
ap·pli·qué
ap·ply
ap·point
ap·poin·tee
ap·point·ive
ap·point·ment
ap·por·tion
ap·por·tion·ment
ap·po·site
ap·po·si·tion
ap·prais·al
ap·praise
ap·pre·cia·ble
ap·pre·ci·ate
ap·pre·ci·a·tion
ap·pre·cia·tive
ap·pre·hend
ap·pre·hen·sion
ap·pre·hen·sive
ap·pren·tice
ap·prise
ap·proach
ap·proach·able
ap·pro·ba·tion
ap·pro·pri·ate
ap·pro·pri·a·tion
ap·prov·able
ap·prov·al
ap·prove
ap·prox·i·mate
ap·prox·i·ma·tion

ap·pur·te·nance
ap·pur·te·nant
apri·cot
a pri·o·ri
apron
ap·ro·pos
ap·ti·tude
aqua·cade
aqua·ma·rine
aqua·plane
aquar·i·um
aquat·ic
aqua·vit
aq·ue·duct
aque·ous
aq·ui·line
ar·a·besque
ar·a·ble
ar·bi·ter
ar·bi·tra·ble
ar·bit·ra·ment
ar·bi·trary
ar·bi·trate
ar·bi·tra·tor
ar·bor
ar·bo·re·al
ar·bo·re·tum
ar·bu·tus
ar·cade
ar·ca·dia
ar·cane
arch
ar·chae·ol·o·gy
ar·cha·ic
arch·an·gel
arch·bish·op
arch·dea·con
arch·di·o·cese
ar·cher
ar·chery

ar·che·type
ar·chi·pel·a·go
ar·chi·tect
ar·chi·tec·ton·ic
ar·chi·tec·tur·al
ar·chi·tec·ture
ar·chive
ar·chi·vist
arch·way
arc·tic
ar·dent
ar·dor
ar·du·ous
ar·ea
are·na
aren't
ar·go·sy
ar·got
ar·gu·able
ar·gue
ar·gu·fy
ar·gu·ment
ar·gu·men·ta·
 tive
ar·id
aright
ar·is·toc·ra·cy
aris·to·crat
arith·me·tic
ar·ma·da
ar·ma·ment
ar·ma·ture
ar·mi·stice
ar·mor
ar·mory
arm-twist·ing
aro·ma
ar·o·mat·ic
around
arouse

ar·raign
ar·raign·ment
ar·range
ar·range·ment
ar·rang·er
ar·ray
ar·rear
ar·rear·age
ar·rest
ar·rest·ing
ar·rhyth·mic
ar·riv·al
ar·rive
ar·riv·ing
ar·ro·gance
ar·ro·gant
ar·ro·gate
ar·row
ar·se·nal
ar·se·nic
ar·son
art de·co
ar·te·ri·al
ar·te·rio·scle·ro·
 sis
ar·tery
ar·te·sian well
art·ful
ar·thrit·ic
ar·thri·tis
ar·ti·choke
ar·ti·cle
ar·tic·u·late
ar·tic·u·la·tion
ar·ti·fact
ar·ti·fice
ar·ti·fi·cial
ar·ti·fi·ci·al·i·ty
ar·til·lery
ar·ti·san

art·ist
ar·tiste
ar·tis·tic
art·ist·ry
art·less
arty
as·bes·tos
as·cend
as·cen·dance
as·cen·dan·cy
as·cen·dant
as·cend·ing
as·cen·sion
as·cent
as·cer·tain
as·cet·ic
as·cribe
as·crip·tion
asep·tic
ashamed
ash·can
ash·en
ashore
aside
as·i·nine
as·i·nine·ly
as·i·nin·i·ty
askance
askew
asleep
aso·cial
as·par·a·gus
as·pect
as·per·i·ty
as·perse
as·per·sion
as·phalt
as·phyx·i·ate
as·phyx·i·a·tion
as·phyx·i·a·tor

as·pic
as·pi·rant
as·pi·rate
as·pi·ra·tion
as·pire
as·pir·er
as·pi·rin
as·sail
as·sas·sin
as·sas·si·nate
as·sault
as·say
as·sem·blage
as·sem·ble
as·sem·bly
as·sem·bly·man
as·sent
as·sent·er
as·sert
as·ser·tion
as·ser·tive
as·sess
as·sess·ment
as·ses·sor
as·set
as·sev·er·ate
as·si·du·ity
as·sid·u·ous
as·sign
as·sig·na·tion
as·sign·ee
as·sign·ment
as·sim·i·la·ble
as·sim·i·late
as·sim·i·la·tion
as·sim·i·la·tive
as·sis·tance
as·sis·tant
as·size
as·so·ci·ate

as·so·ci·a·tion
as·so·cia·tive
as·sort
as·sort·ed
as·sort·ment
as·suage
as·suag·ing
as·sume
as·sum·ing
as·sump·tion
as·sur·ance
as·sure
as·sured·ly
as·sur·er
as·ter·isk
astern
asth·ma
asth·mat·ic
as·tig·mat·ic
astig·ma·tism
as·ton·ish
as·ton·ish·ment
as·tound
as·tound·ing
as·tral
astray
astride
as·trin·gent
as·trol·o·ger
as·trol·o·gy
as·tro·naut
as·tron·o·mer
as·tro·nom·i·cal
as·tute
asun·der
asy·lum
asym·met·ric
athe·ism
athe·ist
athe·is·tic

ath·lete
ath·let·ic
ath·let·ics
athwart
atin·gle
at·las
at·mo·sphere
at·mo·spher·ic
atom·ic
at·om·is·tic
at·om·ize
at·om·iz·er
aton·al
atone
atone·ment
atro·cious
atroc·i·ty
at·ro·phy
at·tach
at·ta·ché
at·tach·ment
at·tack
at·tain
at·tain·able
at·tain·ment
at·taint
at·tempt
at·tend
at·ten·dance
at·ten·dant
at·ten·tion
at·ten·tive
at·ten·u·ate
at·ten·u·a·tion
at·test
at·tic
at·tire
at·ti·tude
at·ti·tu·di·nize

at·tor·ney
at·tor·ney-at-law
at·trac·tion
at·trac·tive
at·trac·tive·ness
at·trib·ut·able
at·tri·bute
at·tri·bu·tion
at·tri·tion
at·tune
atyp·i·cal
au·burn
auc·tion
auc·tion·eer
au·da·cious
au·dac·i·ty
au·di·bil·i·ty
au·di·ble
au·di·bly
au·di·ence
au·dio
au·dio-lin·gual
au·di·ol·o·gy
au·di·om·e·ter
au·dio·vi·su·al
au·dit
au·di·tion
au·di·tor
au·di·to·ri·um
au·ger
aug·ment
aug·men·ta·tion
au gra·tin
au·gur
au·gu·ry
au·gust
au jus
auld lang syne
au na·tu·rel

aunt
au·re·ole
au re·voir
au·ri·cle
au·ric·u·lar
au·ro·ra bo·re·al·is
aus·pic·es
aus·pi·cious
aus·tere
aus·tere·ly
aus·ter·i·ty
au·tar·chy
au·then·tic
au·then·ti·cate
au·thor
au·thor·i·tar·i·an
au·thor·i·ta·tive
au·thor·i·ty
au·tho·ri·za·tion
au·tho·rize
au·tism
au·tis·tic
au·to·bahn
au·to·bi·og·ra·phy
au·to·bus
au·to·cade
au·toc·ra·cy
au·to·crat
au·to·crat·ic
au·to·graph
au·to·mate
au·to·mat·ic
au·to·ma·tion
au·tom·a·tism
au·tom·a·ton
au·to·mo·bile
au·to·mo·tive
au·ton·o·mous
au·ton·o·my

au·top·sy
au·to·stra·da
au·to·sug·ges·
 tion
au·tumn
aux·il·ia·ry
avail·abil·i·ty
avail·able
av·a·lanche
avant-garde
av·a·rice
av·a·ri·cious
av·a·tar
avenge
av·e·nue
av·er·age
averse
aver·sion
avert
avi·ary
avi·a·tion
avi·a·tor
avi·a·trix
av·id
avid·ity
avi·on·ics
av·o·ca·do
av·o·ca·tion
avoid
avoid·ance
av·oir·du·pois
avouch
avow·al
avun·cu·lar
await
awak·en
award
awash
aweigh

awe·some
aw·ful
awk·ward
aw·ning
awry
ax·el
ax·i·al
ax·i·om
ax·i·om·at·ic
ax·is
ax·le
aza·lea
az·i·muth
azure

B

bab·ble
bab·bler
ba·boon
ba·bush·ka
ba·by·ing
ba·by·ish
ba·by-sit
ba·by-sit·ter
bac·ca·lau·re·ate
bac·ca·rat
bac·cha·nal
bac·cha·na·lia
bac·chic
bach·e·lor
ba·cil·lus
back·ache
back·bite
back·bone
back·drop
back·er

back·fire
back·gam·mon
back·ground
back·hand
back·hoe
back·ing
back·lash
back·log
back·slide
back·stage
back·stop
back·swing
back·track
back·ward
back·yard
ba·con
bac·te·ria
bac·te·ri·al
bac·te·ri·ol·o·gist
bac·te·ri·ol·o·gy
badge
bad·ger
ba·di·nage
bad·min·ton
bad-mouth
baf·fle
baf·fle·ment
bag·a·telle
ba·gel
bag·gage
bag·gy
bag·man
bag·pipe
ba·guette
bai·liff
bai·li·wick
bails·man
baize
bak·ery

bak·ing pow·der
bak·ing so·da
bal·a·lai·ka
bal·ance
bal·co·ny
bald
bald·ish
bald·ly
bal·der·dash
bale·ful
balk
bal·kan·ize
balky
bal·lad
bal·lade
bal·last
ball bear·ing
bal·le·ri·na
bal·let
bal·let·o·mane
bal·lis·tic mis·sile
bal·lis·tics
bal·loon
bal·loon·ist
bal·lot
bal·ly·hoo
balm
balmy
ba·lo·ney
bal·sam
bal·us·trade
bam·boo
bam·boo·zle
ba·nal
ba·nal·i·ty
ba·nana
ban·dage
ban·dag·ing
ban·dan·na
band·box

ban·deau
ban·dit
ban·dit·ry
band·mas·ter
bands·man
band·stand
band·wag·on
ban·dy
ban·dy-legged
bane·ful
ban·gle
ban·ish
ban·ish·ment
ban·is·ter
ban·jo
bank·rupt
bank·rupt·cy
ban·ner
banns
ban·quet
ban·shee
ban·tam
ban·ter
ban·yan
bap·tism
bap·tis·mal
bap·tis·tery
bap·tize
bar·bar·ian
bar·bar·ic
bar·ba·rism
bar·bar·i·ty
bar·ba·rous
bar·be·cue
barbed
bar·bell
bar·ber
bar·ber·ry
bar·ber·shop
bar·bi·tu·rate

bar·ca·role
bare·back
bare·faced
bare·foot
bar·fly
bar·gain
barge
bar·hop
bari·tone
bark
bar·keep·er
bar·ley
bar·maid
bar·man
bar mitz·vah
bar·na·cle
barn·storm
barn·yard
baro·graph
ba·rom·e·ter
bar·on
bar·on·ess
bar·on·et
bar·on·et·cy
ba·ro·ni·al
bar·ony
ba·roque
ba·rouche
barque
bar·rack
bar·racks bag
bar·ra·cu·da
bar·rage
barred
bar·rel
bar·rel·ful
bar·ren
bar·rette
bar·ri·cade
bar·ri·er

bar·ring
bar·ris·ter
bar·room
bar·row
bar·tend·er
bar·ter
bar·ware
bas·al
ba·salt
base
based
base·ball
base·board
base·ment
bash·ful
bash·ful·ly
bash·ful·ness
ba·sic
ba·si·cal·ly
ba·sil
ba·sil·i·ca
bas·i·lisk
ba·sin
bas·i·net
bas·ing
ba·sis
bask
bas·ket
bas·ket·ball
bas·ket·ful
bas·ket·ry
bas mitz·vah
bas-re·lief
bass
bas·set hound
bas·si·net
bas·so
bas·soon
bass viol
bass·wood

bas·tard
bas·tard·ize
baste
bast·ed
bas·tille
bast·ing
bas·tion
batch
bate
bath
bathe
bath·er
ba·thet·ic
ba·thos
bath·robe
bath·room
bath·tub
bathy·sphere
ba·tik
ba·tiste
ba·ton
bat·tal·ion
bat·ted
bat·ten
bat·ter
bat·tery
bat·tle
bat·tle·ment
bat·tle·ship
bat·ty
bau·ble
baux·ite
bawd
bawd·i·ly
bawdy
bawl
bay·ber·ry
bay·o·net
bay·ou
bay rum

ba·zaar
ba·zoo·ka
beach
beach·comber
beach·head
beachy
bea·con
bead·ing
bea·dle
beady
bea·gle
bea·ker
be-all and end-
    all
beam
bean
bean·ie
bear·able
beard
beard·less
bear·er
bear·ing
bear·ish
bear·skin
beast
beast·li·ness
beast·ly
beat·en
beat·er
be·atif·ic
be·at·i·fi·ca·tion
be·at·i·fy
beat·ing
be·at·i·tude
beat·nik
beau
beau geste
beau·te·ous
beau·ti·cian
beau·ti·fi·ca·tion

beau·ti·fi·er
beau·ti·ful
beau·ti·ful·ly
beau·ti·fy
beau·ty
beau·ty shop
beaux arts
bea·ver
be·bop
be·calm
be·cause
beck·on
be·cloud
be·come
be·com·ing
be·daub
be·daz·zle
bed·bug
bed·ded
bed·ding
be·deck
be·dev·il
be·dev·il·ment
bed·fel·low
be·di·zen
bed·lam
bed·ou·in
be·drag·gle
bed·rid·den
bed·rock
bed·side
bed·spread
bed-wet·ting
beech
beech·nut
beef·eat·er
beef·steak
beefy
bee·hive
bee·keep·er

bee·line
beery
bees·wax
bee·tle
be·fall
be·fit·ting
be·fog
be·fore·hand
be·friend
be·fud·dle
be·get
be·get·ter
beg·gar
beg·gar·ly
beg·ging
be·gin·ner
be·gin·ning
be·gone
be·gor·ra
be·grime
be·grudge
be·guile
be·guine
be·half
be·have
be·hav·ior
be·hav·ior·al·ly
be·hav·ior·ism
be·head
be·he·moth
be·hest
be·hind
be·hold·en
be·hoove
beige
be·la·bor
be·lat·ed
be·lay
belch
be·lea·guer

bel·fry
be·lie
be·lief
be·liev·able
be·lieve
be·lit·tle
bel·la·don·na
bell·boy
belle
belles let·tres
bell·hop
bel·li·cose
bel·li·cos·i·ty
bel·lig·er·ence
bel·lig·er·en·cy
bel·lig·er·ent
bell·man
bel·low
bel·lows
bell·weth·er
bel·ley·ache
be·long·ing
be·loved
be·med·aled
be·moan
bench
be·neath
ben·e·dict
bene·dic·tion
bene·fac·tion
bene·fac·tor
ben·e·fice
be·nef·i·cence
be·nef·i·cent
ben·e·fi·cial
ben·e·fi·cia·ry
be·nev·o·lence
be·nev·o·lent
be·night·ed
be·nign

be·nig·nan·cy
be·nig·nant
be·numb
ben·zene
be·queath
be·queath·al
be·quest
be·rate
be·reave
be·reave·ment
be·reft
be·ret
be·rib·boned
ber·ried
ber·ry
ber·serk
berth
be·seech
be·set
be·set·ting
be·side
be·sides
be·siege
be·smear
be·smirch
be·speak
be·spec·ta·cled
bes·tial
bes·ti·al·i·ty
bes·ti·ary
be·stir
be·stow
be·stow·al
be·strew
best-sell·er
be·take
bete noire
be·tray
be·tray·al
be·troth

be·troth·al
bet·ter·ment
be·tween·times
be·twixt and
   be·tween
bev·el
bev·er·age
bevy
be·wail
be·ware
be·whis·kered
be·wil·der·ment
be·witch
be·yond
be·zel
bi·an·nu·al
bi·as
bi·ased
bi·be·lot
bi·ble
bib·li·cal
bib·li·og·ra·pher
bib·li·og·ra·phy
bib·lio·phile
bib·u·lous
bi·cam·er·al
bi·car·bon·ate
bi·cen·te·na·ry
bi·cen·ten·ni·al
bi·ceps
bick·er
bi·cus·pid
bi·cy·cle
bid·da·ble
bid·der
bid·dy
bi·det
bi·en·ni·al
bi·en·ni·um
bier

bi·fo·cal
bi·fur·cate
bi·fur·ca·tion
big·a·mous
big·a·my
big·gish
bight
big·ot
big·ot·ed
big·ot·ry
bike
bi·ki·ni
bi·la·bi·al
bi·lat·er·al
bile
bilge
bi·lin·gual
bil·ious
bilk
bill·board
bil·let
bil·let-doux
bil·liards
bill·ing
bil·lings·gate
bil·lion·aire
bil·low
bil·lowy
bil·ly goat
bi·mod·al
bi·month·ly
bi·na·ry
bin·au·ral
bind·er
bind·ery
bind·ing
binge
bin·go
bin·na·cle
bin·oc·u·lar

bi·no·mi·al
bio·chem·is·try
bio·de·grad·able
bi·og·ra·pher
bio·graph·i·cal
bi·og·ra·phy
bi·o·log·i·cal
bi·ol·o·gy
bi·on·ic
bi·op·sy
bi·ot·ic
bi·par·ti·san
bi·ped
bi·plane
bi·po·lar
birch
bird·er
bird-watch·er
birth·day
birth·mark
birth·place
birth·rate
birth·right
birth·stone
bis·cuit
bi·sect
bi·sec·tor
bi·sex·u·al
bish·op
bish·op·ric
bi·son
bisque
bi·state
bis·tro
bitch
bitchy
bit·ing
bit·ter·ly
bit·ter·sweet
bi·tu·mi·nous

bi·valve
bi·var·i·ate
biv·ouac
bi·week·ly
bi·year·ly
bi·zarre
blab·ber
blab·ber·mouth
black·ball
black belt
black·ber·ry
black·bird
black·en
black·guard
black·ing
black·jack
black·list
black·mail
black-mar·ket
black·out
black·smith
black-tie
black·top
blad·der
blade
blah
blam·able
blame
blame·wor·thy
blanch
blanc·mange
bland
blan·dish
blan·dish·ment
blan·ket
blare
blar·ney
bla·sé
blas·pheme
blas·phe·mous

blas·phe·my
blast
blast-off
bla·tan·cy
bla·tant
blath·er
blath·er·skite
blaze
blaz·er
blaz·ing
bla·zon
bleach
bleak
bleary
bleat
bleed
bleep
blem·ish
blench
blend
bless·ed
bless·ing
blight
blind
blind·fold
blind·ly
blind·ness
blink
blin·tze
blip
bliss·ful
bliss·ful·ly
blis·ter
blithe
blithe·some
blitz
blitz·krieg
bliz·zard
bloat·ed
blob

bloc
block
block·ade
block·age
block·bust·er
block·head
blond
blond·ish
blood
blood·cur·dling
blood·hound
blood·less
blood·mo·bile
blood·shed
blood·shot
blood·stock
blood·suck·er
bloody
bloom·ing
bloop·er
blos·som
blotch
blot·ter
blouse
blou·son
blow-by-blow
blow·hard
blown
blow·out
blow·sy
blow·torch
blowy
blub·ber
blud·geon
blue·beard
blue·bell
blue·ber·ry
blue·bird
blue chip
blue-col·lar

blue·fish
blue-pen·cil
blue·print
blue-rib·bon
blues
blue·stock·ing
bluesy
bluff
bluff·ness
blu·ing
blu·ish
blun·der
blun·der·buss
blunt
blur
blurb
blur·ring
blur·ry
blurt
blush
blus·ter
blus·tery
boa
boar
board·er
board·ing·house
board·room
board·walk
boast
boast·ful
boast·ful·ly
boat·er
boats·man·ship
boat·swain
bobbed
bob·bin
bob·ble
bob·by
bob·by-sox·er
bob·cat

bob·sled
boc·cie
bo·de·ga
bod·ice
bodi·less
bodi·ly
bod·ing
body·guard
bo·gey
bo·gey·man
bog·gle
bo·gus
bo·he·mi·an
boil·er
bois·ter·ous
bold·face
bo·le·ro
bol·lix
bo·lo·gna
bo·lo·ney
bol·she·vism
bol·ster
bo·lus
bom·bard
bom·bar·dier
bom·bast
bom·ba·zine
bombed
bo·na fide
bo·na fi·des
bo·nan·za
bon·bon
bond·age
bond·ed
bonds·man
bone·less
bone-dry
bone·head
bon·fire
bon·ho·mie

bon mot
bon·net
bon·sai
bo·nus
bon vi·vant
bon voy·age
bony
boob·oi·sie
boo-boo
boo·by prize
boo·dle
boo·gie-woo·gie
book·bind·ery
book·ie
book·ish
book·keep·er
book·let
book·mak·er
book·sell·er
book·store
boo·mer·ang
boon·docks
boon·dog·gle
boor·ish
boost·er
boo·tee
booth
boot·leg
boot·lick
boo·ty
booze
bo·rac·ic acid
bo·rax
bor·del·lo
bor·der
bor·der·line
bore·dom
bo·ric ac·id
bor·ing
borne

bor·ough
bor·row
borscht
bor·zoi
bo·som
bos·sa no·va
bossy
bo·tan·i·cal
bot·a·nist
bot·a·nize
bot·a·ny
botch
both·er
both·er·ation
both·er·some
bot·tle
bot·tle·neck
bot·tling
bot·tom·less
bot·u·lism
bou·clé
bou·doir
bouf·fant
bough
bouil·la·baisse
bouil·lon
boul·der
bou·le·vard
bounc·er
bounc·ing
bouncy
bound·ary
bound·er
bound·less
boun·te·ous
boun·ti·ful
boun·ty
bou·quet
bour·bon
bour·geois

bour·geoi·sie
bour·geon
bout
bou·tique
bou·ton·niere
bo·vine
bowd·ler·ize
bowed
bow·el
bow·er
bow·ie knife
bow·knot
bow·legged
bow·ler
bowl·ing
bow·sprit
bow tie
box·car
box·ing
boxy
boy·cott
boy·friend
boy·ish·ly
brace
brace·let
bra·cer
brac·ing
brack·et
brack·ish
brad
brag·ga·do·cio
brag·gart
brag·ger
brag·ging
braid
braid·ing
braille
brain·storm·ing
brainy
braise

brake	breath	bril·liant
brake·man	breathe	brim·ful
brak·ing	breath·er	brim·stone
bram·ble	breath·ing	brin·dled
bran·dish	breath·less	brink·man·ship
brand-new	breath·less·ly	briny
bran·dy	breath·tak·ing	bri·oche
brash	breathy	bri·quette
bras·sard	breech	bris·ket
bras·se·rie	breed·ing	brisk·ly
bras·siere	breezy	bris·tle
brassy	breth·ren	bris·tling
brat·ty	bre·vet	britch·es
brat·wurst	bre·via·ry	brit·tle
bra·va·do	brev·i·ty	broach
brave·ly	brew·er	broad·cast
brav·ery	brew·ery	broad·en
bra·vo	bri·ar	broad·loom
bra·vu·ra	bribe	broad-mind·ed
brawl	brib·ery	broad·side
brawn	bric-a-brac	bro·cade
brawn·i·er	brick·bat	broc·co·li
brawny	brick·lay·er	bro·chette
bray	brick·work	bro·gan
bra·zen	brid·al	brogue
bra·zier	bride·groom	broil·er
breach	brides·maid	bro·ken
bread-and-but·ter	bridge·able	bro·ken·heart·ed
breadth	bridge·work	bro·ker
break·able	bri·dle	bro·ker·age
break·age	bri·dling	bro·mide
break·down	brief·case	bro·mid·ic
break·fast	brief·ing	bron·chi·al
break-in	bri·er	bron·chi·tis
break·neck	bri·gade	bron·co
break·through	brig·a·dier	bronze
break·up	brig·and	brooch
break·wa·ter	bright·en	brood
breast	bril·liance	brood·er
breast·stroke	bril·lian·cy	broom·stick

broth
broth·el
broth·er·hood
broth·er-in-law
broth·er·li·ness
brougham
brou·ha·ha
brow·beat
brown·ie
brown·ish
browse
bruise
bruis·er
brunch
bru·net
brunt
brushed
brush·fire
brush-off
brusque
brus·que·rie
brus·sels sprout
bru·tal
bru·tal·i·ty
bru·tal·ize
brute
brut·ish
bub·ble
bub·bly
bu·bon·ic plague
buc·ca·neer
buck·et
buck·et·fuls
buck·le
buck·skin
buck·wheat
bu·col·ic
Bud·dhism
bud·dy
bud·get

budg·ing
buf·fa·lo
buff·er
buf·fet
buf·foon
buf·foon·ery
bug·a·boo
bugged
bug·gy
bu·gle
bu·gler
build·er
built
built-in
bul·bous
bulge
bulg·ing
bulk·head
bulk·i·ness
bulky
bull·dog
bull·doz·er
bul·let
bul·le·tin
bull·fight·er
bul·lion
bull·ish
bull·ock
bull's-eye
bul·ly
bul·wark
bum·ble
bum·ble·bee
bum·per
bump·i·ly
bump·kin
bump·tious
bumpy
bun·dle
bun·ga·low

bung·hole
bun·gle
bun·gler
bun·gling
bun·ion
bun·ker
bun·kum
Bun·sen burn·er
bun·ting
buoy
buoy·an·cy
bur·den
bur·den·some
bu·reau·cra·cy
bu·reau·crat
bur·geon
bur·gher
bur·glar
bur·glar·ize
bur·glary
buri·al
bur·ied
buri·er
bur·lap
bur·lesque
bur·ly
bur·nish
bur·noose
burp
bur·ro
bur·row
bur·sar
burse
bur·si·tis
burst
bury
bus·boy
bush·el
bush·ing
bushy

busi·ly
busi·ness
busi·ness·like
busi·ness·man
busi·ness·wom·
　an
bus·ing
bust·er
bus·tle
busy·body
busy·work
butch·er
butch·ery
but·ler
butt
butte
but·ter·cup
but·ter·fly
but·ter·scotch
butt·in·sky
but·tock
but·ton
but·tress
bux·om
bux·om·ness
buy
buy·ing
buz·zard
buzz·er
buzz·word
by-and-by
by and large
bye
bye-bye
by-elec·tion
by·gone
by·law
by·line
by·pass
by·path

by-prod·uct
by·stand·er
by·street
by·way
by·word

C

ca·bal
ca·ba·la
ca·bana
cab·a·ret
cab·bage
cab·by
cab·driv·er
cab·in
cab·i·net
ca·ble
ca·ble·gram
ca·ble TV
ca·boo·dle
ca·boose
cab·ri·o·let
cac·cia·to·re
cache
ca·chet
cack·le
ca·coph·o·nous
ca·coph·o·ny
cac·tus
ca·dav·er
ca·dav·er·ous
cad·die
cad·dy
ca·dence
ca·den·za
ca·det
cadge

cad·re
ca·du·ceus
ca·fé
caf·e·te·ria
caf·feine
caf·tan
ca·gey
ca·gi·ness
cairn
cais·son
cai·tiff
ca·jole
cal·a·boose
cal·a·mine
ca·lam·i·tous
ca·lam·i·ty
cal·ci·fi·ca·tion
cal·ci·fy
cal·ci·mine
cal·ci·um
cal·cu·la·ble
cal·cu·late
cal·cu·lat·ing
cal·cu·la·tion
cal·cu·la·tor
cal·cu·lus
cal·dron
cal·en·dar
calf
cal·i·ber
cal·i·brate
cal·i·bra·tion
cal·i·co
cal·i·per
cal·is·then·ics
calk
call·able
call·er
cal·lig·ra·pher
cal·lig·ra·phy

call·ing
cal·li·ope
cal·lous
cal·low
call-up
cal·lus
calm
ca·lo·ric
cal·o·rie
cal·o·rif·ic
cal·o·rim·e·ter
ca·lum·ni·ate
ca·lum·ni·ous
cal·um·ny
cal·va·ry
calve
calves
ca·lyp·so
ca·lyx
ca·ma·ra·de·rie
cam·ber
cam·bric
cam·el
ca·mel·lia
cam·eo
cam·era
cam·i·sole
cam·ou·flage
cam·paign
cam·paign·er
cam·pa·nile
camp·er
cam·phor
cam·phor·ate
camp·site
cam·pus
cam·shaft
can
Ca·na·di·an

ca·naille
can·a·lize
can·a·pé
ca·nard
ca·nary
ca·nas·ta
can·can
can·cel
can·cel·able
can·celed
can·cel·la·tion
can·cer
can·cer·ous
can·croid
can·de·la·bra
can·des·cent
can·did
can·di·da·cy
can·di·date
can·di·da·ture
can·died
can·dle
can·dle·wick
can·dor
can·dy strip·er
ca·nine
can·is·ter
can·ker
can·ker·ous
canned
can·nery
can·ni·bal
can·ni·bal·ize
can·ni·ness
can·ning
can·non
can·non·ade
can·not
can·ny

ca·noe
ca·noed
ca·noe·ing
can·on
ca·non·i·cal
ca·non·i·cals
can·on·ist
can·on·ize
can·o·py
cant
can't
can·ta·loupe
can·tan·ker·ous
can·tan·ker·ous·
   ness
can·ta·ta
can·teen
can·ter
can·ti·cle
can·ti·le·ver
can·to
can·ton
can·ton·ment
can·tor
can·vas
can·vass
can·yon
ca·pa·bil·i·ty
ca·pa·ble
ca·pa·cious
ca·pac·i·tate
ca·pac·i·tor
ca·pac·i·ty
ca·per
cap·ful
cap·il·lar·i·ty
cap·il·lary
cap·i·tal
cap·i·tal·ism

cap·i·tal·ist
cap·i·tal·iza·tion
cap·i·tal·ize
cap·i·tol
ca·pit·u·late
ca·pit·u·la·tion
ca·po
ca·pon
ca·pric·cio
ca·price
ca·pri·cious
Cap·ri·corn
cap·size
cap·stan
cap·stone
cap·sule
cap·sul·ize
cap·tain
cap·tion
cap·tious
cap·ti·vate
cap·tive
cap·tiv·i·ty
cap·tor
cap·ture
ca·pu·chin
car·a·bi·neer
car·a·cul
ca·rafe
car·a·mel
car·at
car·a·van
car·a·vel
car·bine
car·bo·hy·drate
car·bol·ic acid
car·bon
car·bon·ate
car·bon di·ox·ide

car·bon·ic
car·bon·ize
car·bon pa·per
car·bon
   tet·ra·chlo·ride
car·bun·cle
car·bu·re·tor
car·cass
car·cin·o·gen
car·ci·no·ma
car·di·ac
car·di·gan
car·di·nal
car·dio·gram
car·dio·graph
car·di·ol·o·gist
car·di·ol·o·gy
ca·reen
ca·reer
care·free
care·ful
care·less
ca·ress
car·et
care·tak·er
care·worn
car·fare
car·ful
car·go
car·i·bou
car·i·ca·ture
car·ies
car·il·lon
ca·ri·o·ca
car·load
car·mine
car·nage
car·nal
car·na·tion

car·ne·lian
car·ni·val
car·ni·vore
car·niv·o·rous
car·ol
car·om
ca·rouse
car·ou·sel
carp
car·pe di·em
car·pen·ter
car·pen·try
car·pet
car·pet·bag·ger
car·pet·ing
car·port
car·rel
car·riage
car·ri·er
car·ri·on
car·rot
car·roty
car·ry·all
car·ry·ing
car·ry·ing-on
car·ry·on
car·ry·out
car·sick
cart·age
carte blanche
car·tel
car·ti·lage
car·ti·lag·i·nous
car·tog·ra·pher
car·ton
car·toon
car·tridge
cart·wheel
carve

carv·en
ca·sa·ba
cas·cade
cas·cad·ing
cas·cara
ca·sein
case·ment
ca·shew
ca·shier
cash·mere
cas·ing
ca·si·no
cas·ket
cas·se·role
cas·sette
cas·sock
cas·ta·net
cast·away
caste
cas·tel·lat·ed
cast·er
cas·ti·gate
cas·tile soap
cas·tle
cast-off
cas·tor
cas·trate
ca·su·al
ca·su·al·ty
ca·su·ist
ca·su·ist·ry
cat·a·clysm
cat·a·comb
cat·a·falque
cat·a·lep·sy
cat·a·log
cat·a·log·er
cat·a·lyst
cat·a·lyt·ic
cat·a·ma·ran

cat·a·pult
cat·a·ract
ca·tarrh
ca·tas·tro·phe
cat·a·stroph·ic
cat·call
catch·all
catch·word
catchy
cat·e·chism
cat·e·chist
cat·e·chize
cat·e·chu·men
cat·e·gor·i·cal
cat·e·go·rize
cat·e·go·ry
ca·ter
cat·er·cor·ner
cat·er·pil·lar
cat·er·waul
cat·fish
ca·thar·sis
ca·thar·tic
ca·the·dral
cath·e·ter
cath·o·lic
Cath·o·lic
cath·o·lic·i·ty
cat·kin
cat·nap
cat·nip
cat·sup
cat·tail
cat·tle
cat·ty
cat·ty-cor·ner
Cau·ca·sian
cau·cus
cau·dal
caught

caul
cau·li·flow·er
caulk
caus·al
cau·sal·i·ty
cau·sa·tion
caus·ative
cause cé·lè·bre
cause·way
caus·tic
cau·ter·i·za·tion
cau·ter·ize
cau·tion
cau·tious
cav·al·cade
cav·a·lier
cav·al·ry
ca·ve·at
cave-in
cav·ern
cav·ern·ous
cav·i·ar
cav·il
cav·i·ty
ca·vort
cay·enne pep·per
cease
cease-fire
cease·less
ce·dar
cede
ce·dil·la
ceil·ing
cel·e·brant
cel·e·brate
ce·leb·ri·ty
ce·ler·i·ty
cel·ery
ce·les·tial
cel·i·ba·cy

cel·i·bate
cel·lar
cel·lo
cel·lo·phane
cel·lu·lar
cel·lu·loid
cel·lu·lose
Celt·ic
ce·ment
cem·e·tery
cen·a·cle
cen·o·bite
cen·o·bit·ic
ceno·taph
cen·ser
cen·sor
cen·so·ri·ous
cen·sor·ship
cen·sur·able
cen·sure
cen·sus
cen·taur
cen·te·nar·i·an
cen·te·na·ry
cen·ten·ni·al
cen·ter
cen·ter·piece
cen·ti·grade
cen·ti·me·ter
cen·ti·pede
cen·tral
cen·trif·u·gal
cen·trip·e·tal
cen·tu·ri·on
cen·tu·ry
ce·phal·ic
ce·ram·ic
ce·re·al
cer·e·bel·lum
ce·re·bral

cer·e·brate
ce·re·brum
cere·ment
cer·e·mo·ni·al
cer·e·mo·ni·ous
cer·e·mo·ny
ce·rise
cer·tain
cer·tain·ty
cer·tif·i·cate
cer·ti·fy
cer·tio·ra·ri
cer·ti·tude
ce·ru·le·an
cer·vi·cal
ce·sar·e·an
ces·sa·tion
ces·sion
cess·pool
ce·ta·cean
chafe
chaff
chaf·ing dish
cha·grin
chain
chair·man
chair·per·son
chair·wom·an
chaise longue
cha·let
chal·ice
chalk
chalky
chal·lenge
chal·leng·er
chal·lis
cham·ber
cham·ber·lain
cham·ber·maid
cham·bray

cha·me·leon
cham·ois
cham·pagne
cham·pi·on
cham·pi·on·ship
chance
chan·cel·lery
chan·cel·lor
chan·cery
chan·cre
chancy
chan·de·lier
change
change·able
change·less
chang·er
chan·nel
chant
chant·er
chan·teuse
chan·tey
chan·ti·cleer
Cha·nu·kah
cha·os
chap·ar·ral
cha·peau
cha·pel
chap·er·on
chap·lain
chapped
chap·ter
char·ac·ter
char·ac·ter·is·tic
char·ac·ter·iza·
  tion
char·ac·ter·ize
cha·rade
char·coal
chard
charge·able

charge-a-plate
char·gé d'af·
  faires
char·i·ot
cha·ris·ma
char·is·mat·ic
char·i·ta·ble
char·i·ty
char·la·tan
char·ley horse
charm·ing
char·ter
char·treuse
char·wom·an
chary
chase
chas·er
chasm
chas·sis
chaste
chas·ten
chas·tise
chas·ti·ty
cha·su·ble
châ·teau
chat·e·laine
chat·tel
chat·ter
chat·ter·box
chat·ty
chauf·feur
chau·tau·qua
chau·vin·ism
cheap·en
cheap·skate
cheat
check
check·book
check·ers

check·mate
check·off
ched·dar
cheeky
cheer·ful
cheer·io
cheer·lead·er
cheer·less
cheery
cheese
cheese·burg·er
cheese·cake
cheesy
chef
chem·i·cal
che·mise
chem·ist
chem·is·try
che·nille
cher·ish
che·root
cher·ry
cher·ry·stone
cher·ub
cher·u·bim
chess
chest·nut
che·va·lier
chev·ron
chewy
chiar·oscu·ro
chic
chi·ca·nery
chi·chi
chick·a·dee
chick·en·heart·ed
chi·cle
chic·o·ry
chide

chief
chief·tain
chief·tain·cy
chif·fon
chif·fo·nier
chig·ger
chi·gnon
chil·blain
child·bear·ing
child·ish
chili
chili con car·ne
chill·er
chilly
chime
chi·me·ra
chi·me·ri·cal
chim·ney
chim·pan·zee
chi·na
chin·chil·la
Chi·nese
chi·noi·se·rie
chintz
chintzy
chip·munk
chip·per
chi·rog·ra·phy
chi·rop·o·dist
chi·ro·prac·tic
chi·ro·prac·tor
chirp
chis·el
chi-square
chit
chi·val·ric
chiv·al·rous
chiv·al·ry
chive

chlo·rine
chlo·ro·form
chlo·ro·phyll
chock
chock-full
choc·o·late
choc·o·laty
choice
choir
choir·boy
choir·mas·ter
choke
chok·ing
chol·era
cho·ler·ic
chomp
choose
choosy
chop·per
chop·py
chop·stick
chop su·ey
cho·ral
cho·rale
chord
chore
cho·reo·graph
cho·re·og·ra·phy
cho·ric
cho·ris·ter
chor·tle
chorus
cho·sen
chow
chow·der
chow mein
chrism
chris·ten
chris·ten·ing

Christ·mas
chro·mat·ic
chrome
chro·mi·um
chro·mo·some
chron·ic
chron·i·cle
chro·nol·o·ger
chro·no·log·i·cal
chro·nol·o·gy
chro·nom·e·ter
chrys·a·lis
chry·san·the·
  mum
chub·by
chuck·le
chuk·ka
chuk·ker
chum·my
chump
chunky
church
church·go·er
church·yard
churl
churl·ish
churn
chute
chut·ney
chutz·pah
ci·bo·ri·um
ci·ca·trix
ci·der
ci·gar
cig·a·rette
cig·a·ril·lo
cinch
cinc·ture
cin·der

cin·e·ma
cin·e·mat·ic
cin·e·ma·tog·ra·
  pher
cin·e·ma·tog·ra·
  phy
cin·na·mon
ci·pher
cir·ca
cir·cle
cir·clet
cir·cu·itous
cir·cu·lar
cir·cu·late
cir·cu·la·tion
cir·cum·cise
cir·cum·ci·sion
cir·cum·fer·ence
cir·cum·flex
cir·cum·lo·cu·
  tion
cir·cum·nav·i·
  gate
cir·cum·scribe
cir·cum·spect
cir·cum·stance
cir·cum·stan·tial
cir·cum·vent
cir·cus
cir·rho·sis
cis·tern
cit·a·del
ci·ta·tion
cite
citi·fy
cit·i·zen
cit·i·zen·ship
cit·ric acid
cit·rine

cit·ron
cit·ro·nel·la
cit·rus
civ·ic
civ·ic-mind·ed
civ·ics
civ·il
ci·vil·ian
ci·vil·i·ty
civ·i·li·za·tion
civ·i·lize
civ·il·ly
civ·vy
clack
claim
claim·ant
clair·voy·ance
clair·voy·ant
clam·ber
clam·mi·ness
clam·my
clam·or
clam·or·ous
clamp
clan·des·tine
clan·gor
clan·gor·ous
clank
clan·nish
clans·man
clap·board
clap·per
clap·trap
clar·et
clar·i·fi·ca·tion
clar·i·fy
clar·i·net
clar·i·on
clar·i·ty
clash

clasp
clas·sic
clas·si·cal
clas·si·cism
clas·si·cist
clas·si·fi·ca·tion
clas·si·fied
clas·si·fi·er
clas·si·fy
class·less
class·mate
classy
clat·ter
clause
claus·tro·pho·bia
clav·i·chord
clav·i·cle
cla·vier
clean·able
clean·ly
clean·ness
cleanse
clear·ance
clear-cut
clear-eyed
clear·head·ed
clear·ing·house
cleat
cleav·age
cleave
cleav·er
clef
cleft
clem·en·cy
clem·ent
clench
cler·gy
cler·ic
cler·i·cal
cler·i·cal·ism

clew
cli·ché
cli·chéd
click
cli·ent
cli·en·tele
cliff
cliff-hang·er
cli·mac·ter·ic
cli·mate
cli·mat·ic
cli·max
climb·er
clinch·er
cling
clin·ic
clin·i·cal
cli·ni·cian
clink
clin·ker
clip·board
clip·per
clip·ping
clique
cli·to·ris
cloak
clob·ber
clock·wise
clock·work
clod·hop·per
clog
clois·ter
clone
close
close·ly
clos·et
clos·ing
clo·sure
cloth
clothe

clothes·line
cloth·ier
clot·ted
clot·ting
clo·ture
cloud·burst
cloud·less
cloudy
clout
clove
clo·ven
clo·ver
clo·ver·leaf
clown·ish
cloy
cloy·ing·ly
club·by
cluck
clue
clump
clum·sy
clung
clunk
clus·ter
clutch
clut·ter
coach
co·ad·ju·tor
co·ag·u·lant
co·ag·u·late
co·alesce
co·ali·tion
coarse
coarse-grained
coarse·ness
coast
coast·line
coat·tail
co·au·thor
coax

co·ax·i·al
co·balt
cob·ble
cob·bler
cob·ble·stone
co·bra
cob·web
co·caine
cock·ade
cock-a-leek·ie
cock·a·too
cocked hat
cock·eyed
cock·le
cock·le·shell
cock·ney
cock·pit
cock·sure
cock·tail
cocky
co·coa
co·co·nut
co·coon
co·cur·ric·u·lar
co·da
cod·dle
code
co·de·fen·dant
co·deine
co·dex
cod·ger
cod·i·cil
cod·i·fy
cod·ling
co·ed
co·ed·i·tor
co·ed·u·ca·tion
co·ef·fi·cient
co·equal
co·erce

co·er·cion
co·er·cive
co·eter·nal
co·eval
co·ex·ist
co·ex·ten·sive
cof·fee
cof·fer
cof·fin
co·gen·cy
co·gent
cog·i·tate
cog·i·ta·tion
co·gnac
cog·nate
cog·ni·tion
cog·ni·tive
cog·ni·zance
cog·ni·zant
cog·no·men
co·gno·scen·te
co·hab·it
co·here
co·her·ent
co·he·sion
co·he·sive
co·hort
coif
coif·feur
coif·feuse
coif·fure
coin·age
co·in·cide
co·in·ci·dence
co·in·ci·dent
co·in·ci·den·tal
co·in·sure
co·ition
co·itus
col·an·der

cold·ly
cole·slaw
col·ic
col·icky
col·i·se·um
col·lab·o·rate
col·lab·o·ra·tor
col·lage
col·lapse
col·lar
col·late
col·lat·er·al
col·la·tion
col·league
col·lect
col·lect·ible
col·lec·tion
col·lec·tive
col·lec·tive·ly
col·lec·tiv·ism
col·lec·tor
col·leen
col·lege
col·le·gial
col·le·gi·al·i·ty
col·le·gian
col·le·giate
col·lide
col·lie
col·li·sion
col·lo·ca·tion
col·lo·qui·al
col·lo·qui·al·ism
col·lo·qui·um
col·lo·quy
col·lu·sion
co·logne
co·lon
col·o·nel
co·lo·nial

co·lo·nial·ism
col·o·nist
col·o·ni·za·tion
col·o·nize
col·on·nade
col·o·ny
col·o·phon
col·or
col·or·ation
col·or·a·tu·ra
col·ored
col·or·ful
col·or·ing
co·los·sal
col·os·se·um
co·los·sus
co·los·to·my
colt·ish
col·umn
co·lum·nar
co·lum·ni·a·tion
col·um·nist
co·ma
co·mak·er
co·ma·tose
comb
com·bat
com·bat·ant
com·bat·ive
com·bi·na·tion
com·bine
com·bin·ing
com·bus·ti·ble
com·bus·tion
co·me·di·an
co·me·di·enne
com·e·dy
come·ly
com·er
co·mes·ti·ble

com·et
come·up·pance
com·fort
com·fort·able
com·fort·er
com·fy
com·ic
com·i·cal
co·mi·ty
com·ma
com·mand
com·man·dant
com·man·deer
com·mand·er
com·mand·ing
com·mand·ment
com·mem·o·rate
com·mem·o·ra·
tion
com·mem·o·ra·
tive
com·mence
com·mence·ment
com·mend
com·men·da·tion
com·men·da·to·ry
com·men·su·ra·
ble
com·men·su·rate
com·ment
com·men·tary
com·men·tate
com·men·ta·tor
com·merce
com·mer·cial
com·mer·cial·ism
com·mer·cial·ize
com·mie
com·min·gle
com·mis·er·ate

com·mis·er·a·tion
com·mis·sar
com·mis·sar·i·at
com·mis·sary
com·mis·sion
com·mis·sion·er
com·mit
com·mit·ment
com·mit·tal
com·mit·tee
com·mit·tee·man
com·mix
com·mode
com·mo·di·ous
com·mod·i·ty
com·mo·dore
com·mon
com·mon·al·i·ty
com·mon·al·ty
com·mon-law
com·mon·place
com·mon·weal
com·mon·wealth
com·mo·tion
com·mu·nal
com·mu·nal·i·ty
com·mune
com·mu·ni·ca·ble
com·mu·ni·cant
com·mu·ni·cate
com·mu·ni·ca·
   tion
com·mu·ni·ca·
   tive
com·mu·ni·ca·tor
com·mu·nion
com·mu·ni·qué
com·mu·nism
com·mu·nist
com·mu·ni·ty

com·mu·nize
com·mu·tate
com·mu·ta·tion
com·mu·ta·tor
com·mute
com·pact
com·pac·tion
com·pan·ion
com·pan·ion·able
com·pan·ion·ate
com·pan·ion·ship
com·pa·ny
com·pa·ra·bil·i·ty
com·pa·ra·ble
com·par·a·tive
com·pare
com·par·i·son
com·part·ment
com·part·men·
   tal·ize
com·pass
com·pas·sion
com·pas·sion·ate
com·pat·i·ble
com·pa·tri·ot
com·peer
com·pel
com·pelled
com·pen·di·ous
com·pen·di·um
com·pen·sate
com·pen·sa·tion
com·pete
com·pe·tence
com·pe·ten·cy
com·pe·tent
com·pe·ti·tion
com·pet·i·tive
com·pet·i·tor
com·pi·la·tion

com·pile
com·pla·cence
com·pla·cen·cy
com·pla·cent
com·plain
com·plain·ant
com·plaint
com·plai·sance
com·plai·sant
com·ple·ment
com·ple·men·tal
com·ple·men·ta·
   ry
com·plete
com·ple·tion
com·plex
com·plex·ion
com·plex·i·ty
com·pli·ance
com·pli·ant
com·pli·cate
com·pli·ca·tion
com·plic·i·ty
com·pli·ment
com·pli·men·ta·
   ry
com·po·nent
com·port
com·pose
com·pos·er
com·pos·ite
com·po·si·tion
com·post
com·po·sure
com·pote
com·pound
com·pre·hend
com·pre·hen·si·
   ble
com·pre·hen·sion

com·pre·hen·sive
com·press
com·press·ible
com·pres·sion
com·prise
com·pro·mise
comp·trol·ler
com·pul·sion
com·pul·sive
com·pul·so·ry
com·punc·tion
com·pu·ta·tion
com·pute
com·put·er
com·put·er·ize
com·rade
com·rad·ery
con·cat·e·na·tion
con·cave
con·cav·i·ty
con·ceal
con·cede
con·ceit
con·ceiv·able
con·ceive
con·cel·e·brant
con·cel·e·brate
con·cen·trate
con·cen·tra·tion
con·cen·tric
con·cept
con·cep·tion
con·cep·tu·al
con·cern
con·cert
con·cert·ed
con·cer·ti·no
con·cer·to
con·ces·sion
con·ces·sion·aire

con·cierge
con·cil·i·ate
con·cise
con·clave
con·clude
con·clu·sion
con·clu·sive
con·coct
con·coc·tion
con·com·i·tant
con·cord
con·cor·dance
con·course
con·crete
con·cu·bine
con·cu·pis·cence
con·cur
con·cur·rence
con·cur·rent
con·cus·sion
con·demn
con·dem·na·tion
con·dem·na·tory
con·den·sa·tion
con·dense
con·dens·er
con·de·scend
con·de·scen·sion
con·dign
con·di·ment
con·di·tion
con·dole
con·do·lence
con·dom
con·do·min·i·um
con·done
con·duce
con·du·cive
con·duct
con·duct·i·bil·i·ty

con·duc·tion
con·duc·tiv·i·ty
con·duc·tor
con·duit
con·fab
con·fab·u·late
con·fec·tion
con·fec·tion·ary
con·fec·tion·ery
con·fed·er·a·cy
con·fed·er·ate
con·fer
con·fer·ence
con·fess
con·fes·sion
con·fes·sor
con·fet·ti
con·fi·dant
con·fi·dante
con·fide
con·fi·dence
con·fi·den·tial
con·fid·ing
con·fig·u·ra·tion
con·fine
con·fine·ment
con·firm
con·fir·ma·tion
con·fis·cate
con·fla·gra·tion
con·flict
con·flu·ence
con·form
con·form·able
con·for·ma·tion
con·for·mi·ty
con·found
con·fra·ter·ni·ty
con·frere
con·front

con·fron·ta·tion
con·fuse
con·fu·sion
con·fu·ta·tion
con·fute
con·ga
con·geal
con·ge·nial
con·glom·er·ate
con·glom·er·a·tion
con·grat·u·late
con·gre·gate
con·gre·ga·tion
con·gress
con·gress·man
con·gress·wom·an
con·gru·ence
con·gru·en·cy
con·gru·ent
con·gru·ity
con·gru·ous
con·jec·tur·al
con·jec·ture
con·join
con·ju·gal
con·ju·gate
con·junc·tion
con·junc·ti·va
con·ju·ra·tion
con·jure
con·jur·er
con·nect
con·nec·tion
con·nec·tive
con·nip·tion
con·niv·ance
con·nive
con·nois·seur

con·no·ta·tion
con·no·ta·tive
con·note
con·nu·bi·al
con·quer
con·quer·or
con·quest
con·san·guin·e·ous
con·san·guin·i·ty
con·science
con·sci·en·tious
con·scious
con·scious·ness
con·script
con·se·crate
con·se·cra·tion
con·sec·u·tive
con·sen·sus
con·sent
con·se·quence
con·se·quent
con·se·quen·tial
con·se·quent·ly
con·ser·va·tion
con·ser·va·tion·ist
con·ser·va·tism
con·ser·va·tive
con·ser·va·tor
con·ser·va·to·ry
con·serve
con·sid·er
con·sid·er·able
con·sid·er·ate
con·sid·er·ation
con·sid·er·ing
con·sign
con·sign·ee
con·sign·ment

con·sist
con·sis·ten·cy
con·sis·tent
con·sis·to·ry
con·so·la·tion
con·sole
con·sol·i·date
con·sol·i·da·tion
con·som·mé
con·so·nant
con·sort
con·sor·tium
con·spic·u·ous
con·spir·a·cy
con·spir·a·tor
con·spir·a·to·ri·al
con·spire
con·sta·ble
con·stab·u·lary
con·stan·cy
con·stant
con·stel·la·tion
con·ster·na·tion
con·sti·pate
con·sti·pa·tion
con·stit·u·en·cy
con·stit·u·ent
con·sti·tute
con·sti·tu·tion
con·sti·tu·tion·al·i·ty
con·sti·tu·tive
con·strain
con·straint
con·strict
con·stric·tion
con·struct
con·struc·tion
con·struc·tive
con·strue

con·sul
con·sul·ate
con·sult
con·sul·tant
con·sul·ta·tion
con·sul·ta·tive
con·sul·tor
con·sum·able
con·sume
con·sum·er
con·sum·mate
con·sum·ma·tion
con·sump·tion
con·tact
con·ta·gion
con·ta·gious
con·tain
con·tain·er
con·tain·er·iza·
   tion
con·tain·er·ize
con·tain·er·ship
con·tain·ment
con·tam·i·nant
con·tam·i·na·tion
con·tem·plate
con·tem·pla·tion
con·tem·pla·tive
con·tem·po·ra·ne·
   ity
con·tem·po·ra·ne·
   ous
con·tem·po·rary
con·tempt·ible
con·temp·tu·ous
con·tend
con·ten·tious
con·test
con·text
con·tex·tu·al

con·ti·gu·ity
con·tig·u·ous
con·ti·nence
con·ti·nent
con·tin·gence
con·tin·gen·cy
con·tin·gent
con·tin·u·al
con·tin·u·ance
con·tin·u·a·tion
con·tin·ue
con·tinu·ing
con·ti·nu·ity
con·tin·u·ous
con·tin·u·um
con·tort
con·tor·tion·ist
con·tour
con·tra·band
con·tra·cep·tion
con·tract
con·tract·ible
con·trac·tion
con·trac·tor
con·trac·tu·al
con·tra·dict
con·tra·dic·to·ry
con·tra·dis·tinc·
   tion
con·tra·in·di·cate
con·tral·to
con·trap·tion
con·tra·ri·ety
con·trari·wise
con·trary
con·trast
con·trasty
con·tra·vene
con·tra·ven·tion
con·tre·temps

con·trib·ute
con·tri·bu·tion
con·trib·u·to·ry
con·trite
con·tri·tion
con·triv·ance
con·trive
con·trived
con·trol
con·trol·ler
con·trol·ment
con·tro·ver·sial
con·tro·ver·sy
con·tro·vert
con·tu·ma·cious
con·tu·ma·cy
con·tu·me·li·ous
con·tume·ly
co·nun·drum
con·va·lesce
con·va·les·cence
con·va·les·cent
con·vec·tion
con·vene
con·ve·nience
con·ve·nient
con·ven·tion
con·verge
con·ver·gence
con·ver·gent
con·ver·sant
con·ver·sa·tion
con·ver·sa·tion·
   al·ist
con·verse
con·ver·sion
con·vert
con·vert·ible
con·vex
con·vey

con·vey·ance
con·vey·er
con·vict
con·vic·tion
con·vince
con·viv·ial
con·vo·ca·tion
con·voke
con·vo·lut·ed
con·vo·lu·tion
con·voy
con·vulse
con·vul·sion
coo
cook·ie
cool·ant
coo·lie
co-op
co·op·er·ate
co·op·er·a·tion
co·op·er·a·tive
co·or·di·nate
co·or·di·na·tion
coo·tie
co·pa·ce·tic
cope
copi·er
co·pi·lot
co·pi·ous
cop-out
cop·per
cop·per·head
cop·ter
cop·u·late
cop·u·la·tive
copy·right
co·quette
co·quett·ish
cor·al
cord·age

cor·dial
cor·dial·i·ty
cor·do·van
cor·du·roy
co·re·li·gion·ist
co·re·spon·dent
cork·screw
cor·mo·rant
corn·cob
cor·nea
cor·ner
cor·ner·back
cor·net
corn·flakes
cor·nice
cor·nu·co·pia
corny
cor·ol·lary
cor·o·nary
cor·o·na·tion
cor·o·ner
cor·o·net
cor·po·ral
cor·po·rate
cor·po·ra·tion
cor·po·re·al
corps
corpse
corps·man
cor·pu·lence
cor·pu·lent
cor·pus·cle
cor·pus de·lic·ti
cor·ral
cor·rect
cor·rec·tor
cor·rec·tive
cor·re·late
cor·re·la·tion
cor·rel·a·tive

cor·re·spond
cor·re·spon·dence
cor·re·spon·dent
cor·ri·dor
cor·ri·gi·ble
cor·rob·o·rate
cor·rob·o·ra·tion
cor·rode
cor·ro·sion
cor·ro·sive
cor·ru·ga·tion
cor·rupt
cor·rup·tion
cor·rup·tive
cor·tege
cor·ti·sone
cor·us·cate
cor·us·ca·tion
co·sign·er
co·sine
cos·met·ic
cos·me·ti·cian
cos·mic
cos·mo·naut
cos·mo·pol·i·tan
cos·mos
co·spon·sor
cos·sack
co-star
cost·ly
cos·tume
cos·tum·er
co·sy
co·te·rie
co·ter·mi·nous
co·til·lion
cot·tage
cot·ton
cot·ton·seed
couch

cou·gar
cough
couldn't
coun·cil
coun·cil·lor
coun·sel
coun·sel·or
coun·sel·or-at-law
count·able
count·down
coun·te·nance
coun·ter·act
coun·ter·claim
coun·ter·clock·
　wise
coun·ter·cul·ture
coun·ter·dem·on·
　stra·tion
coun·ter·es·pi·o·
　nage
coun·ter·feit
coun·ter·foil
coun·ter·mand
coun·ter·pane
coun·ter·part
coun·ter·point
coun·ter·pose
coun·ter·pro·duc·
　tive
coun·ter·sign
count·ess
count·less
coun·tri·fied
coun·try
coun·try·side
coup de grace
coup d'etat
cou·pé
cou·ple
cou·plet

cou·pon
cour·age
cou·ra·geous
cou·ri·er
course
court
cour·te·ous
cour·te·san
cour·te·sy
court·ier
cous·in
cou·ture
cou·tu·ri·er
cove
cov·e·nant
cov·er·age
cov·er·all
cov·er·let
co·vert
cov·et
cov·et·ous
cov·ey
cow·ard·ice
cow·ard·li·ness
cow·er
cowl·ing
cow·shed
cox·comb
cox·swain
coy·ote
co·zy
crab·bed
crab·by
crack·er
crack·er·jack
crack·ling
crack·pot
cra·dle
crafts·man
crafty

crag·gy
cramp
cran·ber·ry
crane
cra·ni·al
cra·ni·um
crank
cranky
cran·ny
crape
crash·ing
crate
cra·ter
cra·vat
crave
cra·ven
crawl·er
cray·fish
cray·on
craze
creaky
cream
crease
cre·ate
cre·ation
cre·ative
cre·ativ·i·ty
cre·ator
crea·ture
crèche
cre·dence
cre·den·tial
cre·den·za
cred·i·ble
cred·it·able
cred·i·tor
cre·du·li·ty
cred·u·lous
creed
creek

creel

creep

creepy

cre·mate

cre·ma·to·ri·um

cre·ma·to·ry

crème de menthe

cren·el·late

cre·o·sote

crepe

crepe de chine

crepe su·zette

crep·i·tate

cre·pus·cu·lar

cre·scen·do

cres·cent

cress

cres·set

crest·fall·en

cre·tin

cre·tin·ism

cre·tonne

cre·vasse

crev·ice

crew·el

crib·bing

crick·et

crim·i·nal

crim·i·nal·i·ty

crim·i·nol·o·gy

crimp

crim·son

cringe

crin·kle

crin·o·line

crip·ple

cri·sis

crisp

criss·cross

cri·te·ri·on

crit·ic

crit·i·cal

crit·i·cism

crit·i·cize

cri·tique

cro·chet

crock·ery

croc·o·dile

cro·cus

crois·sant

crone

crook·ed

croon·er

crop·per

cro·quet

cro·quette

cro·sier

cross-eyed

cross-file

cross-in·dex

cross·ing

cross-legged

cross-pur·pose

cross·road

cross·wise

crotch

crotch·et

crotch·ety

crouch

croup

crou·pi·er

crou·ton

crowd

crow's nest

cru·cial

cru·ci·ble

cru·ci·fix

cru·ci·fix·ion

cru·ci·fy

crud

cru·di·ty

cru·el·ty

cru·et

cruise

cruis·er

crul·ler

crum·ble

crum·bly

crum·my

crum·ple

crunch

cru·sade

cruse

crus·ta·cean

crusty

crux

cry·ba·by

crypt

cryp·tic

cryp·to·gram

cryp·tog·ra·pher

crys·tal

crys·tal·line

crys·tal·lize

cub·by·hole

cu·bi·cle

cub·ism

cuck·oo

cu·cum·ber

cud·dle

cud·gel

cui·sine

cul-de-sac

cu·li·nary

cul·mi·nate

cul·mi·na·tion

cu·lotte

cul·pa·bil·i·ty

cul·pa·ble

cul·prit

cul·ti·vate
cul·ti·va·tor
cul·tur·al
cul·ture
cul·vert
cum·ber·some
cu·mu·la·tive
cu·ne·i·form
cun·ning
cup·ful
cu·pid·i·ty
cu·po·la
cur·able
cu·rate
cu·ra·tive
cu·ra·tor
cur·dle
cure-all
cur·few
cu·rio
cu·ri·os·i·ty
cu·ri·ous
curli·cue
curly
cur·mud·geon
cur·rant
cur·ren·cy
cur·rent
cur·ric·u·lar
cur·ric·u·lum
cur·ry
cur·sive
cur·so·ry
curt
cur·tail
cur·tain
curt·sy
cur·va·ceous
cur·va·ture
curve

cur·vi·lin·ear
cush·ion
cushy
cus·tard
cus·to·di·al
cus·to·di·an
cus·to·dy
cus·tom·ary
cus·tom-built
cus·tom·er
cus·tom·ize
cut-and-dried
cu·ta·ne·ous
cut·away
cute·sy
cu·ti·cle
cut·ie
cut·lass
cut·lery
cut·let
cut·throat
cut·ting
cy·ber·na·tion
cy·ber·net·ic
cy·ber·net·ics
cy·cle
cy·clist
cy·clone
cy·clo·ra·ma
cyg·net
cyl·in·der
cy·lin·dri·cal
cym·bal
cyn·ic
cyn·i·cal
cyn·i·cism
cy·no·sure
cy·press
cyst
czar

cza·ri·na
Czech

D

dab·ber
dab·ble
dab·bler
dab·bling
da·cha
dachs·hund
dac·tyl
da·da
da·da·ism
da·do
daf·fo·dil
daf·fy
daft
dag·ger
da·guerre·o·type
dahl·ia
dai·ly
dain·ti·er
dain·ty
dai·qui·ri
dairy
dairy·maid
dairy·man
da·is
dai·sy
dal·li·ance
dal·ly
dal·ma·tian
dam·age
dam·ag·ing
dam·a·scene
dam·ask
damn

dam·na·ble
dam·na·tion
dam·na·to·ry
damned
damnd·est
damn·ing
damp·en
dam·sel
dam·son
dance
dan·de·li·on
dan·der
dan·di·fy
dan·dle
dan·druff
dan·dy
dan·ger·ous
dan·gle
dan·seur
dan·seuse
dap·per
dap·ple
dare·dev·il
dare·say
dark·en
dar·ling
darned
dash·board
da·shi·ki
das·tard
das·tard·ly
da·ta
da·ta pro·ces·sor
date·line
da·tive
da·tum
daub
daugh·ter
daugh·ter-in-law
daunt

dau·phin
dav·en·port
da·vit
daw·dle
daw·dler
day·bed
day-care
day·dream
day·light
day·time
daze
daz·zle
dea·con
dea·con·ess
de·ac·ti·vate
dead-air space
dead·beat
dead·en
dead-end
dead·ened
dead·en·ing
dead·head
dead·li·er
dead·line
dead·lock
dead·pan
dead·weight
dead·wood
de·aer·ate
deaf·en
deaf-mute
deal·er·ship
deal·ing
dean·ery
dean's list
dearth
death
death·less
death·ly
de·ba·cle

de·bar
de·bark
de·base
de·bat·able
de·bate
de·bauch
de·bauch·ee
de·bauch·ery
de·ben·ture
de·bil·i·tate
de·bil·i·ty
deb·it
deb·o·nair
de·bone
de·bouch
de·brief
de·bris
debt
debt·or
de·bunk
de·but
deb·u·tant
deb·u·tante
de·cade
dec·a·dence
dec·a·den·cy
dec·a·dent
de·caf·fein·ate
deca·gon
de·cal
de·cal·ci·fi·ca·
    tion
de·cal·ci·fy
deca·logue
de·camp
de·cant
de·cant·er
de·cap·i·tate
de·cath·lon
de·cay

de·cease
de·ce·dent
de·ceit
de·ceit·ful
de·ceiv·able
de·ceive
de·cel·er·ate
de·cen·cy
de·cen·ni·al
de·cent
de·cen·tral·iza·
  tion
de·cen·tral·ize
de·cep·tion
de·cep·tive
de·cer·ti·fy
deci·bel
de·cide
de·cid·ing
de·cid·u·ous
dec·ile
dec·i·mal
dec·i·mate
de·ci·pher
de·ci·sion
de·ci·sive
deck·hand
de·claim
de·clam·a·to·ry
dec·la·ra·tion
de·clar·a·tive
de·clar·a·to·ry
de·clare
dé·clas·sé
de·clas·si·fy
de·clen·sion
dec·li·na·tion
de·cline
de·cliv·i·ty
de·coct

de·coc·tion
de·code
dé·col·le·tage
dé·col·le·té
de·com·mis·sion
de·com·press
de·con·ges·tant
de·con·ges·tion
de·con·se·crate
de·con·tam·i·nate
de·con·trol
de·cor
dec·o·rate
dec·o·ra·tion
dec·o·ra·tive
dec·o·ra·tor
dec·o·rous
de·co·rum
de·coy
de·crease
de·cree
de·crep·it
de·crep·i·tude
de·cry
de·dans
ded·i·cate
ded·i·ca·tion
de·duce
de·duct·ible
de·duc·tion
de·duc·tive
dee·jay
de-em·pha·size
deep·en
deep-root·ed
deep-seat·ed
de-es·ca·late
de·face
de fac·to
def·a·ma·tion

de·fame
de·fault
de·feat·ist
def·e·cate
de·fect
de·fec·tion
de·fec·tive
de·fend
de·fen·dant
de·fend·er
de·fense
de·fen·si·ble
de·fen·sive
de·fer
def·er·ence
def·er·ent
def·er·en·tial
de·fer·ral
de·ferred
de·fi·ance
de·fi·ant
de·fi·cien·cy
de·fi·cient
def·i·cit
de·fi·er
de·file
de·fin·able
de·fine
def·i·nite
def·i·ni·tion
de·fin·i·tive
de·flate
de·fla·tion
de·flect
de·flec·tion
de·flow·er
de·fog
de·fo·li·ant
de·fo·li·ate
de·formed

de·for·mi·ty
de·fraud
de·fray
de·frock
de·frost
deft
de·funct
de·fuse
de·fy
de·gen·er·a·cy
de·gen·er·ate
de·grad·able
deg·ra·da·tion
de·grade
de·grad·ed
de·grad·ing
de·gree
de·horn
de·hu·man·ize
de·hu·mid·i·fy
de·hy·drate
de·hy·dra·tion
de·hyp·no·tize
de·ice
de·i·fi·ca·tion
de·i·fy
deign
de·ism
de·ist
de·i·ty
dé·jà vu
de·ject
de·ject·ed
de·jec·tion
de ju·re
de·lay
de·lec·ta·ble
de·lec·ta·tion
del·e·gate
del·e·ga·tion

de·lete
del·e·te·ri·ous
de·le·tion
delft
de·lib·er·ate
de·lib·er·a·tion
del·i·ca·cy
del·i·cate
del·i·ca·tes·sen
de·li·cious
de·light
de·light·ful
de·light·ful·ness
de·light·some
de·lim·it
de·lin·eate
de·lin·ea·tion
de·lin·quen·cy
de·lin·quent
del·i·quesce
de·lir·i·ous
de·lir·i·um
de·lir·i·um tre·
   mens
de·liv·er
de·liv·er·ance
de·liv·ery
de·louse
del·ta
de·lude
del·uge
de·lu·sion
de·lu·sive
de·luxe
delve
dem·a·gog·ic
dem·a·gogue
dem·a·gogu·ery
dem·a·gogy
de·mand

de·mand·ing
de·mar·cate
de·mean
de·mean·or
de·ment·ed
de·men·tia prae·
   cox
de·mer·it
de·mesne
de·mil·i·ta·rize
demi·monde
de·mise
demi·tasse
de·mo·bi·lize
de·moc·ra·cy
dem·o·crat
dem·o·crat·ic
de·moc·ra·tize
de·mo·graph·ic
de·mog·ra·phy
dem·oi·selle
de·mol·ish
de·mo·li·tion
de·mon
de·mo·ni·ac
de·mon·stra·ble
dem·on·strate
dem·on·stra·tion
de·mon·stra·tive
dem·on·stra·tor
de·mor·al·ize
de·mote
de·mot·ic
de·mount
de·mur
de·mure
de·mur·ral
de·mur·rer
de·nat·u·ral·ize
de·na·tured

de·ni·al
den·i·grate
den·im
den·i·zen
de·nom·i·nate
de·nom·i·na·tion
de·nom·i·na·tor
de·no·ta·tion
de·no·ta·tive
de·note
de·noue·ment
de·nounce
de no·vo
dense
den·si·ty
den·tal
den·ti·frice
den·tist
den·tist·ry
den·ti·tion
den·ture
de·nu·cle·ar·ize
de·nude
de·nun·ci·a·tion
de·ny
de·odor·ant
de·odor·ize
de·part
de·part·ment
de·part·men·tal·ize
de·par·ture
de·pend
de·pend·abil·i·ty
de·pend·able
de·pen·dence
de·pen·den·cy
de·pen·dent
de·per·son·al·ize
de·pict

dep·i·late
de·pil·a·to·ry
de·plane
de·plete
de·plor·able
de·plore
de·ploy
de·po·nent
de·pop·u·late
de·port
de·port·able
de·por·ta·tion
de·por·tee
de·port·ment
de·pos·it
de·pos·i·tary
de·po·si·tion
de·pos·i·to·ry
de·pot
de·prave
de·prav·i·ty
dep·re·cate
dep·re·ca·to·ry
de·pre·ci·ate
de·pre·ci·a·tion
de·press
de·pres·sion
de·pres·sor
de·pri·va·tion
de·prive
depth
dep·u·ta·tion
dep·u·tize
dep·u·ty
de·rail
de·range
der·by
de·reg·u·la·tion
der·e·lict
der·e·lic·tion

de·ride
de ri·gueur
de·ri·sion
de·ri·sive
der·i·va·tion
de·riv·a·tive
de·rive
der·ma·tol·o·gist
der·ma·tol·o·gy
de·rog·a·to·ry
der·rick
der·ri·ere
der·vish
de·sa·li·nate
des·cant
de·scend
de·scen·dant
de·scent
de·scribe
de·scrip·tion
de·scrip·tive
des·e·crate
des·e·cra·tion
de·seg·re·gate
de·seg·re·ga·tion
des·ert
de·ser·tion
de·serve
des·ha·bille
des·ic·cant
des·ic·cate
de·sid·er·a·tum
de·sign
des·ig·nate
des·ig·na·tion
de·sir·abil·i·ty
de·sir·able
de·sire
de·sir·ous
de·sist

des·o·late
des·o·la·tion
de·spair
des·per·a·do
des·per·ate
des·per·a·tion
de·spi·ca·ble
de·spise
de·spite
de·spite·ful
de·spoil
de·spon·dence
de·spon·den·cy
des·pot
des·pot·ic
des·sert
de·sta·bi·lize
des·ti·na·tion
des·ti·ny
des·ti·tute
des·ti·tu·tion
de·stroy
de·stroy·er
de·struct
de·struc·ti·ble
de·struc·tion
de·struc·tive
de·sue·tude
des·ul·to·ry
de·tach
de·tach·ment
de·tail
de·tain
de·tain·er
de·tect
de·tec·tion
de·tec·tive
de·tec·tor
dé·tente
de·ten·tion

de·ter
de·ter·gent
de·te·ri·o·rate
de·te·ri·o·ra·tion
de·ter·min·able
de·ter·mi·nant
de·ter·mi·na·tion
de·ter·mine
de·ter·rence
de·ter·rent
de·test
de·test·able
de·tes·ta·tion
det·o·nate
det·o·na·tion
det·o·na·tor
de·tour
de·tox·i·cate
de·tract
de·trac·tion
det·ri·ment
det·ri·men·tal
de·tri·tus
deuce
de·val·u·ate
de·val·u·a·tion
dev·as·tate
dev·as·ta·tion
de·vel·op
de·vel·op·er
de·vel·op·ment
de·vi·ant
de·vi·ate
de·vi·a·tion
de·vi·a·tion·ist
de·vice
dev·il
dev·il·ish
dev·il·ment
de·vi·ous

de·vis·al
de·vise
de·void
de·vo·lu·tion
de·volve
de·vote
dev·o·tee
de·vo·tion
de·vour
de·vout
dewy
dex·ter·i·ty
dex·ter·ous
di·a·be·tes
di·a·bet·ic
di·a·ble·rie
di·a·bol·ic
di·ab·o·lism
di·ac·o·nate
di·a·crit·i·cal
di·a·dem
di·aer·e·sis
di·ag·nose
di·ag·no·sis
di·ag·nos·tic
di·ag·o·nal
di·a·gram
di·al
di·a·lect
di·a·lec·tic
di·a·lec·ti·cian
di·aled
di·a·logue
di·am·e·ter
di·a·met·ric
di·a·mond
di·a·pa·son
di·a·per
di·aph·a·nous
di·a·phragm

di·ar·rhea
di·a·ry
di·as·po·ra
dia·ther·my
dia·ton·ic
di·a·tribe
dice
dic·ey
di·chot·o·mous
di·chot·o·my
dic·tate
dic·ta·tion
dic·ta·tor
dic·ta·to·ri·al
dic·ta·tor·ship
dic·tion
dic·tio·nary
dic·tum
di·dac·tic
did·dle
die·sel
di·etary
di·etet·ic
di·eti·tian
dif·fer
dif·fer·ence
dif·fer·ent
dif·fer·en·tial
dif·fer·en·ti·ate
dif·fer·en·ti·a·
  tion
dif·fer·ent·ly
dif·fi·cult
dif·fi·cul·ty
dif·fi·dence
dif·fi·dent
dif·fuse
dif·fu·sion
dif·fu·sive

dif·fu·sive·ness
di·ges·tion
di·ges·tive
dig·gings
dig·it
dig·i·tal
dig·i·tal·is
dig·ni·fied
dig·ni·fy
dig·ni·tary
di·gress
di·gres·sion
di·gres·sive
di·he·dral
di·lap·i·date
di·late
di·la·tion
dil·a·to·ry
di·lem·ma
dil·et·tante
dil·et·tan·tism
dil·i·gence
dil·i·gent
dil·ly
di·lute
di·lu·tion
di·men·sion
di·min·ish
dim·i·nu·tion
di·min·u·tive
dim·mer
dim·ple
dim·wit
dim-wit·ted
di·nette
din·ghy
din·ky
din·ner·ware
di·no·saur

di·oc·e·san
di·o·cese
di·ora·ma
diph·the·ria
diph·thong
diph·thong·iza·
  tion
diph·thong·ize
di·plo·ma
di·plo·ma·cy
dip·lo·mat
dip·lo·mate
dip·lo·mat·ic
dip·per
dire
di·rect
di·rec·tion
di·rec·tive
di·rect·ly
di·rec·tor·ate
di·rec·to·ry
dirge
di·ri·gi·ble
dirndl
dirt·i·er
dirt·i·ness
dirty
dis·abil·i·ty
dis·able
dis·abuse
dis·ad·van·tage
dis·ad·van·taged
dis·ad·van·ta·
  geous
dis·af·fect
dis·af·fil·i·ate
dis·agree·able
dis·ap·pear
dis·ap·point

dis·ap·point·
  ment
dis·ap·pro·ba·
  tion
dis·ap·prov·al
dis·ap·prove
dis·arm·ing
dis·ar·range
dis·as·sem·ble
dis·as·so·ci·ate
di·sas·ter
dis·avow
dis·band
dis·bar
dis·be·lief
dis·be·lieve
dis·burse
dis·burse·ment
dis·card
dis·cern
dis·cern·ment
dis·charge
dis·ci·ple
dis·ci·pli·nar·i·an
dis·ci·plin·ary
dis·ci·pline
dis·claim
dis·claim·er
dis·close
dis·clo·sure
dis·col·or·ation
dis·com·bob·u·
  late
dis·com·fi·ture
dis·com·mode
dis·com·pose
dis·con·cert
dis·con·nect
dis·con·so·late

dis·con·tent
dis·con·tinu·ance
dis·con·tin·ue
dis·con·ti·nu·ity
dis·con·tin·u·ous
dis·cord
dis·cor·dance
dis·cor·dan·cy
dis·cor·dant
dis·co·theque
dis·count
dis·count·able
dis·cour·age
dis·cour·age·
  ment
dis·course
dis·cour·te·ous
dis·cov·er
dis·cred·it
dis·cred·it·able
dis·creet
dis·crep·an·cy
dis·crep·ant
dis·crete
dis·cre·tion
dis·cre·tion·ary
dis·crim·i·nate
dis·crim·i·na·tion
dis·crim·i·na·to·
  ry
dis·cur·sive
dis·cus
dis·cuss
dis·cus·sant
dis·cus·sion
dis·dain
dis·dain·ful
dis·ease
dis·em·bark

dis·em·body
dis·em·bow·el
dis·en·chant
dis·en·cum·ber
dis·en·fran·chise
dis·en·gage
dis·en·tan·gle
dis·es·tab·lish
dis·fa·vor
dis·fig·ure
dis·func·tion
dis·gorge
dis·grace
dis·grun·tle
dis·guise
dis·gust
dis·gust·ful
dis·gust·ing
dis·ha·bille
di·shev·el
dis·hon·est
dis·hon·or
dis·hon·or·able
dis·il·lu·sion
dis·in·cli·na·tion
dis·in·cline
dis·in·fect
dis·in·fec·tant
dis·in·gen·u·ous
dis·in·her·it
dis·in·te·grate
dis·in·te·gra·tion
dis·in·ter
dis·in·ter·est
dis·in·ter·est·ed
dis·joint·ed
dis·junc·tive
disk
dis·like

dis·lo·cate
dis·lo·ca·tion
dis·lodge
dis·loy·al
dis·mal
dis·man·tle
dis·may
dis·may·ing·ly
dis·miss
dis·miss·al
dis·mount
dis·obe·di·ence
dis·obe·di·ent
dis·obey
dis·or·der
dis·or·ga·nized
dis·own
dis·par·age
dis·pa·rate
dis·par·i·ty
dis·pas·sion·ate
dis·patch
dis·pel
dis·pens·able
dis·pen·sa·ry
dis·pen·sa·tion
dis·pense
dis·perse
dis·per·sion
dispir·it·ed
dis·place
dis·place·ment
dis·play
dis·please
dis·plea·sure
dis·pos·able
dis·pos·al
dis·po·si·tion
dis·pos·sess
dis·pro·por·tion

dis·pro·por·tion·
  ate
dis·prove
dis·pu·tant
dis·pu·ta·tion
dis·pu·ta·tious
dis·qual·i·fi·ca·
  tion
dis·qual·i·fy
dis·qui·et
dis·qui·si·tion
dis·re·gard
dis·re·mem·ber
dis·re·pair
dis·rep·u·ta·ble
dis·re·pute
dis·re·spect
dis·re·spect·able
dis·robe
dis·rupt
dis·sat·is·fac·tion
dis·sat·is·fac·to·
  ry
dis·sat·is·fy
dis·sect
dis·sect·ed
dis·sec·tion
dis·sem·ble
dis·sem·i·nate
dis·sen·sion
dis·sent
dis·sent·er
dis·ser·ta·tion
dis·ser·vice
dis·si·dent
dis·sim·i·lar
dis·si·pate
dis·si·pa·tion
dis·so·ci·ate
dis·so·ci·a·tion

dis·sol·u·ble
dis·so·lute
dis·so·lu·tion
dis·solve
dis·so·nance
dis·so·nant
dis·spir·it
dis·suade
dis·sua·sion
dis·taff
dis·tain
dis·tance
dis·tant
dis·taste
dis·taste·ful
dis·tem·per
dis·tend
dis·ten·sion
dis·till
dis·til·late
dis·til·la·tion
dis·till·er
dis·till·ery
dis·tinct
dis·tinc·tion
dis·tinc·tive
dis·tin·gué
dis·tin·guish
dis·tort
dis·tor·tion
dis·tract
dis·trac·tion
dis·traint
dis·trait
dis·traught
dis·tress
dis·trib·ute
dis·tri·bu·tion
dis·trib·u·tive
dis·trib·u·tor

dis·trict
dis·trust
dis·trust·ful
dis·turb
dis·tur·bance
dis·uni·ty
dis·use
dith·er
dith·y·ramb
dit·to
dit·ty
di·uret·ic
di·ur·nal
di·va·gate
di·va·ga·tion
di·van
di·var·i·cate
di·var·i·ca·tion
di·verge
di·ver·gence
di·ver·gen·cy
di·ver·gent
di·vers
di·verse
di·ver·si·fy
di·ver·sion
di·ver·sion·ist
di·ver·si·ty
di·vert
di·ver·tisse·ment
di·vest
di·ves·ti·ture
di·vide
div·i·dend
div·i·na·tion
di·vin·i·ty
di·vis·i·bil·i·ty
di·vis·i·ble
di·vi·sion
di·vi·sive

di·vi·sor
di·vorce
di·vor·cée
di·vorce·ment
div·ot
di·vulge
div·vy
diz·zi·ness
diz·zy
do·cent
doc·ile
dock·age
dock·et
doc·tor·ate
doc·tri·naire
doc·trin·al
doc·trine
doc·u·ment
doc·u·men·ta·ry
doc·u·men·ta·
   tion
dod·der
dodg·er
do·do
dog·ger·el
dog·gie bag
dog·gy
dog·ma
dog·mat·ic
dog·ma·tism
dog·nap
do-good·er
doi·ly
dol·drums
dole·ful
dol·lop
dol·ly
dol·men
do·lor·ous
dol·phin

do·main
do·mes·tic
do·mes·ti·cate
do·mes·tic·i·ty
dom·i·cile
do·mi·cil·i·ary
dom·i·nance
dom·i·nate
dom·i·na·tion
dom·i·neer·ing
do·min·ion
dom·i·no
do·nate
do·na·tion
don·key
don·nish
don·ny·brook
doo·dad
doo·dle
doo·hick·ey
doom·say·er
dope·ster
dop·ey
dor·man·cy
dor·mant
dor·mer
dor·mi·to·ry
dor·sal
dos·age
do-si-do
dos·sier
dot·age
dot·ty
dou·ble
dou·ble-bar·reled
dou·ble-breast·ed
dou·ble-cross
dou·ble date
dou·ble en·ten·
   dre

dou·blet
doubt·ful
douche
dough
dough·nut
dough·ty
dour
douse
dove·tail
dow·a·ger
dowdy
dow·el
down·grade
down·hill
down·pour
down·right
down·stage
down-the-line
down-to-earth
dow·ry
dowse
dox·ol·o·gy
doy·en
dra·co·ni·an
draft
drafts·man
drag·net
drag·on
dra·goon
drag race
drag racing
drain·age
drake
dra·ma
dra·mat·ic
dra·mat·ics
dra·ma·tis
  per·so·nae
dra·ma·tist
dra·ma·ti·za·tion

dra·ma·tize
dra·ma·tur·gy
drap·ery
dras·tic
draught
drawl
dray·man
dread·ful
dread·nought
dreamy
drea·ry
dredge
dress·er
dress·mak·er
dress·mak·ing
drib·ble
drib·let
dried-up
dri·er
dri·est
dril·ling
drill·mas·ter
drink·able
drip-dry
drip·less
drip·ping
drip·py
drive-in
driv·el
driv·en
drive·way
driv·ing
driz·zle
droll·ery
drom·e·dary
drone
droopy
drop·out
drop·per
drop·si·cal

drop·sy
drosh·ky
dross
drought
drowse
drowsy
drudg·ery
drudg·ing
drug·gist
dru·id
drunk·ard
drunk·en
druth·ers
du·al·ism
du·al·i·ty
du·al-pur·pose
du·bi·ety
du·bi·ous
du·bi·ta·ble
du·cal
duc·at
duch·ess
duchy
duck·ling
ducky
duct
duc·tile
dud·geon
du·el
du·en·na
duf·fel
duf·fer
dul·cet
dul·ci·mer
dull·ard
dull·ish
dulls·ville
dumm·kopf
dum·my
dun·der·head

dun·geon
dun·nage
du·plex
du·pli·cate
du·pli·ca·tion
du·pli·ca·tor
du·plic·i·tous
du·plic·i·ty
du·ra·ble
du·ra·tion
du·te·ous
du·ti·able
du·ti·ful
dwell·ing
dwin·dle
dyb·buk
dyed-in-the-wool
dy·ing
dy·nam·ic
dy·na·mism
dy·na·mite
dy·nas·ty
dys·en·tery
dys·func·tion
dys·pep·tic
dys·tro·phy

E

ea·ger
ea·ger·ly
ea·gle
ea·glet
ear·ache
ear·drum
ear·ful
ear·ing
earl

ear·li·er
ear·lobe
ear·ly
ear·mark
ear·muff
earn
ear·nest
earn·ings
ear·phone
ear·ring
ear·shot
ear·split·ting
earth·en
earth·en·ware
earth·ly
earth·quake
earth·shak·ing
earth·ward
earth·worm
earthy
ear·wax
ea·sel
ease·ment
eas·i·ly
eas·i·ness
east·er·ly
east·ern
east·ern·most
east·ward
easy·go·ing
eat·able
eat·ery
eat·ing
eau de co·logne
eaves
eaves·drop
ebb tide
eb·o·ny
ebul·lience
ebul·lien·cy

ebul·lient
eb·ul·li·tion
ec·cen·tric
ec·cen·tric·i·ty
ec·cle·si·as·tic
ec·cle·si·as·ti·cal
ec·cle·si·as·ti·cism
ec·cle·si·ol·o·gy
ec·dys·i·ast
ech·e·lon
echo
ech·oed
ech·oes
echo·ing
echo·la·lia
éclair
éclat
eclec·tic
eclec·ti·cism
eclipse
eclip·tic
ec·logue
ecol·o·gist
ecol·o·gy
eco·nom·ic
eco·nom·ics
econ·o·mist
econ·o·mize
econ·o·my
ecru
ec·sta·sy
ec·stat·ic
ec·to·mor·phic
ec·to·plasm
ec·u·men·i·cal
ec·u·men·i·cism
ecu·me·nism
ec·ze·ma
ed·dies

ed·dy
edel·weiss
edge
edge·ways
edge·wise
edg·ing
edgy
edict
ed·i·fi·ca·tion
ed·i·fice
ed·i·fy
ed·it
edi·tion
ed·i·tor
ed·i·to·ri·al
ed·i·to·ri·al·ize
ed·u·ca·ble
ed·u·cate
ed·u·ca·tion
ed·u·ca·tion·ist
ed·u·ca·tive
ed·u·ca·tor
educe
eel
e'er
ee·rie
ee·ri·ly
ee·ri·ness
ef·face
ef·fect
ef·fec·tive
ef·fec·tu·al
ef·fec·tu·al·ly
ef·fec·tu·ate
ef·fem·i·na·cy
ef·fem·i·nate
ef·fer·ent
ef·fer·vesce
ef·fer·ves·cence

ef·fer·ves·cent
ef·fete
ef·fi·ca·cious
ef·fi·ca·cy
ef·fi·cien·cy
ef·fi·cient
ef·fi·gy
ef·flo·res·cence
ef·flu·ence
ef·flu·ent
ef·flu·vi·um
ef·fort
ef·fort·ful
ef·fron·tery
ef·ful·gence
ef·ful·gent
ef·fuse
ef·fu·sion
ef·fu·sive
egal·i·tar·i·an
egal·i·tar·i·an·
 ism
egg·head
egg·nog
egg·plant
egg roll
egg·shell
ego·cen·tric
ego·ism
ego·ist
ego·is·tic
ego·ma·ni·ac
ego·tism
ego·tist
ego·tis·tic
ego·tis·ti·cal
ego-trip
egre·gious
egress

egret
ei·der·down
eigh·teen
eigh·teenth
eight·fold
eighth
eight·ies
eight·i·eth
eighty
ei·ther
ejac·u·late
ejac·u·la·tion
ejac·u·la·to·ry
eject
ejec·tor
eke
eked
ek·ing
elab·o·rate
elab·o·ra·tion
élan
élan vi·tal
elapse
elas·tic
elas·tic·i·ty
elas·ti·cized
elate
ela·tion
el·bow
el·der
el·der·ly
elect
elec·tion
elec·tion·eer
elec·tive
elec·tor
elec·tor·al
elec·tric
elec·tri·cian

elec·tric·i·ty
elec·tri·fied
elec·tri·fy
elec·tri·fy·ing
elec·tro·car·dio·gram
elec·tro·cute
elec·trode
elec·trol·y·sis
elec·tro·lyte
elec·tro·mag·net
elec·tron
elec·tron·ic
elec·tro·plate
elec·tro·type
elec·tu·ary
el·ee·mos·y·nary
el·e·gance
el·e·gan·cy
el·e·gant
ele·gi·ac
el·e·gize
el·e·gy
el·e·ment
el·e·men·tal
el·e·men·ta·ry
el·e·phant
el·e·phan·ti·a·sis
el·e·phan·tine
el·e·vate
el·e·va·tion
el·e·va·tor
elev·en
elev·enth
elf·in
elf·ish
elic·it
elic·i·tor
elide

el·i·gi·ble
elim·i·nate
elim·i·na·tor
elim·i·na·to·ry
eli·sion
elite
elit·ism
elix·ir
elk
el·lipse
el·lip·sis
el·lip·tic
el·lip·ti·cal
el·o·cu·tion
el·o·cu·tion·ist
elon·gate
elon·ga·tion
elope
el·o·quence
el·o·quent
else·where
elu·ci·date
elu·ci·da·tor
elude
elu·sive
elu·vi·um
elves
ely·sian
ema·ci·ate
em·a·nate
em·a·na·tion
eman·ci·pate
eman·ci·pa·tion
eman·ci·pa·tor
eman·ci·pa·to·ry
emas·cu·late
emas·cu·la·tor
em·balm
em·balm·er

em·bank·ment
em·bar·go
em·bar·goes
em·bark
em·bar·ka·tion
em·bar·rass
em·bar·rass·ing·ly
em·bar·rass·ment
em·bas·sy
em·bat·tle
em·bed
em·bed·ded
em·bed·ding
em·bed·ment
em·bel·lish
em·bel·lish·ment
em·ber
em·bez·zle
em·bez·zler
em·bit·ter
em·blaze
em·bla·zon
em·blem
em·blem·at·ic
em·bod·ied
em·bodi·ment
em·body
em·body·ing
em·bold·en
em·bo·lism
em·bo·lus
em·bon·point
em·boss
em·bou·chure
em·bowed
em·bow·eled
em·brace

em·brace·able
em·brac·ing
em·bra·sure
em·bro·cate
em·bro·ca·tion
em·broi·der
em·broi·dery
em·broil
em·bryo
em·bry·ol·o·gist
em·bry·ol·o·gy
em·bry·on·ic
em·cee
em·ceed
em·cee·ing
emend
emen·date
emen·da·tion
em·er·ald
emerge
emer·gence
emer·gen·cy
emer·gent
emer·i·tus
em·ery
emet·ic
em·i·grant
em·i·grate
émi·gré
em·i·nence
em·i·nent
emir
emir·ate
em·is·sary
emis·sion
emit
Em·my
emol·lient
emol·u·ment
emote

emot·ing
emo·tion
emo·tion·al
emo·tion·al·ism
emo·tion·less
emo·tive
em·pa·thet·ic
em·pa·thize
em·pa·thy
em·per·or
em·pha·sis
em·pha·size
em·phat·ic
em·phy·se·ma
em·pire
em·pir·ic
em·pir·i·cal
em·pir·i·cism
em·place
em·place·ment
em·plane
em·ploy
em·ploy·able
em·ploy·abil·i·ty
em·ploy·ee
em·ploy·ment
em·po·ri·um
em·pow·er
em·press
em·prise
emp·ti·ness
emp·ty
em·pur·ple
em·py·re·an
em·u·late
em·u·la·tion
em·u·la·tor
em·u·lous
emul·si·fi·er
emul·si·fy

emul·sion
en·able
en·act
en·act·ment
enam·el
enam·el·ware
en·am·or
en bloc
en·camp
en·camp·ment
en·cap·su·late
en·case·ment
en·ceinte
en·ce·phal·ic
en·ceph·a·lit·ic
en·ceph·a·li·tis
en·chant
en·chant·ment
en·chant·ress
en·chi·la·da
en·chi·rid·i·on
en·ci·pher
en·cir·cle
en·clasp
en·clave
en·clit·ic
en·close
en·clo·sure
en·code
en·co·mi·um
en·com·pass
en·core
en·coun·ter
en·cour·age
en·croach
en·crust
en·crus·ta·tion
en·cum·ber
en·cum·brance
en·cyc·li·cal

en·cy·clo·pe·dia
en·cy·clo·pe·dic
en·dan·ger
en·dear·ment
en·deav·or
en·dem·ic
en·dem·i·cal·ly
en·dive
end·less
en·do·crine
en·do·cri·nol·o·gy
en·dog·e·nous
en·dog·e·ny
en·dorse
en·dors·ee
en·dorse·ment
en·dors·er
en·dow
en·dow·ment
en·due
en·dur·able
en·dur·ance
en·dure
en·dur·ing
en·e·ma
en·e·my
en·er·get·ic
en·er·get·i·cal·ly
en·er·gize
en·er·giz·er
en·er·gy
en·er·vate
en·er·va·tion
en·fant ter·ri·ble
en·fee·ble
en·fee·ble·ment
en·fi·lade
en·fold
en·force
en·fran·chise

en·gage
en·gag·ed
en·gage·ment
en·gag·ing
en·gen·der
en·gine
en·gi·neer
en·gi·neer·ing
en·gorge
en·graft
en·grave
en·grav·ing
en·gross
en·gross·ing
en·gulf
en·hance
enig·ma
enig·mat·ic
enig·mat·i·cal
en·join
en·joy
en·joy·ment
en·kin·dle
en·large
en·large·ment
en·light·en
en·light·en·ment
en·list
en·liv·en
en masse
en·mesh
en·mi·ty
en·no·ble
en·nui
enor·mi·ty
enor·mous
enough
en pas·sant
en·plane
en prise

en·quire
en·rage
en·rapt
en·rap·ture
en·rich
en·robe
en·roll
en·roll·ment
en·sconce
en·sem·ble
en·shrine
en·shroud
en·sign
en·slave
en·slave·ment
en·snare
en·snarl
en·sue
en·sure
en·tab·la·ture
en·tail
en·tan·gle
en·tan·gle·ment
en·tente
en·ter
en·ter·ic
en·ter·i·tis
en·ter·prise
en·ter·pris·ing
en·ter·tain
en·ter·tain·ing
en·ter·tain·ment
en·thrall
en·throne
en·thuse
en·thu·si·asm
en·thu·si·ast
en·thu·si·as·tic
en·thy·meme
en·tice

en·tice·ment
en·tire
en·tire·ty
en·ti·tle
en·ti·tle·ment
en·ti·tling
en·ti·ty
en·tomb
en·to·mol·o·gy
en·tou·rage
en·tr'acte
en·trails
en·train
en·trance
en·trant
en·trap
en·treat
en·treaty
en·tre·chat
en·trée
en·trench
en·tre·pre·neur
en·tre·pre·neur·ial
en·trust
en·try
en·try·way
en·twine
enu·mer·ate
enu·mer·a·tor
enun·ci·ate
en·ure·sis
en·vel·op
en·ve·lope
en·ven·om
en·vi·able
en·vi·ous
en·vi·ron
en·vi·ron·ment

en·vi·ron·men·tal·ly
en·vi·ron·men·tal·ism
en·vi·ron·men·tal·ist
en·vi·rons
en·vis·age
en·vi·sion
en·voi
en·voy
en·vy
en·zyme
eon
ep·au·let
épée
epergne
ephe·bic
ephed·rine
ephem·er·al
ep·ic
ep·i·cene
epi·cen·ter
ep·i·cure
ep·i·cu·re·an
ep·i·cu·re·an·ism
epi·cy·cle
ep·i·dem·ic
ep·i·de·mi·ol·o·gy
epi·der·mal
epi·der·mis
epi·glot·tis
ep·i·gram
ep·i·gram·mat·ic
ep·i·graph
ep·i·lep·sy
ep·i·lep·tic
ep·i·logue
epiph·a·nous

epiph·a·ny
epis·co·pa·cy
epis·co·pal
Epis·co·pa·lian
epis·co·pate
ep·i·sode
ep·i·sod·ic
ep·i·ste·mic
epis·te·mol·o·gy
epis·tle
epis·to·lary
ep·i·taph
ep·i·thet
epit·o·me
epit·o·mize
e plu·ri·bus unum
ep·och
ep·och·al
ep·ode
ep·onym
epon·y·mous
ep·oxy
equa·ble
equa·bly
equal
equal·i·ty
equal·ize
equal·iz·er
equal·ly
equa·nim·i·ty
equate
equa·tion
equa·tor
equa·to·ri·al
equer·ry
eques·tri·an
eques·tri·enne
equi·an·gu·lar

equi·dis·tant
equi·lat·er·al
equil·i·brate
equil·i·bra·tion
equil·i·bra·tor
equi·li·brist
equi·lib·ri·um
equine
equi·noc·tial
equi·nox
equip
eq·ui·page
equip·ment
equi·poise
equi·prob·a·ble
eq·ui·ta·ble
eq·ui·ta·tion
eq·ui·ty
equiv·a·lence
equiv·a·len·cy
equiv·a·lent
equiv·o·cal
equiv·o·cate
erad·i·cate
erad·i·ca·tion
erad·i·ca·tor
erase
eras·er
era·sure
erect
erec·tile
erec·tion
erec·tor
er·e·mite
er·mine
erode
erod·ing
erog·e·nous
ero·sion

ero·sive
erot·ic
erot·i·ca
erot·i·cism
er·rand
er·rant
er·ra·ta
er·rat·ic
er·ra·tum
er·ro·ne·ous
er·ror
erst·while
eruc·ta·tion
er·u·dite
er·u·di·tion
erupt
erup·tion
erup·tive
ery·sip·e·las
es·ca·drille
es·ca·late
es·ca·la·tion
es·ca·la·tor
es·cap·able
es·ca·pade
es·cape
es·cap·ee
es·cap·ing
es·cap·ism
es·car·got
es·ca·role
es·carp·ment
es·cha·to·log·i·cal
es·cha·tol·o·gy
es·chew
es·cort
es·cri·toire
es·crow
es·cutch·eon

Es·ki·mo
esoph·a·gus
es·o·ter·ic
es·pa·drille
es·pal·ier
es·pe·cial
es·pi·al
es·pi·o·nage
es·pla·nade
es·pous·al
es·pouse
espres·so
es·prit de corps
es·py
es·quire
es·say
es·say·ist
es·sence
es·sen·tial
es·sen·tial·ism
es·sen·ti·al·i·ty
es·sen·tial·ly
es·tab·lish
es·tab·lish·ment
es·ta·mi·net
es·tate
es·teem
es·ti·ma·ble
es·ti·mate
es·ti·ma·tion
es·ti·ma·tor
es·top
es·top·pel
es·trange
es·tu·ary
esu·ri·ent
éta·gère
et al
et·cet·era

etch
etch·ing
eter·nal
eter·ni·ty
ether
ethe·re·al
ethe·re·al·ly
ether·ize
eth·ic
eth·i·cal
eth·i·cist
eth·nic
eth·nic·i·ty
eth·no·cen·tric
eth·nol·o·gy
ethos
eti·o·late
eti·ol·o·gy
et·i·quette
étude
et·y·mo·log·i·cal
et·y·mol·o·gy
eu·ca·lyp·tus
Eu·cha·rist
eu·chre
eu·clid·e·an
eu·gen·ic
eu·gen·i·cist
eu·gen·ics
eu·lo·gize
eu·lo·gy
eu·nuch
eu·phe·mism
eu·phe·mis·ti·cal·ly
eu·pho·ny
eu·pho·ria
eu·phu·ism
eu·re·ka
Eu·ro·dol·lar

Eu·ro·pe·an
eu·ryth·mics
eu·tha·na·sia
eu·then·ics
evac·u·ate
evac·u·a·tion
evac·u·ee
evade
eval·u·ate
ev·a·nesce
ev·a·nes·cence
ev·a·nes·cent
evan·gel
evan·gel·i·cal
evan·ge·lism
evan·ge·list
evan·ge·lize
evap·o·rate
evap·o·ra·tion
evap·o·ra·tor
eva·sion
eva·sive
even·hand·ed
eve·ning
event
event·ful
even·tu·al
even·tu·al·i·ty
even·tu·ate
ev·er·glade
ev·er·green
ev·er·last·ing
ev·er·more
ev·ery
ev·ery·body
ev·ery·day
ev·ery·man
ev·ery·one
ev·ery·place
ev·ery·thing

ev·ery·where
ev·ery which way
evict
ev·i·dence
ev·i·dent
ev·i·den·tial
ev·i·dent·ly
evil
evil·do·er
evil·do·ing
evil-mind·ed
evince
evis·cer·ate
evo·ca·tion
evoc·a·tive
evoke
evo·lu·tion
evolve
ew·er
ex·ac·er·bate
ex·act
ex·ac·tion
ex·ac·ti·tude
ex·act·ly
ex·ag·ger·ate
ex·alt
ex·al·ta·tion
ex·am
ex·a·men
ex·am·i·na·tion
ex·am·ine
ex·am·in·er
ex·am·ple
ex·arch
ex·as·per·ate
ex·as·per·a·tion
ex ca·the·dra
ex·ca·vate
ex·ca·va·tion
ex·ca·va·tor

ex·ceed
ex·cel
ex·cel·lence
ex·cel·len·cy
ex·cel·lent
ex·cel·si·or
ex·cept
ex·cep·tion
ex·cep·tion·able
ex·cep·tion·al
ex·cerpt
ex·cess
ex·ces·sive
ex·ces·sive·ly
ex·change
ex·change·able
ex·che·quer
ex·cise
ex·cit·able
ex·ci·ta·tion
ex·cite
ex·cite·ment
ex·cit·er
ex·claim
ex·cla·ma·tion
ex·clam·a·to·ry
ex·clud·able
ex·clude
ex·clu·sion
ex·clu·sive
ex·com·mu·ni·
cate
ex·co·ri·ate
ex·cre·ment
ex·cres·cence
ex·cre·ta
ex·cre·tion
ex·cru·ci·at·ing
ex·cul·pate
ex·cul·pa·to·ry

ex·cur·sion
ex·cur·sion·ist
ex·cur·sive
ex·cus·able
ex·cus·ably
ex·cu·sa·to·ry
ex·cuse
ex·cus·ing
ex·e·cra·bly
ex·e·crate
ex·e·cra·tion
ex·e·cute
ex·e·cu·tion
ex·ec·u·tive
ex·ec·u·tor
ex·ec·u·trix
ex·e·ge·sis
ex·e·get·ist
ex·em·plar
ex·em·pla·ry
ex·em·pli·fy
ex·empt
ex·emp·tion
ex·er·cise
ex·ert
ex·er·tion
ex·e·unt
ex·hal·ant
ex·ha·la·tion
ex·hale
ex·haust
ex·haust·ible
ex·haus·tion
ex·haus·tive
ex·hib·it
ex·hi·bi·tion
ex·hi·bi·tion·ism
ex·hil·a·rate
ex·hil·a·ra·tion
ex·hort

ex·hor·ta·tion
ex·hor·ta·tive
ex·hor·ta·to·ry
ex·hume
ex·i·gence
ex·i·gen·cy
ex·i·gent
ex·i·gu·ity
ex·ig·u·ous
ex·ile
ex·ist
ex·is·tence
ex·is·tent
ex·is·ten·tial
ex·is·ten·tial·ism
ex·o·dus
ex of·fi·cio
ex·og·a·my
ex·on·er·ate
ex·or·bi·tant
ex·or·cise
ex·or·cism
ex·or·di·um
ex·o·ter·ic
ex·ot·ic
ex·panse
ex·pan·si·ble
ex·pan·sion
ex·pan·sive
ex·pa·ti·ate
ex·pa·tri·ate
ex·pec·tance
ex·pec·tan·cy
ex·pec·tant
ex·pec·ta·tion
ex·pec·to·rant
ex·pec·to·rate
ex·pe·di·ence
ex·pe·di·en·cy
ex·pe·di·ent

ex·pe·dite
ex·pe·dit·er
ex·pe·di·tion
ex·pe·di·tion·ary
ex·pe·di·tious
ex·pel
ex·pelled
ex·pend
ex·pend·able
ex·pen·di·ture
ex·pense
ex·pen·sive
ex·pe·ri·ence
ex·pe·ri·en·tial
ex·per·i·ment
ex·per·i·ment·er
ex·per·i·men·tal
ex·pert
ex·per·tise
ex·pi·a·ble
ex·pi·ate
ex·pi·a·tion
ex·pi·ra·tion
ex·pi·ra·to·ry
ex·pire
ex·plain
ex·pla·na·tion
ex·plan·a·to·ry
ex·ple·tive
ex·pli·ca·ble
ex·pli·cate
ex·plic·it
ex·plode
ex·ploit
ex·ploi·ta·tion
ex·plo·ra·tion
ex·plor·ative
ex·plor·ato·ry
ex·plore
ex·plo·si·ble

ex·plo·sion
ex·plo·sive
ex·po·nent
ex·po·nen·tial
ex·port
ex·por·ta·tion
ex·pose
ex·po·sé
ex·po·si·tion
ex·pos·i·to·ry
ex post fac·to
ex·pos·tu·late
ex·post·tu·la·tion
ex·po·sure
ex·pound
ex·press
ex·pres·sion
ex·pres·sion·less
ex·pres·sive
ex·pres·sive·ness
ex·press·ly
ex·pro·pri·ate
ex·pro·pri·a·tion
ex·pul·sion
ex·punge
ex·pur·gate
ex·qui·site
ex·tant
ex·tem·po·ra·ne·
  ity
ex·tem·po·ra·ne·
  ous
ex·tem·po·rary
ex·tem·po·re
ex·tem·po·ri·za·
  tion
ex·tem·po·rize
ex·tend
ex·ten·si·ble
ex·ten·sion

ex·ten·sive
ex·ten·sive·ly
ex·tent
ex·ten·u·ate
ex·ten·u·a·tion
ex·te·ri·or
ex·ter·mi·nate
ex·ter·mi·na·tor
ex·ter·nal
ex·tinct
ex·tinc·tion
ex·tin·guish
ex·tin·guish·er
ex·tir·pate
ex·tol
ex·tort
ex·tor·tion
ex·tor·tion·ate
ex·tract
ex·trac·tion
ex·tra·cur·ric·u·
  lar
ex·tra·dit·able
ex·tra·dite
ex·tra·di·tion
ex·tra·mar·i·tal
ex·tra·mu·ral
ex·tra·ne·ous
ex·traor·di·nari·
  ly
ex·traor·di·nary
ex·trap·o·late
ex·tra·sen·so·ry
ex·tra·ter·ri·to·
  ri·al·i·ty
ex·trav·a·gance
ex·trav·a·gant
ex·trav·a·gan·za
ex·tra·ver·sion
ex·tra·vert

ex·treme
ex·trem·ism
ex·trem·i·ty
ex·tri·cate
ex·trin·sic
ex·trude
ex·tru·sion
ex·tru·sive
ex·u·ber·ance
ex·u·ber·ant
ex·ude
ex·ult
ex·ul·tant
ex·ul·ta·tion
eye·brow
eyed
eye·ful
eye·lash
eye-open·er
eye·sight
eye·wash
eye·wit·ness
ey·rie

F

fa·ble
fab·ric
fab·ri·cate
fab·u·lous
fa·cade
face·less·ness
face-off
face-sav·ing
fac·et
fa·ce·ti·ae
fa·ce·tious
fa·cia

fa·cial
fa·cies
fac·ile
fa·cil·i·tate
fa·cil·i·ta·tion
fa·cil·i·ty
fac·ing
fac·sim·i·le
fac·tion
fac·tious
fac·ti·tious
fac·ti·tive
fac·tor
fac·to·ri·al
fac·to·ry
fac·to·tum
fac·tu·al
fac·ul·ta·tive
fac·ul·ty
fade·away
fa·er·ie
fag·got
Fahr·en·heit
fa·ience
faille
fail·ure
faint·heart·ed
fair·ground
fair·ish
fair·ly
fair shake
fair-trade
fair·way
fair-weather
fairy
fairy·land
fairy-tale
fait ac·com·pli
faith·ful
faith·less

fa·kir
fal·con
fal·con·er
fal·con·ry
fal·la·cious
fal·la·cy
fal·li·bil·i·ty
fal·li·ble
fal·lo·pi·an tube
fal·low
fal·set·to
fals·ie
fal·si·fy
fal·si·ty
fal·ter
famed
fa·mil·ial
fa·mil·iar·i·ty
fa·mil·iar·ize
fam·i·ly
fam·ine
fam·ish
fa·mous
fa·nat·ic
fa·nat·i·cism
fan·ci·er
fan·ci·ful
fan·ci·ly
fan·ci·ness
fan·cy
fan·dan·go
fan·fare
fan·light
fan·ny
fan·ta·sia
fan·ta·size
fan·tasm
fan·tas·tic
fan·ta·sy
far·away

farce
far·ceur
far·ci·cal
fare-thee-well
far·fetched
fa·ri·na
far·i·na·ceous
farm·er
faro
far·ra·go
far·ri·er
far·row
far·sight·ed
far·ther
far·thing
fas·ces
fas·cia
fas·ci·nate
fas·ci·na·tion
fas·ci·na·tor
fas·cism
fas·cist
fash·ion
fash·ion·able
fas·ten
fas·tid·i·ous
fa·tal
fa·tal·ism
fa·tal·i·ty
fa·tal·ly
fat·ed
fate·ful
fa·ther
fa·ther-in-law
fa·ther·land
fath·om
fath·om·less
fa·tigue
fat·ly
fat·so

fat·ten
fat·ty
fa·tu·ity
fat·u·ous
fau·bourg
fau·cet
fault
faulty
faun
fau·na
fau·vism
faux pas
fa·vor
fa·vor·able
fa·vor·ite
fa·vor·it·ism
fawn
fe·al·ty
fear·ful
fear·some
fea·si·ble
feast
feath·er
feath·er·bed
feath·er·bed·ding
feath·er·ing
feath·er·weight
feath·ery
fea·ture
fe·brile
fe·cal
fe·ces
feck·less
fec·u·lent
fe·cund
fe·cun·date
fed·er·al
fed·er·ate
fed·er·a·tion
fe·do·ra

fee·ble
feed·back
feel·er
feel·ing
feign
feint
feisty
fe·lic·i·tate
fe·lic·i·ta·tion
fe·lic·i·tous
fe·lic·i·ty
fe·line
fel·low·man
fel·low·ship
felo-de-se
fel·on
fe·lo·ni·ous
fel·o·ny
fe·male
fem·i·nine
fem·i·nin·i·ty
fem·i·nism
fem·i·nize
femme fa·tale
fe·mur
fence
fen·es·trat·ed
fen·es·tra·tion
fen·nel
fe·ral
fe·ria
fer·ment
fer·men·ta·tion
fern
fe·ro·cious
fe·roc·i·ty
fer·ret
fer·rous
fer·rule
fer·ry

fer·tile
fer·til·i·ty
fer·til·iza·tion
fer·til·ize
fer·ule
fer·vent
fer·vid
fer·vor
fes·cue
fes·ti·val
fes·tive
fes·tiv·i·ty
fes·toon
fe·tal
fetch·ing
fet·id
fe·tish
fet·lock
fet·ter
fet·tle
fet·tuc·ci·ne
fe·tus
feud
feu·dal
fe·ver·ish
fe·ver·ous
fey
fi·an·cé
fi·an·cée
fi·an·chet·to
fi·as·co
fi·at
fi·ber
fi·ber·glass
fi·bril·la·tion
fi·broid
fi·brous
fib·u·la
fiche
fick·le

fic·tion
fic·tion·al·ize
fic·ti·tious
fic·tive
fid·dle-fad·dle
fid·dling
fi·del·i·ty
fid·get
fid·gety
fi·du·cial
fi·du·cia·ry
fief
fief·dom
fiend
fiend·ish
fierce
fi·ery
fi·es·ta
fife
fifth
fif·ty
fif·ty-fif·ty
fight
fig·ment
fig·u·ra·tion
fig·u·ra·tive
fig·ure
fig·u·rine
fil·a·ment
fil·bert
filch
fi·let
fi·let mi·gnon
fil·ial
fil·i·bus·ter
fil·i·gree
fil·ing
Fil·i·pi·no
fil·let
fill·ing

fil·lip
fil·ly
film·dom
filmy
fil·ter
fil·ter·able
filth
filthy
fil·trate
fil·tra·tion
fi·na·gle
fi·nal
fi·na·le
fi·nal·ist
fi·nal·i·ty
fi·nal·ize
fi·nance
fi·nan·cial
fi·nan·cier
fine·ly
fin·ery
fines herbes
fi·nesse
fin·est
fin·ger·ing
fin·ger·nail
fin·ger·print
fin·i·al
fin·i·cal
fin·icky
fi·nis
fin·ish
fi·nite
fin·ny
fir·ing
fir·ma·ment
first
first·ly
fis·cal
fish·able

fish-and-chips
fish·ery
fish-eye
fishy
fis·sion
fis·sion·able
fis·sure
fist·ful
fist·ic
fist·i·cuffs
fit·ful
fit·ting
fiv·er
fix·ate
fix·a·tion
fix·a·tive
fixed
fix·er
fix·i·ty
fix·ture
fizz
fiz·zle
fjord
flab·ber·gast
flab·by
flac·cid
fla·con
fla·gel·lant
flag·el·late
flag·el·la·tion
flag·ging
fla·gi·tious
flag·on
fla·grance
fla·grant
fla·gran·te
  de·lic·to
flail
flair
flak

flaky
flam·be
flam·beau
flam·boy·ance
flam·boy·an·cy
flam·boy·ant
fla·men·co
flam·ing
fla·min·go
flam·ma·bil·i·ty
flam·ma·ble
flange
flank·er
flan·nel
flan·nel·ette
flap·doo·dle
flap·jack
flap·per
flare
flar·ing
flash·back
flash·er
flash·ing
flashy
flat·foot
flat·ten
flat·ter
flat·tery
flat·tish
flat·u·lence
flat·u·len·cy
flat·u·lent
flaunt
flau·tist
fla·vor
fla·vor·ful
fla·vor·some
flaw·less
flax·en
flax·seed

flay
flea
fledge
fledg·ling
fleece
fleecy
fleshed
flesh·i·ness
flesh·ly
fleshy
fleur-de-lis
flex·i·bil·i·ty
flex·i·ble
flib·ber·ti·gib·bet
flick·er
fli·er
flighty
flim·flam
flim·sy
flinch
flint·lock
flinty
flip-flop
flip·pan·cy
flip·pant
flip·per
flip side
flir·ta·tious
flitch
flit·ter
float·er
floc·cu·late
floc·cu·lent
flock·ing
floe
floor·age
floor·ing
floo·zy
flop·over
flop·py

flo·ral
flo·res·cence
flo·ret
flo·ri·cul·ture
flor·id
flo·rist
flossy
flo·ta·tion
flo·til·la
flot·sam
flounce
flouncy
floun·der
flour·ish
flout
flow·chart
flow·er
flow·ery
flown
fluc·tu·ate
flue
flu·en·cy
flu·ent
fluffy
flu·id
flu·id·i·ty
fluke
fluky
flunk
flu·o·resce
flu·o·res·cence
flu·o·res·cent
flu·o·ri·date
flu·o·ride
flu·o·ri·nate
flu·o·rine
flu·o·ro·scope
flur·ry
flus·ter
flut·ing

flut·ter
fly·able
fly·blown
fly·by
fly-by-night
fly·er
fly·ing
fly·over
foamy
fo·cal
fo·cal·ize
fo'·c'sle
fo·cus
fod·der
foe·man
fog·gy
fo·gy
foi·ble
foie gras
foist
fold·er
fol·de·rol
fo·liage
fo·li·ate
fo·li·a·tion
fo·lio
folk·lore
folksy
fol·li·cle
fol·low·er
fol·low·ing
fol·low-up
fol·ly
fo·ment
fo·men·ta·tion
fon·dle
fond·ly
fon·due
fool·ery
fool·har·dy

fool·ish
fool·ish·ness
fools·cap
foot·age
foot·ing
foo·tle
foot·lights
foot·note
foot·race
foot·wear
foot·work
fop·pery
fop·pish
for·age
for·ay
for·bear
for·bear·ance
for·bid
for·bid·dance
for·bid·ding
for·bode
force·ful
for·ceps
forc·ible
fore-and-aft
fore·arm
fore·bear
fore·bode
fore·bod·ing
fore·cast
fore·cast·ing
fore·cas·tle
fore·close
fore·clo·sure
fore·doom
fore·fa·ther
fore·fend
fore·fin·ger
fore·front
fore·gath·er

fore·go
fore·go·ing
fore·gone
fore·hand
fore·head
for·eign
for·eign·ism
fore·know
fore·la·dy
fore·land
fore·leg
fore·lock
fore·man
fore·mast
fore·most
fore·noon
fo·ren·sic
fore·or·dain
fore·run
fore·run·ner
fore·see
fore·shad·ow
fore·shore
fore·short·en
fore·sight
fore·skin
for·est
fore·stall
for·est·er
for·est·ry
fore·taste
fore·tell
fore·thought
for·ev·er
for·ev·er·more
fore·warn
for·feit
for·fei·ture
for·fend

forge
forg·er
forg·ery
for·get
for·get·ful
for·get-me-not
for·get·ta·ble
for·give
for·giv·ing
for·go
for·lorn
for·mal
for·mal·ly
form·al·de·hyde
for·mal·ism
for·mal·i·ty
for·mal·ize
for·mat
for·ma·tion
for·ma·tive
for·mer
for·mer·ly
form·fit·ting
form·ful
For·mi·ca
for·mi·da·ble
for·mu·la
for·mu·late
for·mu·la·tion
for·ni·cate
for·ni·ca·tion
for·sake
for·sooth
for·swear
for·sworn
for·syth·ia
forte
forth·com·ing
forth·right

for·ti·fi·ca·tion
for·ti·fi·er
for·ti·fy
for·tis·si·mo
for·ti·tude
fort·night
for·tress
for·tu·itous
for·tu·ity
for·tu·nate
for·ty
for·ty-nin·er
fo·rum
for·ward
for·wards
fosse
fos·sil
fos·sil·ize
fou·lard
foul·ing
foul line
foul·ly
foul up
foun·da·tion
found·ling
found·ry
foun·tain
foun·tain·head
four-flush
four·fold
four·ra·gère
four·some
four·teen
fourth
fowl
foxy
foy·er
fra·cas
frac·tion

frac·tion·al
frac·tion·ate
frac·tious
frac·ture
frag·ile
frag·ment
frag·men·tary
frag·men·tate
frag·men·tize
fra·grance
fra·gran·cy
fra·grant
frail·ty
frame-up
frame·work
fram·ing
franc
fran·chise
fran·chi·see
fran·chi·sor
fran·gi·ble
fran·gi·pane
frank·furt·er
frank·in·cense
frank·ly
fran·tic
frap·pe
fra·ter·nal
fra·ter·ni·ty
frat·er·nize
frat·ri·cide
Frau
fraud
fraud·u·lence
fraud·u·lent
fraught
fräu·lein
fraz·zle
freak·ish

freak-out
freaky
freck·le
free·bie
free·dom
free-fall
free-for-all
free·hand·ed
free·heart·ed
free·hold
free-lance
free·ma·son·ry
free·style
free·way
free·wheel
freeze-dry
freez·er
freight
freight·age
freight·er
french fry
fre·net·ic
fren·zied
fren·zy
fre·quen·cy
fre·quent
fre·quen·ta·tive
fre·quent·ly
fres·co
fresh·en
fresh·et
fresh·man
fret·ful
fret·saw
fret·work
fri·a·ble
fri·ar
fri·ary
fric·as·see

fric·tion
fric·tion·al
friend·ly
fri·er
frieze
frig·ate
fright·en
fright·ful
frig·id
fri·gid·i·ty
fringe
frip·pery
frisk·i·ly
frisky
frit·ter
fri·vol·i·ty
friv·o·lous
friz·zle
frol·ic
frol·ic·some
front·age
fron·tal
fron·tier
fron·tiers·man
fron·tis·piece
front-line
frost·bite
frost·bit·ing
frost·ing
frosty
frost·i·ly
frothy
fro·ward
frow·sy
fro·zen dai·qui·ri
fruc·ti·fi·ca·tion
fruc·ti·fy
fru·gal
fruit·er·er

fruit·ful
fru·ition
fruit·less
frumpy
frus·trate
frus·trat·ed
frus·trat·ing
frus·tra·tion
fuch·sia
fud·dy-dud·dy
fudge
fu·el
fu·gi·tive
fugue
füh·rer
ful·crum
ful·fill
ful·gent
fu·lig·i·nous
full-fledged
ful·mi·nate
ful·mi·nat·ing
ful·some
fum·ble
fu·mi·gate
func·tion
func·tion·al
func·tion·ary
fun·da·men·tal
fun·da·men·tal·
  ism
fun·da·men·tal·
  ist
fu·ner·al
fu·ne·ra·al
fun·gi·cide
fun·go
fun·gous
fun·gus
fu·nic·u·lar

fun·nel
fur·bish
fur·cate
fur·ca·tion
fu·ri·ous
fur·long
fur·lough
fur·nace
fur·nish
fur·ni·ture
fu·ror
fu·rore
fur·ri·er
fur·ring
fur·row
fur·ry
fur·ther·ance
fur·ther·more
fur·ther·most
fur·thest
fur·tive
fu·ry
furze
fu·se·lage
fus·ible
fu·sil·ier
fu·sil·lade
fu·sion
fu·sion·ist
fuss·bud·get
fuss·pot
fussy
fus·tian
fus·ty
fu·tile
fu·til·i·ty
fu·tur·ism
fu·tur·is·tic
fu·tu·ri·ty
fuzzy

G

gab
gab·ar·dine
gab·ber
gab·ble
gab·by
gab·fest
ga·ble
ga·bled
gad·about
gad·fly
gad·get
gad·get·ry
gad·wall
Gael·ic
gaff
gaffe
ga·ga
gage
gag·gle
gag·man
gag·ster
gai·ety
gai·ly
gain·ful
gain·say
gait
gait·ed
gai·ter
ga·la
ga·lac·tic
gal·an·tine
gal·a·vant
gal·axy
gal Fri·day
gall
gal·lant
gal·lant·ry

gal·le·on
gal·lery
gal·ley
gal·li·cism
gal·li·cize
gal·li·mau·fry
gal·li·na·ceous
gall·ing
gal·li·vant
gal·lon
gal·lop
gal·lop·er
gal·lows
gall·stone
Gal·lup poll
ga·loot
ga·lore
ga·losh
ga·lumph
gal·van·ic
gal·va·nize
gam·bier
gam·bit
gam·ble
gam·bol
game·ly
games·man·ship
game·some
gam·ing
gam·mon
gam·ut
gamy
gan·der
gang·er
gan·gling
gan·gli·on
gang·plank
gan·grene
gang·ster
gang·way

gan·try
gape
gap·er
ga·rage
garb
gar·bage
gar·ban·zo
gar·ble
gar·çon
gar·den
gar·de·nia
gar·gan·tuan
gar·gle
gar·goyle
gar·ish
gar·land
gar·lic
gar·licky
gar·ment
gar·ner
gar·net
gar·nish
gar·nish·ee
gar·nish·ment
gar·ni·ture
gar·ri·son
gar·rote
gar·ru·li·ty
gar·ru·lous
gar·ter
gas·con·ade
gas·eous
gas·eous·ness
gash
gas·ket
gas·o·line
gasp
gas·sy
gas·tric
gas·tri·tis

gas·tro·nome
gas·tro·nom·ic
gate-crash·er
gate·keep·er
gate·way
gath·er
gath·er·er
gath·er·ing
gauche
gau·che·rie
gaud·ery
gaud·i·ness
gaudy
gauge
gaunt
gaunt·let
gauze
gav·el
ga·votte
gawk
gawky
gay·ety
gayly
ga·ze·bo
ga·zelle
gaz·et·teer
gaz·pa·cho
gear
gear·ing
gear·shift
geese
gee-whiz
gee·zer
ge·fil·te fish
Ge·hen·na
gei·sha
gel·a·tin
ge·lat·i·nous
geld·ing
gel·id

gel·ig·nite
gem·i·nate
Gem·i·ni
gem·ol·o·gist
gem·ol·o·gy
ge·müt·lich·keit
gen·darme
gen·dar·mer·ie
gen·der
gene
ge·ne·al·o·gist
ge·ne·al·o·gy
gen·era
gen·er·al
gen·er·a·lis·si·mo
gen·er·al·ist
gen·er·al·i·ty
gen·er·al·iza·tion
gen·er·al·ize
gen·er·al·ly
gen·er·ate
gen·er·a·tion
gen·er·a·tive
gen·er·a·tor
ge·ner·ic
gen·er·os·i·ty
gen·er·ous
gen·e·sis
ge·net·ic
ge·net·ics
ge·nial
ge·nial·ly
ge·nie
gen·i·tal
gen·i·ta·lia
gen·i·tive
ge·nius
geno·cide
genre
gen·teel

gen·tian
gen·tile
gen·til·i·ty
gen·tle
gen·tle·man
gen·tle·ness
gen·tle·wom·an
gen·try
gen·u·flect
gen·u·ine
ge·nus
geo·cen·tric
geo·de·sic
ge·od·e·sy
geo·det·ic
ge·og·ra·pher
geo·graph·ic
ge·og·ra·phy
geo·log·ic
ge·ol·o·gy
geo·met·ric
geo·me·tri·cian
ge·om·e·try
geo·pol·i·tics
geor·gette
ge·ra·ni·um
ger·bil
ge·ri·at·ric
ger·i·a·tri·cian
ge·ri·at·rics
ge·ri·a·trist
ger·man
Ger·man
ger·mane
ger·mi·cid·al
ger·mi·cide
ger·mi·nal
ger·mi·nate
ge·ron·tic
ger·on·tol·o·gist

ger·on·tol·o·gy
ger·ry·man·der
ger·und
ge·run·dive
ge·stalt
ge·sta·po
ges·tate
ges·ta·tion
ges·tic·u·late
ges·tic·u·la·tion
ges·ture
ge·sund·heit
get-to·geth·er
gew·gaw
gey·ser
ghast·ly
ghat
gher·kin
ghet·to
ghost
ghost·ly
ghoul
gi·ant
gi·ant·ism
gib·ber
gib·ber·ish
gib·bet
gib·bon
gib·bous
gibe
gid·dap
gid·dy
gi·gan·tesque
gi·gan·tic
gi·gan·tism
gig·gle
gig·o·lo
gild·ing
gilt
gim·crack

gim·crack·ery
gim·let
gim·mick
gim·mick·ry
gimp
gin·ger
gin·ger·ly
ging·ham
gin·seng
gi·raffe
gird·er
gir·dle
girl·ie
girl·ish
girth
gist
giv·en
giz·mo
giz·zard
gla·cial
gla·cier
glad·den
glad·i·a·tor
glad·i·o·la
glad·i·o·lus
glam·or·ize
glam·or·ous
glam·our
glance
glanc·ing
gland
glan·du·lar
glar·ing
glass·ine
glassy
glau·co·ma
glau·cous
glaze
gla·zier
glaz·ing

gleam
glebe
glee·some
glib
glide
glid·er
glim·mer
glimpse
glint
glis·ten
glit·ter
gloam·ing
gloat
glob·al
glob·al·ism
globe
glob·u·lar
glob·ule
gloom
gloomy
glo·ri·fy
glo·ri·ous
glo·ry
gloss
glos·sa·ry
glossy
glot·tal
glove
glow
glow·er
glox·in·ia
glu·cose
glue
glued
glu·ing
glum
glu·ta·mate
glu·ten
glu·ti·nous
glut·ton

glut·ton·ous
glut·tony
glyc·er·in
gnarl
gnash
gnat
gnaw
gneiss
gnome
gno·mic
gnos·ti·cism
gnu
go·er
goad
goal·ie
goal·keep·er
goal line
go-around
goat
goa·tee
gob·ble
gob·ble·dy·gook
go-be·tween
gob·let
go-cart
god-aw·ful
god·child
god·dess
god·fa·ther
God-fear·ing
god·for·sak·en
god·head
god·less
god·ly
god·moth·er
god·par·ent
god·send
god·son
go-get·ter
gog·gle

gog·gle-eyed
go-go
go·ings-on
goi·ter
gold·brick
gold dig·ger
gold·en
golden age
gold·en·rod
gold·finch
gold·fish
gold·smith
go·lem
golf·er
Go·li·ath
gol·li·wog
gon·do·la
gon·do·lier
gon·er
gon·or·rhea
goo·ber
good-bye
good-for-noth·ing
good-heart·ed
good-hu·mored
good-look·ing
good·ly
good-na·tured
good·will
goody-goody
goofy
goo-goo
goo·ney
goose·ber·ry
go·pher ball
gore
gorge
gor·geous
gor·get
gor·gon

go·ril·la
gor·man·dize
gorse
gos·ling
gos·pel
gos·pel·er
gos·sa·mer
gos·sip
gos·sipy
Goth·ic
gouache
Gou·da
gouge
gou·lash
gourd
gour·mand
gour·met
gout
gov·ern
gov·ern·ess
gov·ern·ment
gov·ern·men·tal
gov·er·nor
gown
goy
goy·im
grab·ber
grab·by
grace·ful
grace·less
gra·cious
grack·le
gra·da·tion
gra·di·ent
grad·u·al
grad·u·al·ism
grad·u·ate
grad·u·a·tion
graf·fi·to
grail

grainy
gram·mar
gram·mat·i·cal
Gram·my
gram·o·phone
gra·na·ry
grand·dad·dy
grand·daugh·ter
grande dame
gran·dee
gran·deur
grand·fa·ther
gran·dil·o·quence
gran·di·ose
grand·ma
grand·moth·er
grand prix
grand-slam
grange
gran·ite
gran·ny
grant·ee
grant-in-aid
gran·u·lar
gran·u·late
gran·u·la·tion
gran·ule
grape·vine
graph·eme
graph·ics
graph·ite
gra·phol·o·gist
gra·phol·o·gy
grap·ple
grasp·ing
grass·hop·per
grassy
grate·ful
grat·i·fi·ca·tion
grat·i·fy

grat·i·fy·ing
gra·tin
grat·ing
gra·tis
grat·i·tude
gra·tu·itous
gra·tu·ity
gra·va·men
grave
grav·el
grav·el·ly
grav·er
grav·i·tate
grav·i·ta·tion
grav·i·ty
gra·vure
gra·vy
gray·ish
graz·ing
grease
grease·paint
greas·i·er
greasy
Great Dane
Gre·cian
greedy
green·ery
green·ish
green·room
Green·wich time
greet·ing
gre·gar·i·ous
Gre·go·ri·an chant
grem·lin
gre·nade
gren·a·dier
gren·a·dine
Gresh·am's law
grew·some
grey·hound

grid·dle
grief
griev·ance
grieve
griev·ous
grill
grille
gri·mace
grime
grimy
grind·er
grind·stone
grin·go
gripe
grippe
gris·ly
grist
gris·tle
gris·tly
grit·ty
griz·zled
griz·zly bear
groan·er
gro·cer
gro·cery
grog·gy
grom·met
groom
groove
groovy
grope
gross·ly
gro·tesque
gro·tes·que·rie
grot·to
grouchy
group dy·na·mics
group·ing
grouse
grout

grov·el
growl·er
grown-up
growth
grub·by
grudge
grudg·ing
gru·el
grue·some
grum·ble
grumpy
Gru·yère
G-string
gua·no
guar·an·tee
guar·an·tor
guar·an·ty
guard
guard·ed
guard·ian
gua·va
gu·ber·na·to·ri·al
guck
guer·don
guern·sey
guer·ril·la
guess·ti·mate
guess·work
guf·faw
guid·able
guid·ance
guide·line
gui·don
guild
guile
guile·less
guil·lo·tine
guilty
guimpe
guin·ea

guinea hen
guise
gui·tar
gulch
gulf
gul·let
gull·ible
gul·ly
gulp
gum·bo
gum·boil
gum·my
gump·tion
gung ho
gunk
gun·nery
gun·ny·sack
gun·wale
gup·py
gur·gle
gu·ru
gush·er
gushy
gus·set
gus·ta·tion
gus·ta·to·ri·al
gus·ta·to·ry
gus·to
gutsy
gut·ter
gut·ter·snipe
gut·tur·al
gut·tur·al·ly
guz·zle
gym·kha·na
gym·na·si·um
gym·nast
gym·nas·tic
gy·ne·coc·ra·cy
gy·ne·col·o·gist

gy·ne·col·o·gy
gyp·sum
gyp·sy
gy·rate
gy·ra·tion
gyre
gy·ro·com·pass
gy·ro·scope
gyve

ha·ba·ne·ra
ha·be·as cor·pus
hab·er·dash·er
hab·er·dash·ery
ha·bil·i·ment
ha·bil·i·tate
hab·it
hab·it·able
ha·bi·tant
hab·i·tat
hab·i·ta·tion
ha·bit·u·al
ha·bit·u·ate
ha·bit·u·a·tion
ha·bi·tué
ha·ci·en·da
hack·ie
hack·le
hack·man
hack·ney
hack·neyed
hack·saw
hack·work
had·dock
Ha·des
hag·gard

hag·gis
hag·gle
ha·gi·og·ra·pher
ha·gi·og·ra·phy
ha·gi·ol·o·gy
ha-ha
hai·ku
hail·stone
hail·storm
hair·breadth
hair·cloth
hair·do
hair·dress·er
hair·fol·li·cle
hair·less
hair·line
hair·piece
hair·pin
hair·rais·ing
hair·styl·ing
hair·styl·ist
hairy
hake
hal·cy·on
half-baked
half-cocked
half-dol·lar
half·heart·ed
half-life
half-mast
half·pen·ny
half-pint
half-truth
half-wit
half-wit·ted
hal·i·but
hal·i·to·sis
hal·le·lu·jah
hall·mark
hal·low

hal·lowed
Hal·low·een
hal·lu·ci·nate
hal·lu·ci·na·tion
hal·lu·ci·na·to·ry
hal·lu·ci·no·gen
ha·lo
hal·ter
halt·ing
hal·vah
halve
halves
hal·yard
ha·mate
ham·burg·er
ham-fist·ed
ham-hand·ed
Ham·il·to·ni·an
ham·let
ham·mer
ham·mer-and-
　tongs
ham·mered
ham·mer·lock
ham·mi·er
ham·mock
ham·my
ham·per
ham·ster
ham·string
hand·bag
hand·ball
hand·bill
hand·book
hand·clasp
hand·craft
hand·cuff
hand·ed·ness
hand-feed
hand·ful

hand·gun
hand·i·cap
hand·i·cap·per
hand·i·craft
hand·i·crafts·
　man
hand·i·ly
hand·ker·chief
han·dle
han·dle·bars
han·dler
han·dling
hand·made
hand·maid·en
hand-me-down
hand·out
hand·rail
hand·saw
hands·breadth
hands-down
hand·set
hand·shake
hands-off
hand·some
hand·spike
hand·spring
hand·stand
hand-to-hand
hand-to-mouth
hand·wo·ven
hand·write
hand·writ·ing
hand·wrought
handy·man
han·gar
hang·dog
hang·er
hang·er-on
hang·ing
hang·man

hang·out
hang·over
hang-up
han·ker
han·ker·ing
han·kie
han·ky-pan·ky
han·som
Ha·nuk·kah
hao·le
ha'·pen·ny
hap·haz·ard
hap·haz·ard·ly
hap·less
hap·pen
hap·pen·ing
hap·pen·stance
hap·pi·ly
hap·pi·ness
hap·py
hap·py-go-lucky
hara-kiri
ha·rangue
ha·rangued
ha·rangu·er
ha·rangu·ing
ha·rass
har·bin·ger
har·bor
har·bor·age
hard-and-fast
hard-bit·ten
hard-boiled
hard·bound
hard-core
hard·cov·er
hard-edge
hard·en
hard·en·ing
hard·fist·ed

hard·hand·ed
hard·head·ed
hard·heart·ed
hard-hit·ting
har·di·hood
har·di·ness
hard-line
hard·ly
hard·ness
hard-nosed
hard-of-hear·ing
hard-shell
hard·ship
hard·tack
hard·top
hard·ware
hard·work·ing
har·dy
hare·brained
hare·lip
har·em
har·i·cot
ha·ri·jan
hari-kari
hark·en
har·le·quin
har·le·quin·ade
har·lot
har·lot·ry
harm·ful
harm·less
har·mon·ic
har·mon·i·ca
har·mon·ics
har·mo·ni·ous
har·mo·ni·um
har·mo·nize
har·ness
harp·er
harp·ist

har·poon
harp·si·chord
har·py
har·ri·dan
har·ried
har·ri·er
har·row
har·ry
harsh
har·um-scar·um
har·vest
har·vest·time
has-been
ha·sen·pfef·fer
hash·ish
hash mark
Ha·sid
Ha·sid·ic
Ha·si·dim
hasn't
hasp
has·sle
has·sock
haste
has·ten
hast·i·ly
hasty
hat·band
hat·box
hatch
hatch·back
hat·check
hatch·ery
hatch·et
hatch·ing
hatch·way
hate
hate·ful
hat·ing
ha·tred

hat·ter
haugh·ty
haul
haul·age
haul·er
haunch
haunt
haut·bois
haute cou·ture
haute cui·sine
hau·teur
haut monde
have·lock
ha·ven
have-not
haven't
hav·er·sack
hav·oc
Ha·wai·ian
hawk
hawk·er
Hawk·eye
hawse
haw·ser
haw·thorn
Haw·thorne
    ef·fect
hay·cock
hay·er
hay fe·ver
hay·fork
hay·loft
hay·mak·er
hay·rack
hay·rick
hay·ride
hay·stack
hay·wire
haz·ard
haz·ard·ous

haze
ha·zel
ha·zel·nut
haz·ing
hazy
head·ache
head·band
head·board
head·cheese
head·dress
head·er
head·first
head·ing
head·lamp
head·land
head·less
head·light
head·line
head·lin·er
head·long
head·mas·ter
head·mis·tress
head-on
head·phone
head·piece
head·quar·ters
head·rest
head·room
head·set
head·shrink·er
head·stone
head·strong
head·wait·er
head·wa·ter
head·way
head wind
head·work
heady
heal·er
health

health·ful
health·i·er
health·i·ly
healthy
hear·ing
hear·ken
hear·say
ev·i·dence
hearse
heart·ache
heart·break·ing
heart·bro·ken
heart·burn
heart·en
heart·felt
heart-free
hearth
hearth·stone
heart·i·ly
heart·land
heart·less
heart·rend·ing
heart·sick
heart·string
heart·throb
heart-to-heart
heart·warm·ing
hearty
heat·er
heath
hea·then
hea·then·ish
heath·er
heath·ery
heat wave
heave
heav·en·ly
heav·en-sent
heav·en·ward
heav·en·wards

heavi·er-than-air
heavi·ly
heavy-hand·ed
heavy·weight
heb·dom·a·dal
He·bra·ic
He·brew
hec·a·tomb
heck·le
hec·tic
hec·to·gram
hec·to·graph
hec·tor
hedge
hedge·hog
hedge·row
he·don·ic
he·do·nism
hee·bie-jee·bies
heed·ful
heed·less
hee-haw
heel
heel-and-toe
heel·er
hefty
he·ge·mo·ny
he·gi·ra
heif·er
heigh-ho
height
height·en
hei·nous
heir
heir·ess
heir·loom
heist
he·li·cal
he·li·cop·ter
he·lio·cen·tric

he·lio·graph
he·lio·trope
he·li·ot·ro·pism
he·li·pad
he·li·port
he·li·um
he·lix
he'll
hell·ben·der
hell-bent
hell·box
Hel·len·ic
Hel·le·nism
Hel·le·nist
hel·le·nize
hell-for-leath·er
hel·lion
hell·ish
hel·lo
hel·los
helm
hel·met
helms·man
hel·ot
help·er
help·ful
help·ing
help·less
help·mate
hel·ter-skel·ter
helve
he·ma·tol·o·gist
he·ma·tol·o·gy
hemi·sphere
hem·line
hem·lock
he·mo·phil·ia
he·mo·phil·i·ac
he·mo·phil·ic

hem·or·rhage
hem·or·rhoid
hem·or·rhoid·al
hemp·en
hem·stitch
hence
hence·forth
hench·man
hen·na
hen·nery
hen·peck
hep·a·ti·tis
hep·cat
hepped up
hep·ta·gon
her·ald
he·ral·dic
her·ald·ry
herb
her·ba·ceous
herb·age
herb·al
herb·al·ist
her·biv·o·rous
Her·cu·le·an
herd·er
herds·man
here·abouts
here·af·ter
he·red·i·tary
he·red·i·ty
here·in
here·in·af·ter
her·e·sy
her·e·tic
he·ret·i·cal
here·to·fore
here·un·der
here·un·to

here·up·on
here·with
her·i·tage
her·i·tor
her·maph·ro·dite
her·met·ic
her·met·i·cal·ly
her·mit
her·mit·age
her·nia
he·ro·ic
her·o·in
her·o·ine
her·o·ism
her·on
her·on·ry
her·ring
her·ring·bone
her·ring gull
her·self
hertz
hes·i·tance
hes·i·tan·cy
hes·i·tant
hes·i·tate
hes·i·ta·tion
hes·sian
het·ero·dox
het·ero·doxy
het·er·o·ge·ne·ity
het·er·o·ge·neous
het·ero·sex·u·al
heu·ris·tic
hexa·gon
hex·ag·o·nal
hex·am·e·ter
hey·day
hi·a·tus
hi·ba·chi

hi·ber·nate
Hi·ber·ni·an
hi·bis·cus
hic·cough
hic·cup
hick·ey
hick·o·ry
hi·dal·go
hid·den
hide·away
hide·bound
hid·eous
hide·out
hie
hi·emal
hi·er·ar·chi·cal
hi·er·ar·chy
hi·er·at·ic
hi·ero·glyph
hi·ero·glyph·ic
hi-fi
hig·gle
hig·gle·dy-pig·gle·dy
high-and-mighty
high·ball
high·boy
high·brow
high chair
high-class
high·er-up
high·fa·lu·tin
high fi·del·i·ty
high fi·nance
high-flown
high-fly·ing
high-grade
high-hand·ed
high-hat

high·land
High·land fling
high·light
high-muck-a-muck
high·ness
high-oc·tane
high-pitched
high-pow·ered
high-pres·sure
high-rise
high·road
high-spir·it·ed
high-strung
high-ten·sion
high-test
high-toned
high·way·man
hi·jack
hike
hik·ing
hi·lar·i·ous
hi·lar·i·ty
hill·bil·ly
hill·ock
hill·side
hilly
Hi·ma·la·yan
him·self
hind
hin·der
Hin·di
hind·most
hind·quar·ter
hin·drance
hind·sight
Hin·du
hinge
hin·ter·land

hipped
hip·pie
Hip·po·crat·ic oath
hip·po·drome
hip·po·pot·a·mus
hire·ling
hir·ing
hir·sute
His·pan·ic
his·pa·nism
his·ta·mine
his·tol·o·gy
his·to·ri·an
his·tor·ic
his·tor·i·cal
his·to·ric·i·ty
his·to·ri·og·ra·pher
his·to·ri·og·ra·phy
his·to·ry
his·tri·on·ic
his·tri·on·ics
hit-and-miss
hit-and-run
hitch
hitch·hike
hith·er
Hit·ler·ism
hit-or-miss
hive
hives
hoa·gie
hoard
hoard·ing
hoar·frost
hoarse
hoars·en
hoary

hoax
hob·ble
hob·ble·de·hoy
hob·by
hob·by·horse
hob·gob·lin
hob·nail
hob·nob
ho·bo
Hob·son's choice
hock·ey
hock·shop
ho·cus-po·cus
hodge·podge
hoe·ing
hog·gish
hogs·head
hog-tie
hog·wash
hog-wild
ho hum
hoi pol·loi
hoist
hoi·ty-toi·ty
ho·key·po·key
ho·kum
hold·ing
hold·ing pat·tern
hold·out
hold·over
hold·up
hol·ey
hol·i·day
ho·li·er
ho·li·er-than-
thou
ho·li·ness
ho·lis·tic
hol·lan·daise
sauce

hol·ler
hol·low
hol·ly
hol·ly·hock
Hol·ly·wood
ho·lo·caust
hol·stein
hol·ster
ho·ly
hom·age
hom·burg
home·body
home·bound
home·com·ing
home eco·nom·ics
home·like
home·ly
home·made
home·mak·er
ho·mer
home·spun
home·stead
home·stretch
home·work
hom·ey
ho·mi·cide
hom·i·let·ic
hom·i·let·ics
hom·i·ly
hom·i·ny
ho·mo·ge·ne·ity
ho·mo·ge·neous
ho·mog·e·ni·za·
tion
ho·mog·e·nize
ho·mog·e·nous
ho·mog·e·ny
ho·mo·graph
ho·mol·o·gous
hom·onym

hom·on·y·mous
ho·mo phone
Ho·mo sa·pi·ens
ho·mo·sex·u·al
ho·mo·sex·u·al·i·
ty
hone
hon·est
hon·es·ty
hon·ey
hon·ey·comb
hon·ey·dew
hon·ey·moon
hon·ey·suck·le
hon·kie
hon·ky-tonk
hon·or·able
hon·o·rar·i·um
hon·or·ary
hon·or·if·ic
hooch
hood·lum
hoo·doo
hood·wink
hoo·ey
hoof·er
hoof·print
hoo·kah
hooked
hook·er
hooky
hoo·li·gan
hoop·la
hoose·gow
Hoo·sier
hoo·te·nan·ny
hope·ful
hope·ful·ly
hope·less
hop·ing

hop·per
hop·ping
hop·scotch
horde
hore·hound
ho·ri·zon
hor·i·zon·tal
hor·mone
hor·net
horn·pipe
horn·swog·gle
horny
ho·rol·o·gy
horo·scope
hor·ren·dous
hor·ri·ble
hor·rid
hor·rif·ic
hor·ri·fy
hor·ror
hor·ror-struck
hors de com·bat
hors d'oeuvre
horse-and-bug·gy
horse·back
horse·fly
horse·hide
horse·laugh
horse·man
horse·rad·ish
hors·ey
hors·ing
hor·ta·tive
hor·ta·to·ry
hor·ti·cul·ture
ho·san·na
ho·siery
hos·pice
hos·pi·ta·ble
hos·pi·ta·bly

hos·pi·tal
hos·pi·tal·i·ty
hos·pi·tal·ize
hos·tage
hos·tel
hos·tel·er
hos·tel·ry
host·ess
hos·tile
hos·til·i·ty
hot·cake
hot·dog
ho·te·lier
ho·tel·man
hot·foot
hot·head
hot·head·ed
hot·ly
hot·shot
hound
hour·glass
hour·ly
house·break
house·bro·ken
house·hold
house·keep·er
house·keep·ing
house·room
house·wares
house·warm·ing
house·wife
hous·ing
hove
hov·el
hov·er
how·be·it
how·dah
how·ev·er
how·it·zer
howl

howl·ing
how·so·ev·er
hoy·den
hua·ra·che
hub·bub
hub·by
hub·cap
hu·bris
huck·le·ber·ry
huck·ster
hud·dle
hue
huffy
huge
hug·ger-mug·ger
hu·la
hul·la·ba·loo
hu·man
hu·mane
hu·man·ism
hu·man·i·tar·i·an
hu·man·i·tar·i·
  an·ism
hu·man·i·ty
hu·man·ize
hu·man·ly
hum·ble
hum·bug
hum·ding·er
hum·drum
hu·mer·al
hu·mer·us
hu·mid
hu·mid·i·fi·er
hu·mid·i·fy
hu·mid·i·stat
hu·mid·i·ty
hu·mi·dor
hu·mil·i·ate
hu·mil·i·at·ing

hu·mil·i·ty
hu·mor·esque
hu·mor·ist
hu·mor·less
hu·mor·ous
hump·back
humped
humph
hump·ty-dump·ty
humpy
hu·mus
hunch
hun·dred
hun·ger
hun·gry
hun·ker
hun·ky-do·ry
hunt·er
hunt·ing
hunt·ress
hunts·man
hur·dle
hur·dy-gur·dy
hurl·ing
hur·ly-bur·ly
hur·rah
hur·ri·cane
hur·ried
hur·ry
hur·ry-scur·ry
hurt·ful
hur·tle
hurt·less
hus·band
hus·band·ry
hush pup·py
husky
hus·sar
hus·sy
hus·tings

hus·tle
hutch
hutz·pah
hy·a·cinth
hy·brid
hy·brid·ize
hy·dran·gea
hy·drant
hy·drate
hy·drau·lic
hy·drau·lics
hy·dro·chlo·ric
  acid
hy·dro·elec·tric
hy·dro·foil
hy·dro·gen
hy·dro·ge·nate
hy·drom·e·ter
hy·dro·pho·bia
hy·dro·plane
hy·dro·pon·ics
hy·dro·stat·ics
hy·drox·ide
hy·e·na
hy·giene
hy·gien·ics
hy·men
hy·me·ne·al
hymn
hym·nal
hype
hy·per·ac·tive
hy·per·bo·la
hy·per·bo·le
hy·per·bol·ic
hy·per·bo·re·an
hy·per·crit·i·cal
hy·per·ki·net·ic
hy·per·son·ic
hy·per·ten·sion

hy·per·thy·roid
hy·phen
hy·phen·ate
hy·phen·at·ed
hyp·noid
hyp·no·sis
hyp·not·ic
hyp·no·tism
hyp·no·tize
hy·po·chon·dria
hy·po·chon·dri·ac
hy·po·chon·dri·a·
  cal
hy·po·chon·dri·a·
  sis
hy·poc·ri·sy
hyp·o·crite
hyp·o·crit·i·cal
hy·po·der·mic
hy·po·der·mis
hy·pos·ta·sis
hy·pos·ta·tize
hy·po·ten·sion
hy·pot·e·nuse
hy·poth·e·cate
hy·poth·e·sis
hy·poth·e·size
hy·po·thet·i·cal
hy·po·thy·roid
hy·po·thy·roid·
  ism
hy·po·ton·ic
hys·sop
hys·ter·ec·to·my
hys·te·ria
hysteric
hys·ter·i·cal
hys·ter·i·cal·ly
hys·ter·ics
hys·ter·ot·o·my

I

iamb
Ibe·ri·an
ibex
ibi·dem
ibis
ice age
ice·berg
ice·bound
ice-cold
ice-cream
iced
ice-skate
ich·thy·ol·o·gy
ici·cle
ic·ing
icky
icon
icon·o·clasm
icon·o·clast
ico·nog·ra·pher
ico·nog·ra·phy
ico·sa·he·dral
ico·sa·he·dron
ic·tus
icy
ID card
ide·al
idea·less
ide·al·ism
ide·al·ist
ide·al·is·tic
ide·al·i·ty
ide·al·ize
ide·al·ly
ide·ate
ide·ation
ide·ation·al

idem
iden·ti·cal
iden·ti·fi·ca·tion
iden·ti·fi·er
iden·ti·fy
iden·ti·ty
ideo·gram
ideo·log·i·cal
ide·ol·o·gy
id·i·o·cy
id·io·graph·ic
id·i·om
id·i·om·at·ic
id·io·syn·cra·sy
id·i·ot
id·i·ot·ic
id·i·o·tism
idle
idol
idol·a·ter
idol·a·trous
idol·a·try
idol·ize
idyll
if·fy
ig·loo
ig·ne·ous
ig·nis fat·u·us
ig·nite
ig·nit·ible
ig·ni·tion
ig·no·ble
ig·no·min·i·ous
ig·no·mi·ny
ig·no·ra·mus
ig·no·rance
ig·no·rant
ig·nore
igua·na
ilex

Il·i·ad
ilk
ill-ad·vised
il·la·tive
ill-bred
il·le·gal
il·leg·i·ble
il·le·git·i·ma·cy
il·le·git·i·mate
ill-fat·ed
ill-fa·vored
ill-got·ten
ill-hu·mored
il·lib·er·al
il·lib·er·al·ly
il·lic·it
il·lim·it·able
il·lit·er·a·cy
il·lit·er·ate
ill-man·nered
ill-na·tured
ill·ness
il·log·ic
il·log·i·cal
ill-sort·ed
ill-tem·pered
ill-treat
il·lume
il·lu·mi·nate
il·lu·mi·na·ti
il·lu·mi·na·tion
il·lu·mine
ill-us·age
ill-use
il·lu·sion
il·lu·sion·ary
il·lu·sive
il·lu·so·ry
il·lus·trate
il·lus·tra·tion

il·lus·tra·tive
il·lus·tri·ous
ill-wish·er
im·age
im·ag·ery
imag·in·able
imag·i·nary
imag·i·na·tion
imag·i·na·tive
imag·ine
im·ag·ism
im·bal·ance
im·be·cile
im·be·cil·i·ty
im·bibe
im·bri·cate
im·bro·glio
im·bue
im·i·ta·ble
im·i·tate
im·i·ta·tion
im·i·ta·tive
im·mac·u·late
im·ma·nence
im·ma·nent
im·ma·te·ri·al
im·ma·te·ri·al·i·ty
im·ma·ture
im·mea·sur·able
im·me·di·a·cy
im·me·di·ate
im·me·di·ate·ly
im·me·mo·ri·al
im·mense
im·men·si·ty
im·men·su·ra·ble
im·merge
im·merse
im·mers·ible

im·mer·sion
im·mi·grant
im·mi·grate
im·mi·nence
im·mi·nent
im·mis·ci·ble
im·mo·bile
im·mo·bi·lize
im·mod·er·ate
im·mod·est
im·mo·late
im·mo·la·tion
im·mor·al
im·mo·ral·i·ty
im·mor·tal
im·mor·tal·i·ty
im·mor·tal·ize
im·mov·able
im·mune
im·mu·ni·ty
im·mu·nize
im·mure
im·mu·ta·ble
im·pact
im·pac·tion
im·pac·tor
im·pair
im·pale
im·pal·pa·ble
im·pan·el
im·part
im·par·tial
im·pass·able
im·passe
im·pas·si·ble
im·pas·sioned
im·pas·sive
im·pa·tience
im·pa·tient
im·peach

im·pec·ca·ble
im·pe·cu·nious
im·ped·ance
im·pede
im·ped·i·ment
im·ped·i·men·ta
im·pel
im·pen·e·tra·bil·i·ty
im·pen·e·tra·ble
im·pen·i·tence
im·pen·i·tent
im·per·a·tive
im·per·cep·ti·ble
im·per·cep·tive
im·per·fect
im·per·fec·tion
im·pe·ri·al
im·pe·ri·al·ism
im·per·il
im·pe·ri·ous
im·per·ish·able
im·per·ma·nence
im·per·me·able
im·per·mis·si·ble
im·per·son·al
im·per·son·ate
im·per·ti·nence
im·per·ti·nent
im·per·turb·able
im·per·vi·ous
im·pet·u·os·i·ty
im·pet·u·ous
im·pe·tus
im·pi·ety
im·pinge
im·pi·ous
imp·ish
im·pla·ca·ble
im·plant

im·plau·si·ble
im·ple·ment
im·pli·cate
im·pli·ca·tion
im·plic·it
im·plore
im·plo·sion
im·ply
im·po·lite
im·pol·i·tic
im·pon·der·a·ble
im·port
im·por·tance
im·por·tant
im·por·ta·tion
im·por·tu·nate
im·por·tune
im·pose
im·pos·ing
im·po·si·tion
im·pos·si·bil·i·ty
im·pos·si·ble
im·post
im·pos·tor
im·pos·ture
im·po·tence
im·po·tent
im·pound
im·pov·er·ish
im·pov·er·ished
im·prac·ti·ca·ble
im·prac·ti·cal
im·pre·cate
im·pre·ca·tion
im·pre·cise
im·preg·na·ble
im·preg·nate
im·pre·sa
im·pre·sa·rio
im·press

im·pres·sion
im·pres·sion·able
im·pres·sion·ist
im·pres·sion·is·
    tic
im·pres·sive
im·pri·ma·tur
im·pri·mis
im·print
im·pris·on
im·prob·a·bil·i·ty
im·prob·a·ble
im·promp·tu
im·prop·er
im·pro·pri·ety
im·prov·able
im·prove
im·prove·ment
im·prov·i·dent
im·pro·vi·sa·tion
im·pro·vise
im·pru·dence
im·pru·dent
im·pu·dence
im·pu·dent
im·pugn
im·pulse
im·pul·sive
im·pu·ni·ty
im·pu·ri·ty
im·pu·ta·tion
im·pute
in·abil·i·ty
in ab·sen·tia
in·ac·ces·si·ble
in·ac·cu·ra·cy
in·ac·tion
in·ac·ti·vate
in·ac·tive
in·ad·e·qua·cy

in·ad·e·quate
in·ad·mis·si·ble
in·ad·ver·tence
in·ad·ver·ten·cy
in·ad·ver·tent
in·ad·vis·able
in·alien·able
in·al·ter·able
in·amo·ra·ta
inane
in·an·i·mate
in·a·ni·tion
inan·i·ty
in·ap·pli·ca·ble
in·ap·po·site
in·ap·proach·able
in·ap·pro·pri·ate
in·apt
in·ap·ti·tude
in·ar·tic·u·late
in·ar·tis·tic
in·as·much as
in·at·ten·tion
in·at·ten·tive
in·au·di·ble
in·au·gu·ral
in·au·gu·rate
in·au·gu·ra·tion
in·aus·pi·cious
in·au·then·tic
in-be·tween
in·bred
in·breed·ing
in·cal·cu·la·ble
in·can·des·cence
in·can·des·cent
in·can·ta·tion
in·ca·pa·ble
in·ca·pac·i·tate
in·ca·pac·i·ty

in·car·cer·ate
in·car·di·na·tion
in·car·na·dine
in·car·nate
in·car·na·tion
in·cau·tious
in·cen·di·a·rism
in·cen·di·ary
in·cense
in·cen·tive
in·cep·tion
in·ces·sant
in·cest
in·ces·tu·ous
in·cho·ate
inch·worm
in·ci·dence
in·ci·dent
in·ci·den·tal
in·ci·den·tal·ly
in·cin·er·ate
in·cin·er·a·tor
in·cip·i·ence
in·cip·i·en·cy
in·cip·i·ent
in·cise
in·ci·sion
in·ci·sive
in·ci·sor
in·ci·ta·tion
in·cite
in·ci·vil·i·ty
in·clem·en·cy
in·clem·ent
in·cli·na·tion
in·cline
in·clin·ing
in·close
in·clude
in·clu·sion

in·clu·sive
in·cog·ni·to
in·co·her·ence
in·co·her·ent
in·com·bus·ti·ble
in·come
in·com·ing
in·com·men·su·
ra·ble
in·com·men·su·
rate
in·com·mu·ni·ca·
ble
in·com·mu·ni·ca·
do
in·com·pa·ra·ble
in·com·pat·i·bil·i·
ty
in·com·pat·i·ble
in·com·pe·tence
in·com·pe·ten·cy
in·com·pe·tent
in·com·plete
in·com·pre·hen·
si·ble
in·com·pre·hen·
sion
in·com·press·ible
in·con·ceiv·able
in·con·clu·sive
in·con·gru·ence
in·con·gru·ent
in·con·gru·ity
in·con·gru·ous
in·con·se·quent
in·con·se·quen·
tial
in·con·sid·er·able
in·con·sid·er·ate
in·con·sis·ten·cy

in·con·sis·tent
in·con·sol·able
in·con·spic·u·ous
in·con·stan·cy
in·con·stant
in·con·test·able
in·con·ti·nence
in·con·trol·la·ble
in·con·tro·vert·
ible
in·con·ve·nience
in·con·ve·nient
in·con·vert·ible
in·con·vinc·ible
in·co·or·di·nate
in·co·or·di·na·
tion
in·cor·po·rate
in·cor·po·rat·ed
in·cor·po·re·al
in·cor·rect
in·cor·ri·gi·ble
in·cor·rupt
in·cor·rupt·ible
in·cor·rup·tion
in·creas·ing·ly
in·cred·i·ble
in·cre·du·li·ty
in·cred·u·lous
in·cre·ment
in·cre·men·tal·
ism
in·crim·i·nate
in·crus·ta·tion
in·cu·bate
in·cu·ba·tion
in·cu·ba·tor
in·cu·bus
in·cul·cate
in·cul·pate

in·cum·ben·cy
in·cum·bent
in·cur
in·cur·able
in·curred
in·cur·sion
in·debt·ed
in·debt·ed·ness
in·de·cen·cy
in·de·cent
in·de·ci·pher·able
in·de·ci·sion
in·de·ci·sive
in·de·co·rous
in·de·fat·i·ga·ble
in·de·fec·ti·ble
in·de·fen·si·ble
in·de·fin·able
in·def·i·nite
in·del·i·ble
in·del·i·ca·cy
in·del·i·cate
in·dem·ni·fi·ca·
  tion
in·dem·ni·fy
in·dent
in·den·ta·tion
in·den·ture
in·de·pen·dence
in·de·pen·dent
in-depth
in·de·scrib·able
in·de·struc·ti·ble
in·de·ter·min·
  able
in·de·ter·mi·nate
in·dex
in·di·cate
in·di·ca·tion
in·dic·a·tive

in·di·ca·tor
in·dict
in·dict·able
in·dict·ment
in·dif·fer·ence
in·dif·fer·ent
in·di·gence
in·dig·e·nous
in·di·gent
in·di·gest·ible
in·di·ges·tion
in·dig·nant
in·dig·na·tion
in·di·go
in·di·rect
in·di·rec·tion
in·dis·cern·ible
in·dis·creet
in·dis·cre·tion
in·dis·pens·able
in·dis·pose
in·dis·po·si·tion
in·dis·put·able
in·dis·sol·u·ble
in·dis·tinct
in·dis·tin·guish·
  able
in·dite
in·di·vid·u·al
in·di·vid·u·al·ism
in·di·vid·u·al·i·ty
in·di·vid·u·al·ize
in·di·vid·u·ate
in·di·vid·u·a·tion
in·di·vis·i·ble
in·doc·tri·nate
in·do·lence
in·do·lent
in·dom·i·ta·ble
in·dorse

in·du·bi·ta·ble
in·duce
in·duce·ment
in·duct
in·duct·ee
in·duc·tion
in·duc·tive
in·dulge
in·dul·gence
in·dul·gent
in·dult
in·du·rate
in·dus·tri·al
in·dus·tri·al·ism
in·dus·tri·al·ist
in·dus·tri·al·ize
in·dus·tri·ous
in·dus·try
in·dwell
in·dwell·ing
ine·bri·ate
in·ebri·ety
in·ed·u·ca·ble
in·ef·fa·ble
in·ef·face·able
in·ef·fec·tive
in·ef·fec·tu·al
in·ef·fi·ca·cious
in·ef·fi·ca·cy
in·ef·fi·cien·cy
in·ef·fi·cient
in·elas·tic
in·el·i·gi·ble
in·eluc·ta·ble
in·ept
in·equal·i·ty
in·eq·ui·ta·ble
in·eq·ui·ty
in·erad·i·ca·ble
in·ert

in·er·tia
in·es·cap·able
in·es·sen·tial
in·es·ti·ma·ble
in·ev·i·ta·bil·i·ty
in·ev·i·ta·ble
in·ev·i·ta·bly
in·ex·act
in·ex·cus·able
in·ex·haust·ible
in·ex·o·ra·ble
in·ex·pe·di·ence
in·ex·pe·di·en·cy
in·ex·pe·di·ent
in·ex·pen·sive
in·ex·pe·ri·ence
in·ex·pert
in·ex·pi·a·ble
in·ex·pli·ca·ble
in·ex·press·ible
in·ex·tin·guish·able
in·ex·tri·ca·ble
in·fal·li·ble
in·fa·mous
in·fa·my
in·fan·cy
in·fan·ti·cide
in·fan·tile
in·fan·til·ism
in·fan·try
in·fat·u·ate
in·fea·si·ble
in·fec·tion
in·fec·tious
in·fe·lic·i·tous
in·fe·lic·i·ty
in·fer·ence
in·fe·ri·or
in·fer·nal

in·fer·no
in·fer·tile
in·fes·ta·tion
in·fi·del
in·fi·del·i·ty
in·fight·ing
in·fil·trate
in·fi·nite
in·fin·i·tes·i·mal
in·fin·i·tive
in·fin·i·tude
in·fin·i·ty
in·fir·ma·ry
in·fir·mi·ty
in·flame
in·flam·ma·ble
in·flam·ma·tion
in·flam·ma·to·ry
in·flat·able
in·fla·tion
in·fla·tion·ary
in·flect
in·flec·tion
in·flex·i·ble
in·flict
in·flic·tion
in·flu·ence
in·flu·en·tial
in·flu·en·za
in·flux
in·form
in·for·mal
in·for·mant
in·for·ma·tion
in·for·ma·tive
in·form·er
in·frac·tion
in·fra dig
in·fran·gi·ble
in·fra·red

in·fra·struc·ture
in·fre·quen·cy
in·fre·quent
in·fringe
in·fringe·ment
in·fu·ri·ate
in·fuse
in·fu·sion
in·ge·nious
in·ge·nue
in·ge·nu·ity
in·gen·u·ous
in·gest
in·glo·ri·ous
in·got
in·grained
in·grate
in·gra·ti·ate
in·gra·ti·at·ing
in·grat·i·tude
in·gre·di·ent
in·gress
in·grown
in·hab·it
in·hab·it·ant
in·ha·la·tion
in·ha·la·tor
in·hal·er
in·har·mo·ni·ous
in·her·ence
in·her·ent
in·her·it
in·her·it·able
in·her·i·tance
in·hib·it
in·hib·i·tive
in·hi·bi·tion
in·hib·i·tor
in·hos·pi·ta·ble
in·hos·pi·tal·i·ty

in·house
in·hu·man
in·hu·mane
in·hu·man·i·ty
in·im·i·cal
in·im·i·ta·ble
in·iq·ui·tous
in·iq·ui·ty
ini·tial
ini·tial·ize
ini·tiate
ini·ti·a·tion
ini·tia·tive
ini·tia·to·ry
in·ject
in·jec·tion
in·ju·di·cious
in·junc·tion
in·jure
in·ju·ri·ous
in·ju·ry
in·jus·tice
in·kling
in·laid
in·lay
in·let
in lo·co pa·ren·
   tis
in·mate
in me·di·as res
in me·mo·ri·am
in-mi·grant
in-mi·grate
in·most
in·nards
in·nate
in·ner
in·ner·vate
in·ning
in·no·cence

in·no·cent
in·noc·u·ous
in·no·vate
in·no·va·tion
in·no·va·tive
in·nu·en·do
in·nu·mer·a·ble
in·oc·u·late
in·oc·u·la·tion
in·of·fen·sive
in·op·er·a·ble
in·op·er·a·tive
in·op·por·tune
in·or·di·nate
in·or·gan·ic
in-per·son
in·put
in·quest
in·qui·etude
in·quire
in·qui·ry
in·qui·si·tion
in·quis·i·tive
in·quis·i·tor
in·road
in·sane
in·san·i·tary
in·san·i·ty
in·sa·tia·ble
in·sa·tiate
in·scribe
in·scrip·tion
in·scru·ta·ble
in·sect
in·sec·ti·cide
in·sec·tiv·o·rous
in·se·cure
in·sem·i·nate
in·sem·i·na·tor
in·sen·sate

in·sen·si·ble
in·sen·si·tive
in·sep·a·ra·ble
in·sert
in·ser·tion
in-ser·vice
in·set
in·sid·er
in·sid·i·ous
in·sight·ful
in·sig·nia
in·sig·nif·i·cance
in·sig·nif·i·cant
in·sin·cere
in·sin·u·ate
in·sin·u·at·ing
in·sin·u·a·tion
in·sip·id
in·si·pid·i·ty
in·sis·tence
in·sis·ten·cy
in·sis·tent
in·so·bri·ety
in·so·far
in·so·lence
in·so·lent
in·sol·u·ble
in·solv·able
in·sol·vent
in·som·nia
in·sou·ci·ance
in·spect
in·spec·tion
in·spec·tor
in·spi·ra·tion
in·spi·ra·to·ry
in·spire
in·spir·ing
in·spis·sate
in·sta·bil·i·ty

in·sta·ble
in·stall
in·stal·la·tion
in·stall·ment
in·stance
in·stan·cy
in·stant
in·stan·ta·neous
in·sti·gate
in·still
in·stinct
in·stinc·tive
in·sti·tute
in·sti·tu·tion
in·sti·tu·tion·al·
    ism
in·sti·tu·tion·al·
    ize
in·struct
in·struc·tion
in·struc·tive
in·struc·tor
in·stru·ment
in·stru·men·tal·
    ist
in·stru·men·tal·i·
    ty
in·stru·men·ta·
    tion
in·sub·or·di·nate
in·sub·stan·tial
in·suf·fer·able
in·suf·fi·cien·cy
in·suf·fi·cient
in·su·lar
in·su·late
in·su·la·tion
in·su·la·tor
in·su·lin
in·sult

in·su·per·a·ble
in·sup·port·able
in·sup·press·ible
in·sur·able
in·sur·ance
in·sure
in·sur·gence
in·sur·gen·cy
in·sur·gent
in·sur·mount·
    able
in·sur·rec·tion
in·tact
in·ta·glio
in·tan·gi·ble
in·te·ger
in·te·gral
in·te·grate
in·te·gra·tion
in·te·gra·tive
in·teg·ri·ty
in·teg·u·ment
in·tel·lect
in·tel·lec·tu·al
in·tel·lec·tu·al·
    ize
in·tel·li·gence
in·tel·li·gent
in·tel·li·gent·sia
in·tel·li·gi·ble
in·tem·per·ance
in·tem·per·ate
in·ten·dant
in·tend·ed
in·tense
in·ten·si·fi·er
in·ten·si·fy
in·ten·si·ty
in·ten·tion
in·ter

in·ter·ac·tion
in·ter ali·a
in·ter·ca·late
in·ter·cede
in·ter·cel·lu·lar
in·ter·cept
in·ter·cep·tion
in·ter·cep·tor
in·ter·ces·sion
in·ter·change
in·ter·change·
    able
in·ter·col·le·giate
in·ter·com·mu·
    ni·cate
in·ter·con·nect
in·ter·con·ti·nen·
    tal
in·ter·cos·tal
in·ter·course
in·ter·cul·tur·al
in·ter·de·nom·i·
    na·tion·al
in·ter·de·part·
    men·tal
in·ter·de·pen·
    dence
in·ter·de·pen·
    den·cy
in·ter·de·pen·
    dent
in·ter·dict
in·ter·dis·ci·plin·
    ary
in·ter·est
in·ter·est·ing
in·ter·face
in·ter·faith
in·ter·fere
in·ter·fer·ence

in·ter·im
in·te·ri·or
in·ter·ject
in·ter·jec·tor
in·ter·jec·tion
in·ter·lard
in·ter·li·brary
in·ter·lin·ear
in·ter·lin·ing
in·ter·lude
in·ter·me·di·ary
in·ter·me·di·ate
in·ter·me·di·a·tion
in·ter·ment
in·ter·mez·zo
in·ter·mi·na·ble
in·ter·min·gle
in·ter·mis·sion
in·ter·mit
in·ter·mit·tent
in·tern
in·ter·nal
in·ter·nal·ize
in·ter·na·tion·al
in·ter·ne·cine
in·tern·ee
in·ter·nist
in·tern·ment
in·ter·nu·cle·ar
in·ter·of·fice
in·ter·pel·late
in·ter·pen·e·trate
in·ter·po·late
in·ter·pose
in·ter·po·si·tion
in·ter·pret
in·ter·pre·ta·tion
in·ter·pre·ta·tive
in·ter·pret·er

in·ter·ra·cial
in·ter·re·late
in·ter·re·li·gious
in·ter·ro·gate
in·ter·rog·a·tive
in·ter·ro·ga·tor
in·ter·rupt
in·ter·rupt·er
in·ter·scho·las·tic
in·ter·sect
in·ter·sec·tion
in·ter·ses·sion
in·ter·sperse
in·ter·stel·lar
in·ter·stice
in·ter·sti·tial
in·ter·twine
in·ter·ur·ban
in·ter·val
in·ter·vene
in·ter·ven·tion·ism
in·ter·view
in·ter·view·ee
in·ter·weave
in·tes·tate
in·tes·ti·nal
in·tes·tine
in·ti·ma·cy
in·ti·mate
in·tim·i·date
in·tim·i·da·tion
in·tinc·tion
in·tol·er·a·ble
in·tol·er·ance
in·tol·er·ant
in·to·nate
in·to·na·tion
in·tone
in·tox·i·cant

in·tox·i·cate
in·tox·i·ca·tion
in·trac·ta·ble
in·tra·mu·ral
in·tran·si·gence
in·tran·si·gent
in·tran·si·tive
in·tra·state
in·tra·uter·ine
in·tra·ve·nous
in·tra·zon·al
in·trep·id
in·tri·ca·cy
in·tri·cate
in·trigue
in·trigu·ing
in·trin·sic
in·tro·duce
in·tro·duc·tion
in·tro·duc·to·ry
in·troit
in·tro·mit
in·tro·spect
in·tro·spec·tion
in·tro·ver·sion
in·tro·vert
in·trude
in·tru·sion
in·tru·sive
in·tu·it
in·tu·ition
in·tu·itive
in·tu·mes·cence
in·tu·mes·cent
in·un·date
in·ure
in·vade
in·val·id
in·val·i·date
in·valu·able

in·vari·able
in·vari·ant
in·va·sion
in·vec·tive
in·veigh
in·vei·gle
in·vent
in·ven·tion
in·ven·tive
in·ven·to·ry
in·verse
in·ver·sion
in·vert
in·ver·te·brate
in·vest
in·ves·ti·gate
in·ves·ti·ture
in·vest·ment
in·vet·er·ate
in·vi·a·ble
in·vid·i·ous
in·vig·o·rate
in·vin·ci·ble
in·vi·o·la·ble
in·vi·o·late
in·vis·i·bil·i·ty
in·vis·i·ble
in·vi·ta·tion
in·vite
in·vit·ing
in·vo·ca·tion
in·voice
in·voke
in·vol·un·tary
in·vo·lute
in·vo·lu·tion
in·volve
in·volve·ment
in·vul·ner·a·ble
in·ward·ly

io·dine
ion·ize
ion·o·sphere
ip·so fac·to
Ira·ni·an
Ira·qi
iras·ci·bil·i·ty
iras·ci·ble
irate
ire·nic
ir·i·des·cence
iris
Irish·ry
irk·some
iron
iron·clad
iron·ing
iron out
iro·ny
Ir·o·quois
ir·ra·di·ance
ir·ra·di·ate
ir·ra·di·a·tion
ir·rad·i·ca·ble
ir·ra·tio·nal
ir·re·claim·able
ir·rec·on·cil·able
ir·re·cov·er·able
ir·re·deem·able
ir·re·duc·ible
ir·re·form·able
ir·re·fra·ga·ble
ir·re·fran·gi·ble
ir·re·fut·able
ir·reg·u·lar
ir·reg·u·lar·i·ty
ir·rel·e·vance
ir·rel·e·van·cy
ir·rel·e·vant
ir·re·li·gious

ir·re·me·di·a·ble
ir·re·mov·able
ir·rep·a·ra·ble
ir·re·place·able
ir·re·press·ible
ir·re·proach·able
ir·re·sist·ible
ir·res·o·lute
ir·re·solv·able
ir·re·spec·tive of
ir·re·spon·si·bil·i·ty
ir·re·spon·si·ble
ir·re·spon·sive
ir·re·triev·able
ir·rev·er·ence
ir·rev·er·ent
ir·re·vers·ible
ir·rev·o·ca·ble
ir·ri·gate
ir·ri·ta·bil·i·ty
ir·ri·ta·ble
ir·ri·tant
ir·ri·tate
ir·ri·ta·tion
ir·rupt
ir·rup·tive
isin·glass
is·land
isle
iso·la·ble
iso·late
iso·la·tion
iso·la·tion·ism
iso·met·ric
iso·met·rics
isos·ce·les
   tri·angle
iso·therm
iso·tope

Is·ra·el
Is·rae·li
Is·ra·el·ite
is·sue
isth·mi·an
isth·mus
Ital·ian
ital·ic
ital·i·cize
itch
item
item·iza·tion
item·ize
it·er·ate
it·er·a·tive
itin·er·an·cy
itin·er·ant
itin·er·ary
it·self
it·ty-bit·ty
I've
ivied
ivo·ry
ivy
Ivy League
iz·zard

J

jab·ber
jab·ber·wocky
ja·bot
jack·al
jack·a·napes
jack·ass
jack·daw
jack·et
jack·ham·mer

jack-in-the-box
jack-in-the-pul·
    pit
jack·knife
jack-of-all-trades
jack-o'-lan·tern
jack·pot
jack·rab·bit
Jack·so·ni·an
Jac·o·be·an
jad·ed
jag·ged
jag·ged·ness
jag·uar
jai alai
jail·bait
jail·bird
jail·break
jail·er
ja·lopy
jal·ou·sie
jam
jamb
jam·ba·laya
jam·bo·ree
jammed
jam·mer
jam·ming
jam ses·sion
Jane Doe
jan·gle
jan·gling
jan·i·tor
Jan·u·ary
Jap·a·nese
jape
jap·ery
jar·di·niere
jar·gon
jas·mine

jas·per
jaun·dice
jaunt
jaun·ty
jav·e·lin
jaw·break·er
jawed
jay
jay·bird
jay·gee
jay·vee
jay·walk
jazz
jazzy
jeal·ous
jeal·ou·sy
jean
jeep
jeer
Je·ho·vah
je·hu
je·june
Je·kyll and Hyde
jel·lied
jellies
jel·ly
jel·ly·fish
jen·net
jen·ny
jeop·ar·dize
jeop·ar·dy
jer·e·mi·ad
jerk·i·ly
jer·kin
jerk·wa·ter
jerky
jer·o·bo·am
jer·ry-built
jer·sey
jest

jest·er
Je·su·it
je·su·it·ic
je·su·it·i·cal
jet
jet·ted
jet·ting
je·té
jet-pro·pelled
jet pro·pul·sion
jet·sam
jet stream
jet·ti·son
jet·ty
jeu d'es·prit
jew·el
jew·el·er
jew·el·ry
Jez·e·bel
jib
jibe
jif·fy
jig
jig·ger
jig·ging
jig·gle
jig·gly
jig·saw
jilt
jim crow
jim-dan·dy
jim·jams
jim·my
jin·gle
jin·go·ism
jin·rik·i·sha
jinx
jit·ney
jit·ter
jit·ter·bug

jit·tery
jiu·jit·su
jive
job
job·ber
job·bery
jock·ey
jock·strap
jo·cose
jo·cos·i·ty
joc·u·lar
jo·cund
jodh·pur
jog·ger
jog·gle
John Doe
John Han·cock
john·ny
john·ny·cake
John·ny-on-the-
    spot
joie de vi·vre
join·der
join·er
join·ery
join·ing
joint
join·ture
joist
joke
jok·ing
jol·li·fi·ca·tion
jol·li·ty
jol·ly
Jol·ly Rog·er
jon·quil
josh
joss
jos·tle
jot

jot·ting
jounce
jouncy
jour·nal
jour·nal·ese
jour·nal·ism
jour·nal·ist
jour·nal·is·tic
jour·ney
jour·ney·man
joust
jo·vial
jowl
joy·ful
joy·ous
joy·ride
joy·stick
ju·bi·lant
ju·bi·lar·i·an
ju·bi·late
ju·bi·la·tion
ju·bi·lee
Ju·da·ic
Ju·da·ica
Ju·da·ism
Ju·deo-Chris·tia
judge
judg·mat·ic
judg·ment
ju·di·ca·to·ry
ju·di·ca·ture
ju·di·cial
ju·di·cia·ry
ju·di·cious
ju·do
jug·ful
jug·ger·naut
jug·gle
jug·gler
jug·glery

jug·u·lar
juice
juic·er
juicy
ju·jit·su
ju·jube
juke·box
ju·lep
ju·li·enne
jum·ble
jum·bo
jump·er
jump suit
jumpy
junc·tion
junc·ture
jun·gle
jun·gle gym
ju·nior
ju·nior·ate
ju·nior col·lege
ju·nior high
school
ju·nior miss
ju·nior var·sity
ju·ni·per
junk
jun·ket
junk·ie
junk mail
junk·yard
jun·ta
ju·rid·i·cal
ju·ris·dic·tion
ju·ris·pru·dence
ju·rist
ju·ror
ju·ry
jus·sive
jus·tice

jus·ti·fi·able
jus·ti·fi·ca·tion
jus·ti·fi·ca·to·ry
jus·ti·fy
jute
ju·ve·nile
ju·ve·nile
de·lin·quen·cy
ju·ve·nil·ia
jux·ta·pose
jux·ta·po·si·tion

K

ka·bob
kad·dish
kaf·fee·klatsch
kaf·tan
kale
ka·lei·do·scope
ka·mi·ka·ze
kan·ga·roo
ka·pell·mei·ster
ka·pok
kap·pa
ka·put
kar·a·kul
kar·at
ka·ra·te
ka·ty·did
kay·ak
kayo
ka·zoo
keel
keel·haul
keel·son
keen
keep·ing

keep·sake
keg·ler
kelp
ken·nel
ke·no
ker·a·to·sis
ker·chief
ker·mis
ker·nel
ker·o·sene
ke·ryg·ma
kes·trel
ketch
ket·tle
Kew·pie
key·board
key·note
key·punch
key·stone
kha·ki
khe·dive
kib·ble
kib·butz
kib·butz·nik
ki·bitz
ki·bitz·er
ki·bosh
kick·back
kick·off
kid
kid·die
kid·ding
kid·nap
kid·ney
kid·skin
kiel·ba·sa
kill·ing
kill·joy
kiln
ki·lo

kilo·cy·cle
ki·lo·gram
ki·lo·hertz
ki·lo·me·ter
ki·lo·watt
kilt
kil·ter
ki·mo·no
kin·der·gar·ten
kin·der·gart·ner
kind·heart·ed
kin·dle
kind·less
kind·li·ness
kin·dling
kind·ly
kin·dred
kine
kin·e·scope
ki·ne·sics
ki·ne·si·ol·o·gy
ki·ne·sis
ki·net·ic
ki·net·ics
kin·folk
king·dom
king·fish·er
King James
  Ver·sion
king·ly
king·mak·er
king·pin
King's En·glish
king·ship
king-size
kink
kinky
kins·folk
kin·ship
kins·man

kins·wom·an
ki·osk
kip·per
kirk
kirsch
kis·met
kitch·en
kitch·en·ette
kitch·en·ware
kite
kith
kit·ing
kitsch
kit·ten
kit·ten·ish
kit·ty
kit·ty-cor·ner
ki·wi
Klee·nex
klep·to·ma·nia
klep·to·ma·ni·ac
klutz
knack
knack·er
knap·sack
knave
knav·ery
knav·ish
knead
knee
knee·cap
kneed
knee-deep
kneel
knell
knick·er·bock·er
knick·ers
knick·knack
knife
knight

knight·hood
knight·ly
knish
knit
knit·ting
knit·wear
knives
knob
knock
knock·down
knock-knee
knock off
knock·out
knock·wurst
knoll
knot
knot·hole
knot·ty
knout
know
know-how
know·ing
know-it-all
knowl·edge
knowl·edge·able
known
know-noth·ing
knuck·le
knuck·le·ball
knurl
kohl·ra·bi
kook
kooky
Ko·ran
ko·sher
kow·tow
kraal
kra·ter
kraut
krem·lin

ku·chen
ku·dos
Ku Klux·er
Ku Klux Klan
kul·tur
küm·mel
kum·quat
kur·to·sis
kvass
ky·mo·graph
ky·pho·sis
ky·rie

L

la·bel
la·bi·al
la·bile
la·bio·den·tal
la·bor
lab·o·ra·to·ry
la·bo·ri·ous
la·bor·ite
la·bur·num
lab·y·rinth
lab·y·rin·thine
lac·er·ate
lac·er·a·tion
lach·ry·mal
lach·ry·mose
lac·ing
lack·a·dai·si·cal
lack·ey
lack·lus·ter
la·con·ic
lac·o·nism
lac·quer
lac·ri·ma·tion

la·crosse
lac·tate
lac·te·al
lac·tic
lac·tose
la·cu·na
la·cu·nar
lacy
lad·der
lad·die
lad·en
la-di-da
ladies' man
ladies' room
lad·ing
la·dle
la·dy·fin·ger
la·dy-in-wait·ing
la·dy·like
la·dy·ship
la·ger
lag·gard
lag·ging
la·gniappe
la·goon
la·gu·na
la·ical
la·icism
la·icize
lain
lair
lais·sez-faire
la·ity
lake·front
lake·shore
lake·side
lal·ly·gag
la·ma
la·ma·sery
lam·baste

lam·bent
lamb·skin
la·mé
la·med
lame duck
la·ment
la·men·ta·ble
la·men·ta·bly
lam·en·ta·tion
la·ment·ed
lam·i·nate
lam·i·na·tion
lamp·light
lam·poon
lance
lan·cet
lan·dau
land·fall
land·fill
land grant
land·la·dy
land·lord
land·lord·ism
land·lub·ber
land·mark
land-of·fice
   busi·ness
land·own·er
land·scape
land·slide
lands·man
lang syne
lan·guage
lan·guid
lan·guish
lan·guor
lan·guor·ous
lanky
lan·o·lin
lan·ta·na

lan·tern
lan·tern jaw
lan·yard
lap·board
la·pel
lap·i·dar·i·an
lap·i·dary
lap·in
la·pis la·zu·li
lap·pet
lapse
lar·ce·nist
lar·ce·nous
lar·ce·ny
larch
lar·der
large·ly
large-scale
lar·gess
lar·go
lar·i·at
larky
lar·va
lar·vi·cide
la·ryn·geal
lar·yn·gec·to·my
la·ryn·ges
lar·yn·gi·tis
lar·yn·gol·o·gy
la·ryn·go·scope
lar·ynx
la·sa·gna
las·civ·i·ous
las·civ·i·ous·ly
la·ser
lash·ings
lass·ie
las·si·tude
las·so
last-ditch

last·ing
latch
latch·et
latch·key
late·com·er
late·ly
la·ten·cy
la·tent
lat·er·al
lat·est
la·tex
lath
lathe
lath·er
lath·ing
Lat·in·ism
la·tin·i·ty
lat·in·ize
lat·ish
lat·i·tude
lat·i·tu·di·nar·i·
    an
la·trine
lat·ter
lat·ter·ly
lat·tice
lat·tice·work
laud
laud·able
laud·abil·i·ty
lau·da·num
lau·da·tion
lau·da·tive
lau·da·to·ry
laugh
laugh·able
laugh·ing·stock
laugh·ter
launch
launch·er

launch·pad
laun·der
laun·der·ette
Laun·dro·mat
laun·dry
lau·re·ate
lau·rel
la·va
la·va·bo
la·va·liere
lav·a·to·ry
lav·en·der
lav·ish
law-abid·ing
law·break·er
law·ful
law·ful·ly
law·giv·er
law·less
law·mak·er
lawn
law·suit
law·yer
lax
lax·a·tive
lax·ity
lax·ly
lay-by
lay·er
lay·ette
lay·man
lay·off
lay·out
lay·over
lay·up
lay·wom·an
la·zi·er
la·zi·ness
la·zy
la·zy·bones

la·zy·ish
la·zy Su·san
leach
lead·en
lead·er
lead·er·ship
lead-in
lead·ing
lead·less
lead·off
lead pen·cil
leads·man
leaf·hop·per
leaf·let
leafy
league
leak·age
leaky
lean·ing
lean-to
leap·frog
learn
learn·ing
lease
lease·hold
leash
least
least·wise
leath·er
leath·ern
leath·er·neck
leath·ery
leave
leav·en
leav·en·ing
leave-tak·ing
leav·ings
le·bens·raum
lech·er
lech·er·ous

lech·ery
lec·tern
lec·tion·ary
lec·tor
lec·ture
le·der·ho·sen
ledge
led·ger
leech
leek
leer
leery
lee·ward
lee·way
left-hand·ed
left-hand·er
left·over
lefty
leg·a·cy
le·gal
le·gal·ese
le·gal·ism
le·gal·ist
le·gal·i·ty
le·gal·ize
leg·ate
leg·a·tee
le·ga·tion
le·ga·to
leg·end
leg·end·ary
leg·end·ry
leg·er·de·main
leg·ging
leg·gy
leg·horn
leg·i·ble
le·gion
le·gion·ary
le·gion·naire

leg·is·late
leg·is·la·tion
leg·is·la·tive
leg·is·la·tor
leg·is·la·ture
le·git·i·ma·cy
le·git·i·mate
le·git·i·ma·tize
leg·man
leg-pull
le·gume
lei·sure
lei·sure·ly
leit·mo·tiv
le·man
lem·ming
lem·on
lem·on·ade
lend-lease
length
length·en
length·ways
length·wise
le·nience
le·nien·cy
le·nient
len·i·tive
len·i·ty
len·tic·u·lar
len·til
le·o·nine
leop·ard
le·o·tard
lep·er
lep·i·dop·ter·ist
lep·re·chaun
lep·ro·sar·i·um
lep·ro·sy
les·bi·an
les·bi·an·ism

lese maj·es·ty
le·sion
les·see
less·en
less·er
les·son
les·sor
lest
le·thal
le·thar·gic
le·thar·gi·cal·ly
leth·ar·gy
le·the
let·ter
let·tered
let·ter·head
let·ter·ing
let·ter-per·fect
let·tuce
leu·ke·mia
le·vant·er
le·vee
lev·el·er
lev·el·head·ed
le·ver·age
le·vi·a·than
lev·i·tate
lev·i·ta·tion
lev·i·ty
levy
lewd
lex·i·cal
lex·i·cog·ra·pher
lex·i·cog·ra·phy
lex·i·con
Lha·sa ap·so
li·a·bil·i·ty
li·a·ble
li·ai·son
li·ar

li·ba·tion
li·bel
li·bel·ous
lib·er·al
lib·er·al·ism
lib·er·al·i·ty
lib·er·al·i·ty
lib·er·al·ize
lib·er·ate
lib·er·a·tion
lib·er·tar·i·an
lib·er·tine
lib·er·ty
li·bid·i·nal
li·bid·i·nous
li·bi·do
li·bra
li·brar·i·an
li·brary
li·bret·tist
li·bret·to
li·cense
li·cens·ee
li·cen·ti·ate
li·cen·tious
li·chee
li·chen
lic·it
lick·e·ty-split
lick·ing
lic·o·rice
lid·less
lie
lieb·frau·milch
lied
lief
liege
lie-in
lien
lieu

lieu·ten·an·cy
lieu·ten·ant
life-and-death
life-force
life-giv·ing
life·guard
life·less
life·like
life·line
life·long
life net
lif·er
life·sav·er
life-size
life span
life·time
lift-off
lig·a·ment
li·gate
lig·a·ture
light·en
ligh·ter
light-fin·gered
light-foot·ed
light-head·ed
light·ing
light·ly
light·ning
light·ship
light·some
light-struck
light·weight
lig·ne·ous
lig·nite
lik·able
like·li·hood
like·ly
like-mind·ed
lik·en
like·ness

like·wise
lik·ing
li·lac
lil·li·pu·tian
lilt·ing
lily-white
li·ma bean
lim·ber
lim·bo
Lim·burg·er
lime·ade
lime·light
li·men
lim·er·ick
lime·stone
lim·i·nal
lim·it·less
lim·i·ta·tion
lim·it·ed
lim·it·ing
limn
lim·ou·sine
lim·pid
limp·ly
lin·age
linch·pin
Lin·coln·i·an
lin·den
lin·dy
lin·eage
lin·eal
lin·ea·ment
lin·ear
line·back·er
lin·en
lin·er
lines·man
line·up
lin·ger
lin·ge·rie

lin·go
ling·on·ber·ry
lin·gua fran·ca
lin·guist
lin·guis·tic
lin·guis·tics
lin·i·ment
lin·ing
link·age
links
link·up
li·no·leum
Li·no·type
lin·seed
lint
lin·tel
li·on·heart·ed
li·on·ize
li·on's share
lipped
lip·py
lip-read
lip-read·ing
lip ser·vice
lip·stick
liq·ue·fac·tion
liq·ue·fy
li·queur
liq·uid
liq·ui·date
li·quor
li·ra
lisle
lisp
lis·some
lis·ten
lis·ten·able
list·ing
list·less
lit·a·ny

li·tchi
li·ter
lit·er·a·cy
lit·er·al
lit·er·ary
lit·er·ate
li·te·ra·ti
lit·er·a·ture
lithe
lithe·some
litho·graph
li·thog·ra·phy
lit·i·gant
lit·i·gate
li·ti·gious
lit·mus
lit·ter
lit·ter·a·teur
lit·ter·bag
lit·ter·bug
lit·tle
lit·tle·neck
lit·to·ral
li·tur·gi·cal
lit·ur·gist
lit·ur·gy
liv·abil·i·ty
liv·able
live-for·ev·er
live-in
live·li·ness
live·long
live·ly
liv·en
liv·er
liv·er·ied
liv·er·ish
liv·er·wurst
liv·ery
live·stock

live wire
liv·id
liv·ing
liz·ard
lla·ma
load·ing
loaf
loam
loan·word
loath
loathe
loath·ing
loath·some
lob·by
lob·by·er
lob·by·ist
lo·be·lia
lob·ster
lob·ster·man
lo·cal
lo·cale
lo·cal·ism
lo·cal·i·ty
lo·cal·ize
lo·cate
lo·ca·tion
loch
loci
locked-in
lock·er
lock·jaw
lock·smith
lock·step
lock, stock, and bar·rel
lo·co·mo·tion
lo·co·mo·tive
lo·cus
lo·cust
lo·cu·tion

lode·star
lode·stone
lodge
lodg·er
lodg·ing
lodg·ment
lofty
log·a·rithm
log·ger
log·ger·head
log·gia
log·ic
log·i·cal
log·i·cal·ly
lo·gi·cian
lo·gis·tics
log·jam
log·roll
lo·gy
loin
loi·ter
loi·ter·er
loll
lol·li·pop
lol·ly·gag
lone·li·ness
lone·ly
lon·er
lone·some
long-ago
lon·ga·nim·i·ty
long-dis·tance
long-drawn-out
lon·gev·i·ty
long·hand
long·ing
long·ish
lon·gi·tude
lon·gi·tu·di·nal
long johns

long-lived
long-play·ing
long-range
long·shore·man
long·sight·ed
long·some
long-stand·ing
long-suf·fer·ing
long-term
long-wind·ed
look-alike
look·er
look·er-on
look-in
loo·ny
loop·hole
loose
loose-joint·ed
loose-leaf
loos·en
loot
lope
lop-eared
lop·sid·ed
lo·qua·cious
lo·quac·i·ty
lo·ran
lord·ly
lor·do·sis
lord·ship
lore
lor·gnette
lor·ry
los·er
loss lead·er
lo·thar·io
lo·tion
lot·tery
lot·to
lo·tus

loud·mouth
loud·ness
loud·speak·er
lough
lounge
louse
lousy
lout
lout·ish
lou·ver
lov·able
love-in
love·less
love·lorn
love·ly
lov·er
love·sick
lov·ing
lov·ing cup
low·born
low·boy
low·brow
low·er
low·er·case
low·er-class
low-grade
low-key
low-lev·el
low·ly
low-ly·ing
low-pro·file
lox
loy·al
loy·al·ist
loy·al·ty
loz·enge
lub·ber
lu·bri·cant
lu·bri·cate
lu·bri·cious

lu·bri·to·ri·um
lu·cent
lu·cid
lu·cid·i·ty
Lu·cite
lucky
lu·cra·tive
lu·cre
lu·cu·bra·tion
Lu·cul·lan
lu·di·crous
luff
lug·gage
lug·ger
lu·gu·bri·ous
luke·warm
lul·la·by
lum·ba·go
lum·bar
lum·ber
lum·ber·jack
lum·ber·yard
lu·mi·nary
lu·mi·nes·cence
lu·mi·nes·cent
lu·mi·nos·i·ty
lu·mi·nous
lum·mox
lump·ish
lumpy
lu·na·cy
lu·nar
lu·na·tic
lun·cheon
lun·cheon·ette
lu·nette
lunge
lung·er
lunk·head
lu·pine

lurch
lure
lu·rid
lus·cious
lush
lus·ter
lust·ful
lus·trous
lusty
lute
lu·te·nist
Lu·ther·an
lux·u·ri·ance
lux·u·ri·ant
lux·u·ri·ate
lux·u·ri·ous
lux·u·ry
ly·cée
ly·ce·um
lye
ly·ing
lymph
lynch
lynx
lynx-eyed
lyre
lyr·ic
lyr·i·cal
lyr·i·cism
lyr·i·cist

ma·ca·bre
mac·ad·am
mac·a·da·mia
    nut
mac·ad·am·ize

mac·a·ro·ni
mac·a·ron·ic
mac·a·roon
Mc·Car·thy·ism
Mc·Coy
mace
ma·cé·doine
mac·er·ate
ma·chete
Ma·chi·a·vel·lian
mach·i·nate
mach·i·na·tion
ma·chine
ma·chine·like
ma·chin·ery
ma·chin·ist
ma·chis·mo
ma·cho
mack·er·el
mack·i·naw
mack·in·tosh
mac·ra·me
mac·ro
mac·ro·cosm
ma·cron
mac·u·late
mac·u·la·tion
mad
mad·am
mad·cap
mad·den
mad·den·ing
mad·der
mad·dest
ma·de·moi·selle
made-up
mad·house
mad·ly
mad·man
mad·ness

Ma·don·na
ma·dras
mad·ri·gal
mad·wom·an
mael·strom
mae·stro
Mae West
Ma·fia
ma·fi·o·so
mag·a·zine
mag·de·len
ma·gen·ta
mag·got
ma·gi
mag·ic
mag·i·cal
ma·gi·cian
mag·is·te·ri·al
mag·is·te·ri·um
mag·is·tra·cy
ma·gis·tral
mag·is·trate
Mag·na Char·ta
mag·na cum
  lau·de
mag·na·nim·i·ty
mag·nan·i·mous
mag·nate
mag·ne·sia
mag·ne·sium
mag·net
mag·net·ic
mag·net·ic flux
mag·ne·tism
mag·ne·tize
mag·ne·tiz·able
mag·ne·to
mag·ne·tom·e·ter
mag·nif·i·cat
mag·ni·fi·ca·tion

mag·nif·i·cence
mag·nif·i·cent
mag·ni·fi·er
mag·ni·fy
mag·nil·o·quence
mag·nil·o·quent
mag·ni·tude
mag·no·lia
mag·num
mag·pie
ma·ha·ra·ja
ma·ha·ra·ni
ma·hat·ma
Mah-Jongg
ma·hog·a·ny
maid·en
maid·en·hood
maid·en·ly
maid·en name
maid-in-wait·ing
mail·able
mail·bag
mail·box
mail·er
mail·man
maim
main·land
main·line
main·ly
main·mast
main·sail
main·sheet
main·spring
main·stay
main·stream
main·tain
main·tain·able
main·te·nance
mai·son·ette
mai·tre d'

mai·tre d'hô·tel
maize
ma·jes·tic
maj·es·ty
ma·jor·do·mo
ma·jor·ette
ma·jor·i·ty
ma·jus·cule
mak·able
make-be·lieve
make-do
mak·er
make·shift
make·up
make-work
mak·ing
ma·ko
mal·adapt·ed
mal·ad·just·ed
mal·ad·just·ment
mal·ad·min·is·ter
mal·adroit
mal·adroit·ly
mal·adroit·ness
mal·a·dy
ma·la·gue·na
mal·aise
mal·a·mute
mal·apert
mal·a·prop
mal·a·prop·ism
mal·ap·ro·pos
ma·lar·ia
mal·a·thi·on
mal·con·tent
mal de mer
mal·dis·tri·bu·
   tion
male·dict
male·dic·tion

male·fac·tion
male·fac·tor
ma·lef·i·cence
ma·lef·i·cent
mal·e·mute
ma·lev·o·lence
ma·lev·o·lent
mal·fea·sance
mal·for·ma·tion
mal·formed
mal·func·tion
mal·ice
ma·li·cious
ma·lign
ma·lig·nance
ma·lig·nan·cy
ma·lig·nant
ma·lig·ni·ty
ma·li·hi·ni
ma·lin·ger
ma·lin·ger·er
mal·lard
mal·lea·ble
mal·let
mal·nour·ished
mal·nu·tri·tion
mal·oc·clu·sion
mal·odor·ous
mal·prac·tice
mal·prac·ti·tio·
   ner
malt
Mal·tese
Mal·thu·sian
mal·treat
mal·ver·sa·tion
ma·ma
mam·bo
mam·mal
mam·ma·ry

mam·mon
mam·moth
mam·my
man-about-town
man·a·cle
man·age
man·age·able
man·age·ment
man·ag·er
ma·ña·na
man·da·mus
man·da·rin
man·date
man·da·to·ry
man·di·ble
man·do·lin
mane
man-eat·er
ma·neu·ver
man·ful
man·ful·ly
man·ga·nate
man·ga·nese
mange
man·ger
man·gle
man·go
man·grove
mangy
man·han·dle
man·hat·tan
man·hole
man·hood
ma·nia
ma·ni·ac
ma·ni·a·cal
man·ic
man·ic-de·pres·
   sive
ma·ni·cot·ti

man·i·cure
man·i·cur·ist
man·i·fest
man·i·fes·ta·tion
man·i·fes·to
man·i·fold
man·i·kin
ma·nila
man·i·ple
ma·nip·u·late
ma·nip·u·la·tion
ma·nip·u·la·tor
man·kind
man·ly
man-made
man·na
manned
man·ne·quin
man·ner
man·ner·ism
man·ner·ly
man·nish
man-of-war
man·or
man·qué
man·sard
manse
man·sion
man·slaugh·ter
man·sue·tude
man·teau
man·tel
man·tel·piece
man·til·la
man·tis·sa
man·tle
man-to-man
man·tra
man·u·al
man·u·fac·ture

man·u·fac·tur·er
man·u·mis·sion
man·u·mit
ma·nure
manu·script
many-sid·ed
ma·ple
map·mak·er
map·ping
mar·a·schi·no
mar·a·thon
ma·raud
mar·ble
mar·bled
mar·ble·ize
mar·ca·site
mar·cel
march
mar·chio·ness
Mar·di Gras
mare
mare's nest
mar·ga·rine
mar·ga·ri·ta
mar·gin
mar·gin·al
mar·gi·na·lia
mar·gue·rite
mari·gold
mar·i·jua·na
ma·rim·ba
ma·ri·na
mar·i·nate
mar·i·ner
mar·i·o·nette
mar·i·tal
mar·i·time
mar·jo·ram
mar·ket·able
mar·ket·ing

mar·ket·place
marks·man
mar·lin
mar·ma·lade
mar·mo·re·al
mar·mo·set
mar·mot
ma·roon
mar·quee
mar·quess
mar·que·try
mar·quise
mar·qui·sette
mar·riage
mar·ried
mar·ron
mar·rons gla·cés
mar·row
mar·row·bone
mar·ry
mar·shal
marsh·mal·low
marshy
mar·su·pi·al
mart
mar·tial
mar·tian
mar·tin
mar·ti·net
mar·tin·gale
mar·ti·ni
mar·tyr
mar·tyr·dom
mar·tyr·ol·o·gy
mar·vel
mar·vel·ous
Marx·ian
Marx·ism
Marx·ism-
   Le·nin·ism

mar·zi·pan
mas·cara
mas·cot
mas·cu·line
mash·er
mask
mas·och·ism
ma·son
Ma·son-Dix·on
  line
Ma·son·ic
ma·son jar
ma·son·ry
masque
mas·quer·ade
mass
mas·sa·cre
mas·sage
mas·seur
mas·seuse
mas·sif
mas·sive
mast
mas·tec·to·my
mas·ter
mas·ter·ful
mas·ter·ly
mas·ter·mind
mas·ter·piece
mas·tery
mast·head
mas·tic
mas·ti·cate
mas·tiff
mast·odon
mas·toid
mas·tur·bate
mat·a·dor
match
match·able

match·less
match·mak·er
mate
ma·te·ri·al
ma·te·ri·al·ism
ma·te·ri·al·i·ty
ma·te·ri·al·iza·
  tion
ma·te·ri·al·ize
ma·té·ri·el
ma·ter·nal
ma·ter·ni·ty
math
math·e·mat·i·cal
math·e·ma·ti·
  cian
math·e·mat·ics
mat·i·nee
ma·tri·arch
ma·tri·ar·chy
ma·tri·ces
ma·tri·cide
ma·tric·u·late
mat·ri·mo·nial
mat·ri·mo·ny
ma·trix
ma·tron
ma·tron·ly
mat·ted
mat·ter
mat·ter-of-fact
mat·ting
mat·tress
mat·u·rate
mat·u·ra·tion
ma·ture
ma·tu·ri·ty
ma·tu·ti·nal
mat·zo
maud·lin

maul
maun·der
mau·so·le·um
mauve
ma·ven
ma·vour·neen
maw
mawk·ish
max·im
max·i·mal
max·i·mize
max·i·mum
may·be
may·fly
may·hap
may·hem
mayn't
may·on·naise
may·or
may·or·al·ty
may·or·ess
maze
ma·zur·ka
mea cul·pa
mead
mead·ow
mead·ow·lark
mea·ger
meal
meal·time
mealy
mealy·bug
mean
mean·ness
me·an·der
mean·ing
mean·ing·ful
mean·ing·less
mean·ly
mea·sles

mea·sly
mea·sur·ably
mea·sure·less
mea·sure·ment
mea·sur·ing
meat
meat·ball
meaty
mec·ca
me·chan·ic
me·chan·i·cal
me·chan·ics
mech·a·nism
mech·a·nis·tic
mech·a·nize
med·al·ist
me·dal·lion
med·dle
med·dle·some
me·dia
me·di·al
me·di·an
me·di·ate
me·di·a·tion
me·di·a·tor
me·dic
med·i·ca·ble
med·ic·aid
med·i·cal
me·di·ca·ment
medi·care
med·i·cate
med·i·ca·tion
me·dic·i·na·ble
me·dic·i·nal
med·i·cine
me·di·eval
me·di·eval·ism
me·di·eval·ist
me·di·o·cre

me·di·oc·ri·ty
med·i·tate
med·i·ta·tive
Med·i·ter·ra·
  nean
med·lar
med·ley
meed
meek
meer·schaum
meet
meet·ing
mega·cy·cle
mega·hertz
mega·lith
meg·a·lo·ma·nia
meg·a·lop·o·lis
mega·phone
mega·ton
me·gil·lah
Meis·sen
mel·an·cho·lia
mel·an·chol·ic
mel·an·choly
mé·lange
mel·ba toast
meld
me·lee
me·lio·rate
me·lio·rism
mel·lif·er·ous
mel·lif·lu·ent
mel·lif·lu·ous
mel·low
me·lo·de·on
me·lod·ic
me·lo·di·ous
melo·dra·ma
melo·dra·mat·ic
mel·o·dy

mel·on
melt
mem·ber
mem·ber·ship
mem·brane
mem·bra·nous
me·mem·to
mem·oir
mem·o·ra·bil·ia
mem·o·ra·ble
mem·o·ran·dum
me·mo·ri·al
me·mo·ri·al·ize
me·mo·ri·ter
mem·o·rize
mem·o·ry
men·ace
mé·nage
me·nag·er·ie
mend
men·da·cious
men·dac·i·ty
Men·del's law
men·di·can·cy
men·di·cant
men·dic·i·ty
men·ha·den
me·nial
men·in·gi·tis
meno·pause
me·no·rah
men·sal
men·stru·ate
men·stru·a·tion
men·su·ra·ble
mens·wear
men·tal
men·tal·i·ty
men·thol
men·tho·lat·ed

men·tion
men·tion·able
men·tor
menu
me·ow
me·phit·ic
mer·can·tile
mer·can·til·ism
mer·ce·nary
mer·cer·ize
mer·chan·dise
mer·chan·dis·ing
mer·chant
mer·ci·ful
mer·ci·ful·ly
mer·ci·less
mer·cu·ri·al
mer·cu·ric
Mer·cu·ro·
　chrome
mer·cu·ry
mer·cy
mere
mer·e·tri·cious
merge
merg·er
me·rid·i·an
me·ringue
me·ri·no
mer·it
mer·i·toc·ra·cy
mer·i·to·ri·ous
mer·maid
mer·man
mer·ri·ment
mer·ry
mer·ry-go-round
mer·ry·mak·ing
me·sa
més·al·li·ance

mes·dames
mes·de·moi·selles
mesh
mes·mer·ism
mes·mer·ize
mess
mes·sage
mes·sen·ger
mes·si·ah
mes·si·an·ic
mes·si·a·nism
mes·sieurs
messy
mes·ti·zo
met·a·bol·ic
me·tab·o·lism
me·tab·o·lize
meta·car·pal
met·al
me·tal·lic
met·al·lur·gy
met·al·ware
meta·mor·phose
meta·mor·pho·sis
met·a·phor
meta·phys·i·cal
meta·phys·ics
me·tas·ta·sis
me·tas·ta·size
me·tath·e·sis
meta·zo·an
mete
me·tem·psy·cho·
　sis
me·te·or
me·te·or·ic
me·te·or·ite
me·ter
meth·a·done
meth·ane

meth·od
me·thod·i·cal
meth·od·ism
meth·od·ist
meth·od·ol·o·gy
Me·thu·se·lah
me·tic·u·lous
mé·tier
me·ton·y·my
met·ric
met·ri·cal
met·ri·ca·tion
met·ro·nome
met·ro·nom·ic
me·trop·o·lis
met·ro·pol·i·tan
met·tle
met·tle·some
mew
me·zu·zah
mez·za·nine
mez·zo-so·pra·no
mi·aow
mi·as·ma
mi·ca
mice
Mick·ey Finn
Mick·ey Mouse
mi·crobe
mi·cro·copy
mi·cro·cosm
mi·cro·fiche
mi·cro·film
mi·cro·groove
mi·crom·e·ter
mi·cro·phone
mi·cro·scope
mi·cro·scop·ic
mi·cro·some
mi·cro·wave

mic·tu·rate
mid·air
mid·day
mid·dle
mid·dle-aged
middle-class
mid·dle·man
mid·dle-of-the
   road
mid·dle school
mid·dle·weight
mid·dling
mid·dy
mid·field
midg·et
midi
mid·land
mid·night
mid·point
mid·riff
mid·sec·tion
mid·ship·man
midst
mid·stream
mid·town
mid·way
mid·week
mid·wife
mien
miff
might
might·i·ly
mightn't
mighty
mi·graine
mi·grant
mi·grate
mi·gra·to·ry
mi·ka·do
mike

mi·la·dy
milch
mil·dew
mile·age
mil·er
mile·stone
mi·lieu
mil·i·tan·cy
mil·i·tant
mil·i·tari·ly
mil·i·ta·rism
mil·i·ta·rize
mil·i·tary
mil·i·tate
mi·li·tia
milk-and-wa·ter
milk·maid
milk·man
milk·sop
milky
Milky Way
mill·age
mil·len·ni·al
mil·len·ni·um
mill·er
mil·let
mil·li·gram
mil·li·li·ter
mil·li·me·ter
mil·li·ner
mil·li·nery
mill·ing
mil·lion
mil·lion·aire
mil·lion·air·ess
mill·pond
mill·stone
mill·stream
mi·lord
Milque·toast

mime
mim·eo·graph
mi·me·sis
mi·met·ic
mim·ic
mim·ic·ry
mi·mo·sa
min·a·ret
mi·na·to·ry
mince
minc·ing
mind
mind-blow·ing
mind·ful
mind·less
mine
min·er·al
min·er·al·ize
min·er·al·o·gy
min·e·stro·ne
min·gle
min·ia·ture
min·ia·tur·ize
mini·bike
mini·bus
mini·car
mini·com·put·er
min·i·mal
min·i·mal·ly
min·i·mize
min·i·mum
min·ing
min·ion
min·is·cule
mini·skirt
min·is·ter
min·is·te·ri·al
min·is·tra·tion
min·is·try
mink

min·now
mi·nor
mi·nor·i·ty
min·ster
min·strel
min·strel·sy
mint·age
mint ju·lep
min·u·end
min·u·et
mi·nus
mi·nus·cule
min·ute
mi·nute·ly
min·ute·man
min·ute steak
mi·nu·tia
minx
mir·a·cle
mi·rac·u·lous
mi·rage
mire
mir·ror
mirth
mirth·ful·ness
mis·ad·ven·ture
mis·aligned
mis·al·li·ance
mis·an·thrope
mis·an·throp·ic
mis·an·thro·py
mis·ap·pli·ca·tion
mis·ap·ply
mis·ap·pre·hend
mis·ap·pro·pri·ate
mis·be·got·ten
mis·be·have
mis·be·lief
mis·be·lieve

mis·be·liev·er
mis·cal·cu·late
mis·car·riage
mis·car·ry
mis·cast
mis·ce·ge·na·tion
mis·cel·la·neous
mis·cel·la·ny
mis·chance
mis·chief
mis·chie·vous
mis·ci·ble
mis·clas·si·fy
mis·con·ceive
mis·con·duct
mis·con·struc·tion
mis·con·strue
mis·count
mis·cre·ant
mis·cre·ate
mis·cue
mis·deal
mis·deed
mis·de·mean·or
mis·di·rect
mis·di·rec·tion
mis·ed·u·cate
mise-en-scène
mi·ser
mis·er·a·ble
mi·ser·ly
mis·ery
mis·es·ti·mate
mis·fea·sance
mis·file
mis·fire
mis·fit
mis·for·tune
mis·giv·ing

mis·gov·ern
mis·guide
mis·han·dle
mis·hap
mish·mash
mis·in·form
mis·in·ter·pret
mis·judge
mis·la·bel
mis·lay
mis·lead
mis·man·age
mis·match
mis·no·mer
mi·sog·a·mist
mi·sog·y·nist
mis·per·ceive
mis·place
mis·play
mis·print
mis·pri·sion
mis·prize
mis·pro·nounce
mis·pro·nun·ci·a·tion
mis·quote
mis·quo·ta·tion
mis·read
mis·rep·re·sent
mis·rule
mis·sal
mis·send
mis·shap·en
mis·sile
mis·sion
mis·sion·ary
mis·sion·er
mis·sive
miss·out
mis·spell

mis·spend
mis·state
mis·step
mis·sus
mist
mis·tak·able
mis·take
mis·tak·en·ly
mis·ter
mis·tle·toe
mis·trans·late
mis·treat
mis·tress
mis·tri·al
mis·trust
misty
misty-eyed
mis·un·der·stand
mis·us·age
mis·use
mite
mi·ter
mit·i·gate
mit·i·ga·tor
mitt
mit·ten
mix·able
mixed
mixed-up
mix·er
mix·ture
mix-up
miz·zen·mast
miz·zle
mne·mon·ic
mne·mon·ics
moan
moat
mobbed
mo·bile

mo·bi·li·za·tion
mo·bi·lize
mob·ster
moc·ca·sin
mo·cha
mock·ing·ly
mock·ery
mock-he·ro·ic
mock-up
mod
mod·al
mo·dal·i·ty
mode
mod·el
mod·er·ate
mo·der·a·to
mod·er·a·tor
mod·ern
mod·ern·ism
mod·ern·is·tic
mod·ern·iza·tion
mod·ern·ize
mod·est
mod·es·ty
mod·i·cum
mod·i·fi·able
mod·i·fi·ca·tion
mod·i·fi·er
mod·i·fy
mod·ish
mo·diste
mod·u·lar
mod·u·late
mod·u·la·tion
mod·ule
mo·dus ope·ran·
  di
mo·dus vi·ven·di
mo·gul
mo·hair

Mo·ham·med·an
moi·ety
moil
moi·ré
moist·en
mois·ture
mois·tur·ize
mo·lar
mo·las·ses
mold·able
mold·er
mold·ing
moldy
mole
mo·lec·u·lar
mol·e·cule
mole·skin
mo·lest
mo·les·ta·tion
mol·li·fy
mol·lusk
mol·ly·cod·dle
Mo·lo·tov
  cock·tail
mol·ten
mo·ment
mo·men·tari·ly
mo·men·tary
mo·ment·ly
mo·men·tous
mo·men·tum
mon·arch
mo·nar·chi·cal
mon·ar·chism
mon·ar·chy
mon·as·te·ri·al
mon·as·tery
mo·nas·tic
mon·au·ral
mon·e·tary

mon·ey
mon·eyed
mon·ey·lend·er
mon·ger
mon·go·lian·ism
mon·gol·ism
Mon·gol·oid
mon·grel
mon·i·ker
mo·nism
mo·ni·tion
mon·i·tor
mon·i·to·ry
monk
mon·key
mon·key wrench
monk·ish
mono·chro·mat·ic
mon·o·cle
mon·oc·u·lar
mono·dra·ma
mo·nog·a·my
mono·gram
mono·graph
mo·nog·y·ny
mono·lin·gual
mono·lith
mono·lith·ic
mono·logue
mono·ma·nia
mo·no·mi·al
mono·nu·cle·o·sis
mo·nop·o·list
mo·nop·o·lize
mo·nop·o·ly
mono·rail
mono·syl·la·ble
mono·the·ism
mono·tone
mo·not·o·nous

mo·not·o·ny
mon·ox·ide
mon·sei·gneur
mon·sieur
mon·si·gnor
mon·soon
mon·ster
mon·stros·i·ty
mon·strous
mon·tage
mon·te
Mon·te Car·lo
Mon·tes·so·ri·an
month
mon·u·ment
mon·u·men·tal
mooch
mood
moody
moo·la
moon·beam
moon·light
moon·lit
moon·shine
moon·stone
moor
moor·age
moor·ing
moose
moot
mope
mopped
mop·pet
mo·raine
mor·al
mo·rale
mor·al·ism
mor·al·is·tic
mo·ral·i·ty
mor·al·ize

mor·al·iza·tion
mo·rass
mor·a·to·ri·um
mo·ray
mor·bid
mor·bid·i·ty
mor·dan·cy
mor·dant
more·over
mo·res
mor·ga·nat·ic
morgue
mor·i·bund
Mor·mon
morn·ing
mo·roc·co
mo·ron
mo·ron·ic
mo·rose
mor·phine
Morse code
mor·sel
mor·tal
mor·tal·i·ty
mor·tal·ly
mor·tar
mor·tar·board
mort·gage
mort·gag·ee
mort·gag·or
mor·ti·cian
mor·ti·fi·ca·tion
mor·ti·fy
mor·tise
mort·main
mor·tu·ary
mo·sa·ic
mo·sey
Mos·lem
mosque

mos·qui·to
mossy
most·ly
mote
mo·tel
mo·tet
moth
moth-eat·en
moth·er
Moth·er Hub·bard
moth·er-in-law
moth·er·ly
moth·er-of-pearl
mo·tif
mo·tile
mo·tion
mo·ti·vate
mo·ti·va·tion
mo·tive
mot juste
mot·ley
mo·tor
mo·tor·cade
mo·tor·cy·cle
mo·tor inn
mo·tor·ist
mot·tle
mot·to
mould
mound
mount
mount·able
moun·tain
moun·tain·eer
moun·tain·ous
moun·tain·side
moun·tainy
moun·te·bank
mourn
mourn·ful

mourn·ing
mouse
mous·er
mous·sa·ka
mousse
mousy
mouth
mouth·ful
mouth·piece
mouth-to-mouth
mouthy
mou·ton
mov·able
mov·abil·i·ty
move·less
move·ment
mov·er
mov·ie
mov·ie·go·er
mow
mown
mox·ie
moz·za·rel·la
Mrs. Grun·dy
mu·ci·lage
mu·ci·lag·i·nous
muck
muck·rake
mu·cous
mu·cus
mud·dle
mud·dy
mud·room
mud·sling·er
muf·fin
muf·fle
muf·fler
mug·ger
mug·gy
mug·wump

Mu·ham·mad·an
mu·lat·to
mul·ber·ry
mulch
mulct
mule
mu·le·teer
mul·ish
mull
mul·let
mul·li·gan stew
mul·li·ga·taw·ny
mul·ti·col·ored
mul·ti·cul·tur·al
mul·ti·di·men·
sion·al
mul·ti·di·rec·
tion·al
mul·ti·dis·ci·plin
ary
mul·ti·fac·et·ed
mul·ti·far·i·ous
mul·ti·fold
mul·ti·lat·er·al
mul·ti·lay·ered
mul·ti·lev·el
mul·ti·lin·gual
mul·ti·mil·lion·
aire
mul·ti·ple
mul·ti·pli·able
mul·ti·pli·ca·tion
mul·ti·plic·i·ty
mul·ti·pli·er
mul·ti·ply
mul·ti·pur·pose
mul·ti·ra·cial
mul·ti·sen·so·ry
mul·ti·tude
mul·ti·tu·di·nou

mum·ble
mum·bo jum·bo
mum·mi·fy
mum·my
mumps
munch
mun·dane
mu·nic·i·pal
mu·nic·i·pal·i·ty
mu·nif·i·cent
mu·ni·tion
mu·ral
mur·der
mur·der·er
mur·der·ous
mu·ri·at·ic acid
murky
mur·mur
mur·mur·ous
mus·ca·tel
mus·cle
mus·cled
mus·co·vite
mus·cu·lar
mus·cu·lar
   dys·tro·phy
mus·cu·la·ture
muse
mu·sette
mu·se·um
mush
mushy
mu·sic
mu·si·cal
mu·si·cale
mu·si·cal·i·ty
mu·si·cian
mu·si·cian·ship
mu·si·col·o·gy
musk

mus·ket
mus·ke·teer
musk·mel·on
musk·rat
Mus·lim
mus·lin
mus·sel
mus·tache
mus·ta·chio
mus·tang
mus·tard
mus·ter
mustn't
musty
mu·ta·ble
mu·tant
mu·ta·tion
mute
mu·ti·late
mu·ti·la·tion
mu·ti·la·tor
mu·ti·neer
mu·ti·nous
mu·ti·ny
mutt
mut·ter
mut·ton
mu·tu·al
mu·tu·al·i·ty
mu·tu·al·ize
muu·muu
muz·zle
my·o·pia
myr·i·ad
myr·mi·don
myrrh
myr·tle
my·self
mys·te·ri·ous
mys·tery

mys·tic
mys·ti·cal
mys·ti·cism
mys·ti·fi·ca·tion
mys·ti·fy
mys·tique
myth
myth·i·cal
myth·o·log·i·cal
my·thol·o·gize
my·thol·o·gy

N

na·bob
na·dir
nag
nagged
nag·ging
na·iad
na·if
nail
na·ive
na·ive·té
na·ked
nam·by-pam·by
name
name·able
name-call·ing
name·less
name·ly
name·sake
nan·ny
nap
na·palm
nape
na·pery

naph·tha
nap·kin
na·po·leon
napped
nap·ping
nar·cis·sism
nar·cis·sus
nar·co·lep·sy
nar·co·sis
nar·cot·ic
nar·rate
nar·ra·tion
nar·ra·tive
nar·row
na·sal
na·sal·ize
na·scen·cy
na·scent
nas·ti·ly
nas·ti·ness
nas·tur·tium
nas·ty
na·tal
na·ta·to·ri·al
na·ta·to·ri·um
na·tion
na·tion·al
na·tion·al·ism
na·tion·al·ist
na·tion·al·is·tic
na·tion·al·i·ty
na·tion·al·iza·
  tion
na·tion·al·ize
na·tion·wide
na·tive
na·tiv·ism
na·tiv·i·ty
nat·ty
nat·u·ral

nat·u·ral·ism
nat·u·ral·ist
nat·u·ral·ize
nat·u·ral·ly
nat·u·ral·ness
na·ture
naught
naugh·ty
nau·sea
nau·se·ate
nau·seous
nau·seous·ness
nau·ti·cal
nau·ti·lus
na·val
na·vel
nav·i·ga·ble
nav·i·gate
nav·i·ga·tion
nav·i·ga·tor
nav·vy
na·vy
na·zi
Na·zi·ism
Na·zism
neap
Ne·a·pol·i·tan
near·by
nearly
near·sight·ed
neat
neat's-foot oil
neb·bish
neb·u·la
neb·u·lous
nec·es·sar·i·ly
nec·es·sary
ne·ces·si·tate
ne·ces·si·tous
ne·ces·si·ty

neck·er·chief
neck·ing
neck·lace
neck·line
neck·tie
ne·crol·o·gy
nec·ro·man·cy
ne·crop·o·lis
nec·rop·sy
nec·tar
nec·tar·ine
née
need·ful
need·ful·ly
need·ful·ness
nee·dle
nee·dle·point
need·less
need·less·ness
nee·dle·work
needn't
needy
ne'er-do-well
ne·far·i·ous
ne·far·i·ous·ness
ne·gate
ne·ga·tion
neg·a·tive
neg·a·tiv·ism
ne·glect
ne·glect·ful
ne·glect·ful·ness
neg·li·gee
neg·li·gence
neg·li·gent
neg·li·gi·ble
ne·go·tia·ble
ne·go·ti·ate
ne·go·ti·a·tion
Ne·gress

ne·gri·tude
Ne·gro
ne·gus
neigh
neigh·bor
neigh·bor·hood
neigh·bor·ly
nei·ther
nel·son
nem·e·sis
neo·clas·sic
neo·co·lo·nial
neo-Freud·ian
neo-im·pres·sion·ism
neo·lith·ic
ne·ol·o·gism
ne·ol·o·gy
ne·on
neo·na·tal
neo·phyte
neo-scho·las·ti·cism
ne·pen·the
neph·ew
ne·phrit·ic
ne·phri·tis
ne plus ul·tra
nep·o·tism
Nep·tune
nerve
nerve·less
nerve-rack·ing
ner·vos·i·ty
ner·vous
nervy
ne·science
nes·tle
nest·ling
neth·er

neth·er·most
neth·er·world
net·ted
net·ting
net·tle
net·tle·some
net·work
neu·ral
neu·ral·gia
neur·as·the·nia
neu·ri·tis
neu·rol·o·gist
neu·rol·o·gy
neu·ro·mus·cu·lar
neu·ro·sis
neu·ro·sur·geon
neu·ro·sur·gery
neu·rot·ic
neu·rot·i·cism
neu·ter
neu·tral
neu·tral·ism
neu·tral·i·ty
neu·tral·iza·tion
neu·tral·ize
neu·tron
nev·er·more
nev·er-nev·er land
nev·er·the·less
new·born
new·com·er
new·el
new·fan·gled
New·found·land
new·ly
new·ly·wed
news·agent
news·boy

news·break
news·cast
news·let·ter
news·mag·a·zine
news·man
news·pa·per
news·wor·thy
newsy
newt
New Year's Day
next-door
nex·us
Ni·ag·a·ra
nib·ble
nice·ly
nice-nel·ly
nice·ty
niche
nick
nick·el
nick·el·ode·on
nick·nack
nick·name
nic·o·tine
nic·o·tin·ic
ni·dus
niece
nif·ty
nig·gard
nig·gard·li·ness
nig·gle
nig·gling
night·cap
night·clothes
night·club
night·dress
night·hawk
night·ie
night·in·gale
night·long

night·ly
night·mare
night·shirt
ni·gri·tude
ni·hil·ism
ni·hil ob·stat
nim·ble
nim·bus
nin·com·poop
nine·fold
nine·teen
nine·ty
nin·ny
nip·ple
nip·py
nir·va·na
ni·sei
nit-pick·ing
ni·trate
ni·tric
ni·tro·gen
ni·trous
nit·ty-grit·ty
nit·wit
no-ac·count
nob·by
No·bel·ist
No·bel prize
no·bil·i·ty
no·ble
no·blesse oblige
noc·tur·nal
noc·turne
noc·u·ous
nod·ding
node
nod·ule
no·el
no-fault
nog·gin

no-hit
noise
noi·some
noisy
no·lo con·ten·de·
re
no·mad
no·mad·ic
no-man's-land
nom de plume
no·men·cla·ture
nom·i·nal
nom·i·nal·ism
nom·i·nate
nom·i·na·tion
nom·i·na·tive
nom·i·na·tor
nom·i·nee
no·mo·thet·ic
non·age
no·na·ge·nar·i·an
non·aligned
non·ca·lo·ric
nonce
non·cha·lance
non·cha·lant
non·com
non·com·ba·tant
non·com·mis·
sioned of·fi·cer
non·com·mit·tal
non·con·cur·
rence
non·con·form
non·con·for·
mance
non·con·form·ist
non·con·for·mi·ty
non·co·op·er·a·
tion

non·co·op·er·a·
tive
non·dairy
non·de·duct·ible
non·de·script
non·de·struc·tive
non·di·rec·tive
non·en·force·able
non·en·ti·ty
none·such
none·the·less
non-eu·clid·e·an
non·fic·tion
non·fic·tion·al
non·flam·ma·ble
non·in·duc·tive
non·in·ter·ven·
tion
non·in·volve·
ment
non·judg·men·tal
non·match·ing
non·me·tal·lic
non·ob·jec·tive
no-non·sense
non·pa·reil
non·par·ti·san
non·per·son
non·plussed
non·pro·duc·tive
non·pro·fes·sion·
al
non·prof·it
non·pro·lif·er·a·
tion
non·read·er
non·re·fund·able
non·rep·re·sen·
ta·tion·al
non·res·i·dent

non·re·sis·tance
non·re·turn·able
non·sec·tar·i·an
non·sense
non·sen·si·cal
non se·qui·tur
non·sig·nif·i·cant
non·skid
non·start·er
non·sup·port
non·ten·ured
non·ver·bal
non·vi·o·lence
non·vi·o·lent
non·white
noo·dle
noon·time
noose
Nor·dic
nor·mal
nor·mal·cy
nor·mal·ize
nor·mal school
nor·ma·tive
normed
north·east·er
north·east·ern
North·east·ern·er
north·east·ward
north·er
north·er·ly
north·ern
north·ern·most
north·west
north·west·ern
North·west·ern·
   er
north·west·ward
nose·bleed
nose·gay

no-show
nos·ing
nos·tal·gia
nos·tril
nos·trum
nosy
no·ta be·ne
no·ta·bil·i·ty
no·ta·ble
no·ta·ri·za·tion
no·ta·rize
no·ta·ry pub·lic
no·tate
no·ta·tion
notch
note·book
not·ed
note·pa·per
note·wor·thy
noth·ing·ness
no·tice
no·tice·able
no·ti·fi·ca·tion
no·ti·fy
no·tion
no·to·ri·ety
no·to·ri·ous
no-trump
not·with·stand·
   ing
nou·gat
nour·ish
nour·ish·ing
nour·ish·ment
nou·veau riche
nov·el
nov·el·ette
nov·el·ist
nov·el·ty
no·ve·na

nov·ice
no·vi·tiate
no·vo·caine
now·a·days
no·where
nox·ious
noz·zle
nu·ance
nub·ble
nub·bly
nu·bile
nu·cle·ar
nu·cle·ate
nu·cle·on
nu·cle·us
nude
nudge
nud·ism
nu·di·ty
nu·ga·to·ry
nug·get
nui·sance
null hy·poth·e·sis
nul·li·fi·ca·tion
nul·li·fy
nul·li·ty
numb
num·ber·less
numb·skull
nu·mer·al
nu·mer·ate
nu·mer·a·tion
nu·mer·a·tor
nu·mer·i·cal
nu·mer·ol·o·gy
nu·mer·ous
nu·mis·mat·ic
nu·mis·mat·ics
num·skull
nun·cio

nup·tial
nurse
nurs·ery
nurs·ery·maid
nurs·ery·man
nurse's aide
nurs·ing
nur·ture
nut-brown
nut·crack·er
nut·meg
nu·tri·ent
nu·tri·ment
nu·tri·tion
nu·tri·tion·ist
nu·tri·tious
nu·tri·tive
nut·shell
nut·ty
nuz·zle
ny·lon
nymph
nym·phet

O

oaf
oaf·ish
oak-leaf clus·ter
oars·man
oa·sis
oat·cake
oath
oat·meal
ob·bli·ga·to
ob·du·ra·cy
ob·du·rate
obe·di·ence

obe·di·ent
obei·sance
obe·lisk
obese
obe·si·ty
obey
ob·fus·cate
Obie
obit
obi·ter dic·tum
obit·u·ary
ob·ject
ob·ject·ti·fy
ob·ject·ti·fi·ca·
    tion
ob·jec·tion
ob·jec·tion·able
ob·jec·tive
ob·jec·tiv·ism
ob·jet d'art
ob·jur·gate
ob·late
ob·la·tion
ob·li·gate
ob·li·ga·tion
oblig·a·to·ry
oblige
oblig·ing
oblique
obliq·ui·ty
oblit·er·ate
obliv·i·on
obliv·i·ous
ob·long
ob·lo·quy
ob·nox·ious
ob·nox·ious·ness
oboe
ob·scene
ob·scen·i·ty

ob·scu·ran·tism
ob·scure
ob·scu·ri·ty
ob·se·qui·ous
ob·se·quy
ob·serv·able
ob·ser·vance
ob·ser·vant
ob·ser·va·tion
ob·ser·va·to·ry
ob·serve
ob·serv·er
ob·sess
ob·ses·sion
ob·ses·sive
ob·sid·i·an
ob·so·les·cence
ob·so·les·cent
ob·so·lete
ob·sta·cle
ob·stet·ric
ob·ste·tri·cian
ob·stet·rics
ob·sti·na·cy
ob·sti·nate
ob·strep·er·ous
ob·strep·er·ous·
    ness
ob·struct
ob·struc·tion
ob·tain
ob·trude
ob·tru·sive
ob·tru·sive·ness
ob·tuse
ob·verse
ob·vi·ate
ob·vi·ous
oc·a·ri·na
oc·ca·sion

oc·ca·sion·al
oc·ci·den·tal
oc·cip·i·tal
oc·clude
oc·clu·sion
oc·cult
oc·cul·ta·tion
oc·cult·ism
oc·cu·pan·cy
oc·cu·pant
oc·cu·pa·tion
oc·cu·pa·tion·al
oc·cu·py
oc·cur
oc·cur·rence
oc·cur·rent
ocean
ocean·ar·i·um
oce·an·ic
ocean·og·ra·phy
oce·lot
o'clock
oc·ta·gon
oc·tag·o·nal
oc·ta·he·dral
oc·ta·he·dron
oc·tane
oc·tave
oc·ta·vo
oc·tet
oc·to·ge·nar·i·an
oc·to·pod
oc·to·pus
oc·to·roon
oc·u·lar
oc·u·list
oda·lisque
odd·ball
odd·i·ty
odd·ly

odd·ment
odds
ode
odi·ous
odi·um
odom·e·ter
odon·tol·o·gy
odor·if·er·ous
odor·ize
odor·less
odor·ous
od·ys·sey
oe·cu·men·i·cal
oe·di·pal
Oe·di·pus
　com·plex
oeu·vre
of·fal
off·beat
off·col·or
of·fend
of·fense
of·fen·sive
of·fer·ing
of·fer·to·ry
off·hand
off·hand·ed·ness
of·fice
of·fi·cer
of·fi·cial
of·fi·cial·dom
of·fi·cial·ese
of·fi·ci·ate
of·fi·cious
off·ing
off-key
off lim·its
off-off-Broad·way
off-sea·son
off·set

off·shoot
off·shore
off·side
off·spring
off·stage
off-the-re·cord
of·ten·times
ogive
ogle
ogre
ohm
oiled
oil·er
oil·skin
oily
oink
oint·ment
okey-doke
okra
old·en
old-fash·ioned
Old Glory
old guard
old·ie
old·ish
Old Nick
old·ster
old-time
ole·ag·i·nous
ole·an·der
oleo·graph
oleo·mar·ga·rine
ol·fac·tion
ol·fac·to·ry
oli·garch
oli·gar·chy
olio
ol·ive
ol·la po·dri·da
olym·pi·ad

Olym·pi·an
Olym·pic Games
om·buds·man
ome·ga
om·elet
omen
om·i·nous
omis·sion
omit
om·ni·bus
om·ni·di·rec·tion·
al
om·nip·o·tence
om·nip·o·tent
om·ni·pres·ence
om·ni·science
om·ni·scient
om·ni·um-gath·
er·um
om·ni·vore
om·niv·o·rous
once-over
on·com·ing
one-armed
ban·dit
one-bag·ger
one-di·men·sion·
al
one-hand·ed
one-horse
one-night stand
one-on-one
one-piece
oner·ous
one·self
one-shot
one-sid·ed
one-up·man·ship
one-way
on·ion

on·ion·skin
on·look·er
on·ly
on·o·mas·tic
on·o·mato·poe·ia
on·o·mato·po·et·
i·cal·ly
on·rush
on·set
on·shore
on·side
on·stage
on-the-job
on·to
on·tog·e·ny
on·to·log·i·cal
on·tol·o·gy
onus
on·ward
on·yx
oo·dles
ooh
oo·long
oomph
oops
ooze
oozy
opac·i·ty
opal
opal·es·cent
opal·es·cence
opal·ine
opaque
op art
open·ness
open-air
open-and-shut
open-cir·cuit
open-end
open·er

open·eyed
open·hand·ed
open-heart
open·ing
open-mind·ed
open-mouthed
open ses·a·me
op·era
op·er·a·ble
opé·ra bouffe
opé·ra co·mique
op·era·go·er
op·er·ant
op·er·ate
op·er·a·tion
op·er·a·tion·al
op·er·a·tive
op·er·a·tor
op·er·et·ta
oph·thal·mic
oph·thal·mol·o·
gist
oph·thal·mol·o·
gy
oph·thal·mo·
scope
opi·ate
opine
opin·ion
opin·ion·at·ed
opin·ion·ative
opi·um
opos·sum
op·po·nent
op·por·tune
op·por·tun·ism
op·por·tu·ni·ty
op·pos·able
op·pose
op·po·site

op·po·si·tion
op·press
op·pres·sion
op·pres·sive
op·pro·bri·ous
op·pro·bri·um
op·pugn
op·ta·tive
op·tic
op·ti·cal
op·ti·cian
op·tics
op·ti·mal
op·ti·mism
op·ti·mize
op·ti·mum
op·tion
op·tion·al
op·tom·e·trist
op·tom·e·try
opt out
op·u·lence
op·u·lent
opus
or·a·cle
orac·u·lar
oral
oral·ly
or·ange
or·ange·ade
or·ange pe·koe
or·ange·ry
or·angy
orate
ora·tion
or·a·tor
or·a·tor·i·cal
or·a·to·rio
or·a·to·ry
orb

or·bic·u·lar
or·bit
or·bit·al
or·chard
or·ches·tra
or·ches·tral
or·ches·trate
or·ches·tra·tion
or·chid
or·dain
or·deal
or·der
or·der·ly
or·di·nal
or·di·nance
or·di·nary
or·di·na·tion
ord·nance
or·don·nance
or·dure
ore
oreg·a·no
or·gan
or·gan·dy
or·gan·ic
or·gan·ism
or·gan·ist
or·ga·ni·za·tion
or·ga·nize
or·ga·niz·er
or·gasm
or·gi·as·tic
or·gy
ori·el
ori·ent
ori·en·tal
ori·en·tal·ism
ori·en·tate
ori·en·ta·tion
or·i·fice

ori·flamme
or·i·gin
orig·i·nal
orig·i·nal·i·ty
orig·i·nate
ori·ole
or·i·son
Or·lon
or·mo·lu
or·na·ment
or·na·men·ta·
  tion
or·nate
or·nery
or·ni·thol·o·gist
or·ni·thol·o·gy
oro·tund
or·phan
or·phan·age
orth·odon·tia
orth·odon·tics
orth·odon·tist
or·tho·dox
or·tho·doxy
or·tho·epy
or·thog·ra·phy
or·tho·pe·dic
or·tho·pe·dics
or·tho·pe·dist
Os·car
os·cil·late
os·cil·la·tion
os·cil·la·tor
os·cil·lo·gram
os·cil·lo·graph
os·cil·lo·scope
os·cu·late
os·cu·la·tion
os·mo·sis
os·mot·ic

os·prey
os·si·fi·ca·tion
os·si·fy
os·ten·si·ble
os·ten·ta·tion
os·ten·ta·tious
os·teo·ar·thri·tis
os·te·ol·o·gy
os·teo·path
os·te·op·a·thy
os·tler
os·tra·cism
os·tra·cize
os·trich
oth·er·wise
oth·er·world·ly
oti·ose
oto·lar·yn·gol·o·gy
ot·ter
ot·to·man
ouch
ought
ounce
our·selves
oust
oust·er
out·age
out-and-out
out·board
out·break
out·burst
out·cast
out·come
out·crop
out·cry
out·dat·ed
out·dis·tance
out·do
out·door

out·doors
out·doors·man
out·doorsy
out·er·coat
out·face
out·field
out·fit
out·fit·ter
out·flank
out·fox
out·gen·er·al
out·go
out·go·ing
out·grow
out·growth
out·guess
out·house
out·ing
out·land·ish
out·last
out·law
out·law·ry
out·lay
out·let
out·line
out·live
out·look
out·ly·ing
out·ma·neu·ver
out·mod·ed
out·num·ber
out-of-bounds
out-of-date
out-of-doors
out-of-pock·et
out-of-the-way
out·pa·tient
out·per·form
out·point
out·put

out·rage
out·ra·geous
ou·tré
out·reach
out·rig·ger
out·right
out·shine
out·side
out·sid·er
out·smart
out·spent
out·spo·ken
out·stand·ing
out·stare
out·strip
out·ward
out·ward-bound
out·ward·ly
out·wear
out·wit
out·worn
ou·zo
oval
ovar·i·an
ova·ry
ovate
ova·tion
ov·en
over·abun·dance
over·achiev·er
over·act
over·ac·tive
over·age
over·all
over·arch·ing
over·awe
over·bear
over·bear·ing
over·board
over·bur·den

over·cap·i·tal·ize
over·cast
over·cau·tious
over·charge
over·coat
over·come
over·com·pen·sa·tion
over·con·fi·dence
over·de·ter·mined
over·de·vel·op
over·do
over·dose
over·draw
over·dress
over·due
over·em·pha·sis
over·es·ti·mate
over·ex·pose
over·fill
over·flow
over·hand
over·hang
over·haul
over·head
over·hear
over·in·dulge
over·kill
over·land
over·lap
over·lay
over·load
over·lord
over·ly
over·much
over·night
over·op·ti·mism
over·pass
over·play

over·pop·u·la·tion
over·pow·er
over·price
over·pro·duce
over·qual·i·fied
over·rate
over·reach
over·re·act
over·rep·re·sent·ed
over·ride
over·ripe
over·rule
over·run
over·seas
over·seer
over·sell
over·sen·si·tive
over·shoe
over·shot
over·sight
over·sim·pli·fy
over·size
over·sleep
over·sold
over·spend
over·state
over·stay
over·stock
over·sub·scribe
over·sup·ply
overt
over·take
over-the-count·er
over·time
over·ture
over·turn
over·view
over·ween·ing

over·weight
over·whelm
over·work
over·wrought
ovu·late
ovule
owe
ow·ing to
owl·et
owl·ish
ox·blood
ox·ford
ox·i·da·tion
ox·ide
ox·i·dize
ox·tail
ox·tongue
ox·y·gen
ox·y·gen·ate
oxy·mo·ron
oyez
oys·ter
oys·ter·man
ozone

P

pab·u·lum
pace
pace·mak·er
pac·er
pace·set·ter
pachy·derm
pachy·der·ma·tous
pach·ys·an·dra
pa·cif·ic
pac·i·fi·ca·tion

pa·cif·i·ca·tor
pa·cif·i·ca·to·ry
pa·cif·i·cism
pac·i·fi·er
pac·i·fism
pac·i·fist
pac·i·fy
pack·age
pack·ag·ing
pack·er
pack·et
pack·horse
pack·ing·house
pact
pad·ded
pad·ding
pad·dle
pad·dle·ball
pad·dle·board
pad·dock
pad·dy
pad·lock
pa·dre
pa·dro·ne
pae·an
pa·el·la
pae·on
pa·gan
pa·gan·ism
page
pag·eant
pag·eant·ry
page boy
pag·i·nal
pag·i·nate
pag·i·na·tion
pag·ing
pa·go·da
paid
pail·ful

pain·kill·er
pain·less
pains·tak·ing
paint·brush
paint·er
paint·ing
pair
pais·ley
pa·ja·ma
pal·ace
pal·a·din
pa·laes·tra
pa·lan·quin
pal·at·able
pal·a·tal
pal·a·tal·iza·tion
pal·a·tal·ize
pal·ate
pa·la·tial
pa·la·ver
pa·laz·zo
pale
pale·face
pa·le·og·ra·phy
Pa·leo·lith·ic
pa·le·on·tol·o·gy
pal·ette
pal·frey
pa·limp·sest
pal·in·drome
pal·ing
pal·i·sade
pal·ish
pall
pal·la·di·um
pall·bear·er
pal·let
pal·lette
pal·liasse
pal·li·ate

pal·lia·tive
pal·lid
pal·lid·ly
pal·lid·ness
pall-mall
pal·lor
pal·ly
palm
pal·mate
palmed
pal·met·to
palm·ist·ry
palmy
pal·o·mi·no
pal·pa·ble
pal·pate
pal·pi·tant
pal·pi·tate
pal·sied
pal·sy
pal·sy-wal·sy
pal·ter
pal·try
pam·pa
pam·per
pam·phlet
pam·phle·teer
pan·a·cea
pa·nache
pan·a·ma
Pan-Amer·i·can
pan·a·tela
pan·cake
pan·chro·mat·ic
pan·cre·as
pan·da
pan·dem·ic
pan·de·mo·ni·um
pan·der
pan·dit

pan·do·ra
Pan·do·ra's box
pane
pan·e·gy·ric
pan·e·gy·rist
pan·el
pan·el·ing
pan·el·ist
pan·han·dle
Pan·hel·len·ic
pan·ic
pan·icked
pan·ick·ing
pan·i·cle
pan·jan·drum
panned
pan·ning
pan·o·plied
pan·o·ply
pan·ora·ma
pan·sy
pant
pan·ta·loon
pan·the·ism
pan·the·on
pan·ther
pant·ie
pant·isoc·ra·cy
pan·to·graph
pan·to·mime
pan·to·mim·ist
pan·try
pants suit
panty hose
panty·waist
pan·zer
pa·pa·cy
pa·pal
pa·pal·ly
pa·pa·raz·zo

pa·pa·ya
pa·per
pa·per·back
pa·per·er
pa·per·hang·er
pa·per-thin
pa·per·weight
pa·per·work
pa·pery
pa·pier-mâ·ché
pa·pil·lon
pa·pist
pa·pist·ry
pa·poose
pa·pri·ka
Pap smear
pa·py·rus
par·a·ble
pa·rab·o·la
par·a·bol·ic
para·chute
para·chut·ist
pa·rade
par·a·digm
par·a·dig·mat·ic
par·a·dis·al
par·a·dise
par·a·di·si·a·cal
par·a·dox
par·a·dox·i·cal
par·af·fin
par·a·gon
para·graph
par·a·keet
par·al·lax
par·al·lel
par·al·lel·ism
par·al·lel·o·gram
pa·ral·y·sis
par·a·lyt·ic

par·a·lyze
para·med·ic
para·med·i·cal
pa·ram·e·ter
para·mil·i·tary
par·am·ne·sia
par·a·mount
par·amour
para·noia
para·noi·ac
para·noid
para·noid
  schiz·o·phre·nia
par·a·pet
par·a·pher·na·lia
para·phrase
para·phras·tic
para·ple·gia
para·pro·fes·sion·
  al
par·a·site
par·a·sit·ic
par·a·sit·ism
par·a·si·tol·o·gy
para·sol
para·troop·er
par·boil
par·cel
par·cel·ing
parch
Par·chee·si
parch·ment
pard·ner
par·don
par·don·able
par·don·er
pare
par·e·go·ric
par·ent
par·ent·age

pa·ren·the·sis
pa·ren·the·size
par·ent·hood
par·ent-teach·er
  as·so·ci·a·tion
par ex·cel·lence
par·fait
pa·ri·ah
par·i·an
pa·ri·etal
pari-mu·tu·el
par·ing
pa·ri pas·su
par·ish
pa·rish·io·ner
par·i·ty
par·ka
Par·kin·son's
  dis·ease
Par·kin·son's
  Law
park·way
par·lance
par·lay
par·ley
par·lia·ment
par·lia·men·tar·i·
  an
par·lia·men·ta·ry
par·lor
par·lous
Par·me·san
par·mi·gia·na
pa·ro·chi·al
pa·ro·chi·al·ism
par·o·dist
par·o·dy
pa·role
pa·rol·ee
par·ox·ysm

par·quet
par·que·try
par·ra·keet
par·ri·cid·al
par·ri·cide
par·rot
par·ry
parse
par·si·mo·ni·ous
par·si·mo·ny
pars·ley
pars·nip
par·son
par·son·age
par·take
part·ed
par·terre
par·the·no·gen·e·
  sis
par·tial
par·tial·i·ty
par·tial·ly
par·tic·i·pant
par·tic·i·pate
par·tic·i·pa·tion
par·tic·i·pa·to·ry
par·ti·cip·i·al
par·ti·ci·ple
par·ti·cle
par·ti-col·ored
par·tic·u·lar
par·tic·u·lar·i·ty
par·tic·u·lar·ize
par·tic·u·lar·ly
part·ing
par·ti·san
par·ti·tion
part·ner
part·ner·ship
par·tridge

part-time
par·tu·ri·ent
par·tu·ri·tion
part·way
par·ty
par·ve·nu
pas de deux
pa·seo
pas·qui·nade
pass·able
pas·sage
pas·sage·way
pas·sé
pas·sen·ger
pass·er·by
pas·ser·ine
pas seul
pas·si·ble
pas·sim
pass·ing
pas·sion
pas·sion·ate
pas·sive
pas·siv·ism
pass·key
Pass·over
pass·port
pas·ta
paste
paste·board
pas·tel
pas·tern
pas·teur·iza·tion
pas·teur·ize
pas·tiche
past·ies
pas·tille
pas·time
past·i·ness
pas·tor

pas·to·ral
pas·tor·ate
pas·tra·mi
past·ry
pas·tur·age
pas·ture
pas·ture·land
pas·tur·ing
pas·ty
patch
patchy
pate
pâ·té
pâ·té de foie gras
pat·en
pa·tent
pat·ent·able
pat·en·tee
pa·ter·fa·mil·i·as
pa·ter·nal
pa·ter·nal·ism
pa·ter·ni·ty
pa·thet·ic
path·find·er
patho·log·i·cal
pa·thol·o·gist
pa·thol·o·gy
pa·thos
path·way
pa·tience
pa·tient
pa·ti·na
pa·tio
pa·tois
pa·tri·arch
pa·tri·ar·chy
pa·tri·cian
pat·ri·cide
pat·ri·mo·ny
pa·tri·ot·ic

pa·tri·o·tism
pa·tris·tic
pa·trol
pa·trol·man
pa·tron
pa·tron·age
pa·tron·ess
pa·tron·ize
pat·ro·nym·ic
pat·sy
pat·ter
pat·tern
pat·ty
pau·ci·ty
paunch
paunchy
pau·per
pau·per·ize
pause
paved
pave·ment
pa·vil·ion
pav·ing
Pav·lov·ian
pawn
pawn·bro·ker
pay·able
pay-as-you-go
pay·ee
pay·er
pay·ment
pay·off
pay·ola
peace
peace·able
peace·ful
peace·keep·ing
peace·mak·er
peace·time
peach

peachy
pea·cock
peaked
peal
pea·nut
pear
pearl
pearly
peas·ant
peas·ant·ry
pease
peat
peb·ble
peb·bly
pe·can
pec·ca·ble
pec·ca·dil·lo
peck·sniff·ian
pecky
pec·to·ral
pe·cu·liar
pe·cu·liar·i·ty
pe·cu·ni·ari·ly
pe·cu·ni·ary
ped·a·gog·ic
ped·a·gog·ics
ped·a·gogue
ped·a·go·gy
ped·al
ped·ant
pe·dan·tic
ped·ant·ry
ped·dle
ped·dler
ped·er·ast
ped·es·tal
pe·des·tri·an
pe·des·tri·an·ism
pe·di·at·ric
pe·di·a·tri·cian

pe·di·at·rics
pe·dic·u·lo·sis
pe·dic·u·lous
ped·i·cure
ped·i·gree
ped·i·ment
pe·dol·o·gy
pe·dom·e·ter
peek·a·boo
peel
peep·er
Peep·ing Tom
peer
peer·age
peer·less
peeve
pee·vish
pee·wee
pegged
pei·gnoir
pe·jo·ra·tive
Pe·king·ese
pe·koe
pe·lag·ic
pelf
pel·i·can
pe·lisse
pel·let
pel·li·cle
pell-mell
pel·lu·cid
pelt
pel·vic
pel·vis
pe·nal
pe·nal·iza·tion
pe·nal·ize
pen·al·ty
pen·ance
pence

pen·chant
pen·cil
pen·cil·ing
pen·dant
pend·ing
pen·du·lous
pen·du·lum
pen·e·tra·ble
pen·e·tra·bil·i·ty
pen·e·trate
pen·e·trat·ing
pen·e·tra·tion
pen·guin
pen·i·cil·lin
pen·in·su·la
pen·i·tence
pen·i·tent
pen·i·ten·tial
pen·i·ten·tia·ry
pen·knife
pen·man·ship
pen·nant
pen·ni·less
pen·non
pen·ny
pen·ny-pinch
pen·ny-wise
pe·nol·o·gy
pen·sion
pen·sion·er
pen·sive
pen·ta·gon
pen·tam·e·ter
pen·tath·lon
pent·house
pe·nult
pen·ul·ti·mate
pen·um·bra
pe·nu·ri·ous
pen·u·ry

pe·on
pe·on·age
pe·o·ny
peo·ple
pep·lum
pep·per
pep·per·mint
pep·pery
pep·py
per·am·bu·late
per·am·bu·la·to·ry
per an·num
per·cale
per cap·i·ta
per·ceiv·able
per·ceive
per·cent
per·cent·age
per·cen·tile
per·cept
per·cep·ti·bil·i·ty
per·cep·ti·ble
per·cep·tion
per·cep·tive
per·cep·tu·al
perch
per·chance
per·cip·i·ent
per·co·late
per·co·la·tor
per·cus·sion
per·cus·sive
per di·em
per·di·tion
per·e·gri·nate
pe·remp·to·ry
pe·ren·ni·al
per·fect
per·fec·ta

per·fect·ibil·i·ty
per·fect·ible
per·fec·tion
per·fec·to
per·fid·i·ous
per·fi·dy
per·fo·rate
per·fo·ra·tion
per·force
per·form
per·form·able
per·for·mance
per·form·er
per·fume
per·fum·ery
per·func·to·ry
per·func·to·ri·ly
per·fuse
per·go·la
per·haps
per·i·gee
peri·he·lion
per·il·ous
pe·rim·e·ter
pe·ri·od
pe·ri·od·ic
pe·ri·od·i·cal
pe·ri·od·ic·i·ty
peri·odon·tics
peri·odon·tist
peri·pa·tet·ic
pe·riph·er·al
pe·riph·ery
peri·phras·tic
peri·scope
per·ish·able
per·ish·ing
peri·to·ni·tis
per·i·win·kle
per·jure

per·jur·er
per·ju·ri·ous
per·ju·ry
perk
perky
per·ma·frost
per·ma·nence
per·ma·nen·cy
per·ma·nent
per·me·abil·i·ty
per·me·able
per·me·ate
per·mis·si·ble
per·mis·sion
per·mis·sive
per·mit
per·mu·ta·tion
per·ni·cious
per·orate
per·ora·tion
per·ox·ide
per·pen·dic·u·lar
per·pe·trate
per·pet·u·al
per·pet·u·ate
per·pe·tu·ity
per·plex
per·plex·i·ty
per·qui·site
per se
per·se·cute
per·se·cu·tion
per·se·ver·ance
per·sev·er·a·tion
per·se·vere
per·si·flage
per·sim·mon
per·sist
per·sis·tence
per·sis·tent

per·snick·e·ty
per·so·na
per·son·able
per·so·na gra·ta
per·son·al
per·son·al·i·ty
per·son·al·ize
per·son·al·ly
per·so·na non
  gra·ta
per·son·i·fi·ca·
  tion
per·son·i·fy
per·son·nel
per·spec·tive
per·spi·ca·cious
per·spic·u·ous
per·spi·ra·tion
per·spire
per·suade
per·sua·sion
per·sua·sive
per·tain
per·ti·na·cious
per·ti·nence
per·ti·nent
per·turb
per·tur·ba·tion
pe·ruse
per·vade
per·va·sive·ness
per·verse
per·ver·sion
per·ver·sive
per·vert
pes·ky
pes·si·mism
pes·si·mis·tic
pest
pes·ter

pes·ti·cide
pes·tif·er·ous
pes·ti·lence
pes·ti·lent
pes·ti·len·tial
pes·tle
pet·al
pe·tard
pe·ter
pe·tite
pe·tit four
pe·ti·tion
pet·it jury
pe·tit mal
pet·it point
pe·trel
pet·ri·fy
pet·rol
pet·ro·la·tum
pe·tro·leum
pet·ti·coat
pet·ti·fog·ger
pet·ti·ness
pet·tish
pet·ty
pet·u·lance
pet·u·lant
pe·tu·nia
pew·ter
pha·eton
pha·lanx
phal·lic
phan·tasm
phan·tas·ma·go·
ria
phan·tasy
phan·tom
phar·i·sa·ic
phar·i·sa·ical
phar·i·sa·ism

phar·i·see
phar·ma·ceu·ti·
cal
phar·ma·cist
phar·ma·col·o·
gist
phar·ma·col·o·gy
phar·ma·cy
phar·ynx
phase
pheas·ant
phe·nom·e·nal
phe·nom·e·non
phi·al
Phi Be·ta Kap·pa
phi·lan·der
phil·an·throp·ic
phi·lan·thro·pist
phi·lan·thro·py
phi·lat·e·list
phi·lat·e·ly
Phil·har·mon·ic
phi·lis·tine
philo·den·dron
phi·log·y·ny
phi·lol·o·gist
phi·lol·o·gy
phi·los·o·pher
philo·soph·ic
phi·los·o·phize
phi·los·o·phy
phil·ter
phle·bi·tis
phle·bot·o·my
phlegm
phleg·mat·ic
phlox
pho·bia
phoe·be
phoe·nix

pho·nate
pho·neme
pho·net·ic
pho·ne·ti·cian
pho·nics
pho·no·graph
pho·nol·o·gy
pho·ny
phoo·ey
phos·phate
phos·pho·res·
cence
phos·pho·res·cent
phos·pho·rus
pho·to·copy
pho·to·elec·tric
pho·to·en·grav·
ing
pho·to·ge·nic
pho·to·graph
pho·tog·ra·pher
pho·to·graph·ic
pho·tog·ra·phy
pho·to·gra·vure
pho·to·jour·nal·
ism
pho·to·off·set
pho·to·stat
pho·to·syn·the·
sis
phras·al
phrase
phrase·ol·o·gy
phras·ing
phre·net·ic
phre·nol·o·gy
phthis·ic
phthi·sis
phy·lac·tery
phy·log·e·ny

phys·ic
phys·i·cal
phys·i·cal·i·ty
phy·si·cian
phys·i·cist
phys·ics
phys·i·og·no·my
phys·i·og·ra·phy
phys·i·o·log·i·cal
phys·i·ol·o·gy
phy·sique
pi·a·nis·si·mo
pi·a·nist
pi·a·no
pi·ano·forte
pi·az·za
pi·ca
pic·a·dor
pic·a·resque
pic·a·yune
pic·ca·lil·li
pic·co·lo
pick·a·back
pick·a·nin·ny
pick·ax
picked
pick·er·el
pick·et
pick·le
pick·pock·et
Pick·wick·ian
picky
pic·nic
pic·nicked
pic·nick·ing
pi·cot
pic·to·graph
pic·to·ri·al
pic·to·ri·al·ly
pic·ture

pic·tur·esque
pid·dle
pid·dling
Pid·gin En·glish |
pie·bald
piece
pièce de ré·sis·
    tance
piece·meal
piece·work
pied·mont
pied pip·er
pier
pierce
pierc·ing
pier glass
pie·ta
pi·etism
pi·etis·tic
pi·ety
pif·fle
pi·geon
pi·geon-toed
pig·gery
pig·gish
pig·gy·back
pig·gy bank
pig·ment
pig·men·ta·tion
pig·pen
pig·skin
pig·sty
pike
pik·er
pi·laf
pi·las·ter
pile
pi·le·at·ed
pile·up
pil·fer

pil·fer·age
pil·grim
pil·grim·age
pil·ing
pil·lage
pil·lar
pil·lion
pil·lo·ry
pil·low
pil·low·case
pi·lot
pi·lot·age
pil·sner
pi·men·to
pi·mien·to
pim·ple
pin·afore
pi·ña·ta
pince-nez
pin·cer
pinch
pinch-hit
pin curl
pin·cush·ion
pine
pine·ap·ple
ping
pin·head
pin·hole
pin·ion
pin·kie
pink·ish
pin·nace
pin·na·cle
pin·nate
pi·noch·le
pin·point
pin·to
pin·up
pi·o·neer

pi·ous
pipe
pipe·ful
pipe·line
pip·ing
pip·pin
pi·quan·cy
pi·quant
pique
pi·ra·cy
pir·ou·ette
pis·ca·to·ri·al
pis·ca·to·ry
pi·scine
pish
pis·ta·chio
pis·tol
pis·ton
pit-a-pat
pitch
pitch-dark
pitch·er
pitch·man
pitch·out
pit·e·ous
pit·fall
pith
pithy
piti·able
piti·ful
piti·less
pi·ton
pit·tance
pit·ted
pit·ter-pat·ter
pi·tu·itary
pity
piv·ot
pivot·able
piv·ot·al

pix·ie
pix·i·lat·ed
piz·za
piz·zazz
piz·ze·ria
piz·zi·ca·to
pla·ca·ble
plac·ard
pla·cate
pla·ca·tive
pla·cat·er
pla·ce·bo
place·ment
plac·id
plack·et
pla·gia·rism
pla·gia·rist
pla·gia·rize
plague
plague·some
plagu·ey
plaice
plaid
plain·ness
plaint
plain·tiff
plain·tive
plait
plane
plan·et
plan·e·tar·i·um
plan·e·tary
plan·gent
plank
plank·ton
plan·ning
plan·tain
plan·ta·tion
plaque
plash

plas·ma
plas·ter
plas·tic
plas·ti·cal·ly
plas·tic·i·ty
plas·ti·cize
plat du jour
plate
pla·teau
plate·let
plat·en
plat·form
plat·ing
plat·i·num
plat·i·tude
plat·i·tu·di·nize
pla·ton·ic
pla·toon
plat·ter
plau·dit
plau·si·bil·i·ty
plau·si·ble
play·back
play·boy
play-by-play
play·ful
play·go·er
play·pen
play·wright
pla·za
plea
plead
pleas·ant
pleas·ant·ry
please
pleas·ing
plea·sur·able
plea·sure
pleat
plebe

ple·be·ian
pleb·i·scite
pledge
ple·na·ry
ple·nip·o·tent
pleni·po·ten·tia·
ry
plen·i·tude
plen·te·ous
plen·ti·ful
plen·ti·tude
plen·ty
ple·num
ple·o·nasm
pleth·o·ra
pleu·ri·sy
Plexi·glas
pli·able
pli·an·cy
pli·ant
pli·ers
plight
plod
plo·sion
plo·ver
plow
plow·share
ploy
pluck
pluck·i·er
pluck·i·ly
plucky
plugged
plug-ug·ly
plum·age
plumb
plumb·er
plume
plum·met
plump

plump·ish
plump·ness
plumy
plun·der
plunge
plunk
plu·per·fect
plu·ral·ism
plu·ral·is·tic
plu·ral·i·ty
plus fours
plush
plushy
plu·toc·ra·cy
plu·vi·al
ply·wood
pneu·mat·ic
pneu·mat·ics
pneu·mo·nia
poach
poach·er
pock·et
pock·mark
po·di·a·try
po·di·um
po·em
po·esy
po·et
po·et·as·ter
po·et·ic
po·et·i·cal
po·et lau·re·ate
po·et·ry
po·grom
poi·gnan·cy
poi·gnant
poin·ci·ana
poin·set·tia
poin·til·lism
pointy

poise
poi·son
poi·son·ous
poke
pok·er
poky
po·lar
po·lar·i·ty
po·lar·iza·tion
po·lar·ize
Po·lar·oid
pole
pole·cat
po·lem·ic
po·le·mist
pole·star
pole vault
po·lice
pol·i·cy
po·lio
pol·ish
po·lit·bu·ro
po·lite
po·li·tesse
pol·i·tic
po·lit·i·cal
pol·i·ti·cian
po·lit·i·cize
po·lit·i·co
pol·i·tics
pol·i·ty
pol·ka
pol·ka dot
pol·lack
pol·len
pol·len·ate
pol·li·nate
pol·li·na·tion
pol·li·wog
poll·ster

pol·lut·ant
pol·lute
pol·lu·tion
po·lo
po·lo·naise
pol·ter·geist
pol·troon
poly·an·dry
poly·chrome
poly·es·ter
po·lyg·a·mous
po·lyg·a·my
poly·glot
poly·glot·ism
poly·gon
poly·graph
po·lyg·y·ny
poly·he·dron
poly·no·mi·al
pol·yp
poly·phon·ic
poly·syl·lab·ic
poly·tech·nic
poly·the·ism
poly·un·sat·u·rat·ed
po·made
po·ma·tum
pome·gran·ate
Pom·er·a·nian
pom·mel
pomp
pom·pa·dour
pom·pa·no
pom-pom
pom·pos·i·ty
pomp·ous
pon·cho
pon·der
pon·der·a·ble

pon·der·ous
pon·gee
pon·iard
pon·ti·fex
pon·tiff
pon·tif·i·cal
pon·tif·i·cate
pon·toon
po·ny
pooch
poo·dle
pooh-pooh
poop
poor·house
poor·ly
poor white
pop art
pop·corn
pope
pop·ery
pop·in·jay
pop·ish
pop·lar
pop·lin
pop-off
pop·py
pop·py·cock
pop·u·lace
pop·u·lar
pop·u·lar·i·ty
pop·u·lar·ize
pop·u·late
pop·u·la·tion
pop·u·list
pop·u·lous
por·ce·lain
por·ce·lain·ize
porch
por·cine
por·cu·pine

pore
por·gy
pork·pie hat
por·nog·ra·pher
por·nog·ra·phy
po·ros·i·ty
po·rous
por·phy·ry
por·poise
por·ridge
por·rin·ger
por·ta·ble
por·tage
por·tal
por·tal-to-por·tal
por·tend
por·tent
por·ten·tous
por·ter
por·ter·age
por·ter·house
port·fo·lio
por·ti·co
por·tiere
por·tion
port·ly
port·man·teau
por·trait
por·trait·ist
por·trai·ture
por·tray
por·tray·al
por·tu·laca
pos·er
po·seur
posh
pos·it
po·si·tion
pos·i·tive
pos·se

pos·sess
pos·ses·sion
pos·ses·sive
pos·si·bil·i·ty
pos·si·ble
pos·sum
post·age
post·al
post·bel·lum
post·card
post-com·mu·nion
post·date
post·er
pos·te·ri·or
pos·ter·i·ty
pos·tern
post·grad·u·ate
post·haste
post hoc
post·hu·mous
post·man
post·mark
post me·ri·di·em
post·mor·tem
post·op·er·a·tive
post·pone
post·pran·di·al
post·script
pos·tu·lan·cy
pos·tu·lant
pos·tu·late
pos·tur·al
pos·ture
po·sy
po·ta·ble
po·tage
po·tas·si·um
po·ta·to
pot·bel·ly

pot·boil·er
po·teen
po·ten·cy
po·tent
po·ten·tate
po·ten·tial
po·ten·ti·al·i·ty
poth·er
po·tion
pot·pour·ri
pot·shot
pot·tage
pot·ted
pot·ter's field
pot·tery
pouch
poul·tice
poul·try
pounce
pound
pound-fool·ish
pour·boire
pout
pov·er·ty
pov·er·ty-strick·en
pow·der
pow·dery
pow·er
pow·er·ful
pow·er·house
pow·wow
prac·ti·ca·bil·i·ty
prac·ti·ca·ble
prac·ti·cal
prac·ti·cal·ly
prac·tice
prac·tic·ing
prac·ti·cum
prac·ti·tio·ner

prag·mat·ic
prag·ma·tism
prai·rie
praise
praise·wor·thy
pra·line
prance
pran·di·al
prank
prank·ish
prank·ster
prate
prat·fall
prat·tle
prat·tler
prawn
prax·is
prayer
prayer·ful
preach
preach·ify
preach·ment
preachy
pre·adapt·ed
pre·ad·o·les·cence
pre·am·ble
pre·ar·range
pre·as·signed
preb·end
preb·en·dary
pre·can·cer·ous
pre·car·i·ous
prec·a·to·ry
pre·cau·tion
pre·cede
pre·ce·dence
pre·ce·dent
pre·ced·ing
pre·cept

pre·cep·tor
pre·cep·to·ry
pre·ces·sion
pre·cinct
pre·ci·os·i·ty
pre·cious
pre·cious·ly
prec·i·pice
pre·cip·i·tan·cy
pre·cip·i·tate
pre·cip·i·ta·tion
pre·cip·i·tous
pré·cis
pre·cise
pre·ci·sion
pre·clude
pre·co·cious
pre·con·ceive
pre·con·cep·tion
pre·con·di·tion
pre·cur·sor
pre·da·tion
pred·a·tor
pre·de·cease
pre·de·ces·sor
pre·des·ti·na·tion
pre·de·ter·mi·na·
tion
pre·de·ter·mine
pred·i·ca·ble
pre·dic·a·ment
pred·i·cate
pre·dict
pre·dic·tion
pre·di·lec·tion
pre·dis·pose
pre·dis·po·si·tion
pred·ni·sone
pre·dom·i·nant
pre·dom·i·nate

pre·emer·gent
pre·em·i·nence
pre·em·i·nent
pre·empt
pre·emp·tive
preen
pre·ex·is·tence
pre·fab·ri·cate
pref·ace
pref·a·to·ry
pre·fect
pre·fec·ture
pre·fer
pref·er·a·ble
pref·er·ence
pref·er·en·tial
pre·fer·ment
pre·fig·u·ra·tion
pre·fig·u·ra·tive
pre·fig·ure
pre·fix
preg·na·ble
preg·nan·cy
preg·nant
pre·hen·sile
pre·hen·sion
pre·his·tor·ic
pre·in·duc·tion
pre·judge
pre·judg·ment
prej·u·dice
prej·u·di·cial
prej·u·di·cious
prel·a·cy
prel·ate
pre·lim·i·nary
pre·lude
pre·mar·i·tal
pre·ma·ture
pre·med·i·cal

pre·med·i·tate
pre·med·i·ta·tion
pre·med·i·ta·tive
pre·mier
pre·mier dan·
seur
pre·miere dan·
seuse
pre·mier·ship
prem·ise
pre·mi·um
pre·mix
pre·mo·ni·tion
pre·mon·i·to·ry
pre·mu·ni·tion
pre·na·tal
pre·oc·cu·pan·cy
pre·oc·cu·pa·tion
pre·oc·cu·pied
pre·or·dain
prep·a·ra·tion
pre·par·a·tive
pre·pa·ra·to·ry
pre·pare
pre·pared·ness
pre·pay
pre·pay·ment
pre·plan
pre·pon·der·ance
pre·pon·der·ant
prep·o·si·tion
pre·pos·sess
pre·pos·ses·sion
pre·pos·ter·ous
pre·po·ten·cy
pre·po·tent
pre·pran·di·al
pre·pub·li·ca·tion
pre-reg·is·tra·
tion

pre·reg·is·ter
pre·req·ui·site
pre·rog·a·tive
pres·age
pre·sanc·ti·fied
pres·by·ter
Pres·by·te·ri·an
pres·by·tery
pre·school
pre·science
pre·scind
pre·scribe
pre·script
pre·scrip·tion
pre·scrip·tive
pres·ence
pres·ent
pre·sent·able
pre·sen·ta·tion
pre·sen·tient
pre·sen·ti·ment
pres·ent·ly
pre·sent·ment
pres·er·va·tion·ist
pre·ser·va·tive
pre·serve
pre·set
pre·shrunk
pre·side
pres·i·den·cy
pres·i·dent
pre·sid·i·um
pre·soak
press
press·ing
pres·sure
pres·sure gauge
pres·sur·iza·tion
pres·sur·ize

pres·ti·dig·i·ta·tion
pres·tige
pres·ti·gious
pres·to
pre·sum·able
pre·sume
pre·sump·tion
pre·sump·tive
pre·sump·tu·ous
pre·sup·pose
pre·tend
pre·tense
pre·ten·sion
pre·ten·tious
pre·ter·nat·u·ral
pre·test
pre·text
pret·ti·fy
pret·ti·ness
pret·ty
pret·zel
pre·vail
prev·a·lence
prev·a·lent
pre·var·i·cate
pre·vent
pre·ven·ta·tive
pre·ven·tive
pre·view
pre·vi·ous
pre·vi·sion
pre·war
prexy
prey
price·less
prick·ly
pride·ful
prie-dieu
priest

priest·hood
priest-rid·den
prig
prig·gish
prim
pri·ma bal·ler·ina
pri·ma·cy
pri·ma don·na
pri·ma fa·cie
pri·mal
pri·mar·i·ly
pri·ma·ry
pri·mate
prim·er
pri·me·val
prim·ing
prim·i·tive
prim·i·tiv·ism
pri·mo·gen·i·tor
pri·mo·gen·i·ture
pri·mor·di·al
primp
prim·rose
prince
prince·dom
prince·li·ness
prince·ly
prin·cess
prin·ci·pal
prin·ci·pal·i·ty
prin·ci·ple
prink
print·able
print·ery
print·out
pri·or
pri·or·ess
pri·or·i·ty
pri·o·ry
prism

pris·mat·ic
pris·on
pris·on·er
pris·sy
pris·tine
pri·va·cy
pri·vate
pri·va·teer
pri·va·tion
priv·a·tive
priv·et
priv·i·lege
priv·i·ly
privy
prix fixe
prize
prize·win·ning
prob·a·bil·i·ty
prob·a·ble
pro·bate
pro·ba·tion
pro·ba·tive
probe
pro·bi·ty
prob·lem
prob·lem·at·ic
pro·bos·cis
pro·ce·dur·al
pro·ce·dure
pro·ceed
pro·cess
pro·cess·ible
pro·ces·sion
pro·ces·sor
pro·claim
proc·la·ma·tion
pro·cliv·i·ty
pro·cras·ti·nate
pro·cre·ate
pro·crus·te·an

proc·tor
proc·u·ra·tor
pro·cure
prod
prod·i·gal
pro·di·gious
prod·i·gy
pro·duce
prod·uct
pro·duc·tion
pro·duc·tive
pro·duc·tiv·i·ty
pro·em
pro·fa·na·tion
pro·fa·na·to·ry
pro·fane
pro·fan·i·ty
pro·fess
pro·fessed·ly
pro·fes·sion
pro·fes·sion·al·ize
pro·fes·sor
pro·fes·so·ri·al
prof·fer
pro·fi·cien·cy
pro·fi·cient
pro·file
prof·it
prof·it·able
prof·i·teer
prof·li·ga·cy
prof·li·gate
pro for·ma
pro·found
pro·fun·di·ty
pro·fuse
pro·fu·sion
pro·gen·i·tor
prog·e·ny
prog·na·thous

prog·no·sis
prog·nos·tic
prog·nos·ti·cate
prog·nos·ti·ca·
    tion
pro·gram
pro·gram·mer
pro·gram·ming
prog·ress
pro·gres·sion
pro·gres·sive
pro·gres·siv·ism
pro·hib·it
pro·hi·bi·tion
pro·hib·i·tive
pro·hib·i·to·ry
proj·ect
pro·jec·tile
pro·jec·tion
pro·jec·tion·ist
pro·jec·tor
pro·lapse
pro·le·gom·e·non
pro·le·tar·i·an
pro·le·tar·i·at
pro·lif·er·ate
pro·lif·er·ous
pro·lif·ic
pro·lix
pro·lix·i·ty
pro·logue
pro·long
pro·lon·gate
pro·lon·ga·tion
prom
prom·e·nade
prom·i·nence
prom·i·nent
pro·mis·cu·i·ty
pro·mis·cu·ous

prom·ise
prom·is·ing
prom·is·so·ry
prom·on·to·ry
pro·mot·er
pro·mo·tion
prompt
prompt·er
promp·ti·tude
pro·mul·gate
pro·nate
prone
prong
pro·noun
pro·nounce
pro·nounce·ment
pro·nounc·ing
pro·nun·ci·a·men·to
pro·nun·ci·a·tion
proof
prop
pro·pae·deu·tic
pro·pa·gan·da
pro·pa·gan·dize
prop·a·gate
prop·a·ga·tor
prop·a·ga·tion
pro·pane
pro·pel
pro·pel·lant
pro·pel·ler
pro·pen·si·ty
prop·er
prop·er·tied
prop·er·ty
proph·e·cy
proph·e·sy
proph·et
pro·phet·ic

pro·phy·lac·tic
pro·phy·lax·is
pro·pin·qui·ty
pro·pi·ti·a·tion
pro·pi·tia·to·ry
pro·pi·tious
pro·po·nent
pro·por·tion
pro·por·tion·al
pro·pos·al
pro·pose
prop·o·si·tion
pro·pound
pro·pri·etary
pro·pri·etor
pro·pri·ety
pro·pul·sion
pro·rate
pro·rogue
pro·sa·ic
pro·sa·i·cal·ly
pro·sce·ni·um
pro·sciut·to
pro·scribe
pro·scrip·tion
prose
pros·e·cute
pros·e·cu·tion
pros·e·cu·tor
pros·e·lyte
pros·e·ly·tism
pros·e·ly·tize
pro·sit
pros·o·dy
pros·pect
pro·spec·tive
pro·spec·tus
pros·per
pros·per·ous
pros·tate

pros·thet·ics
pros·ti·tute
pros·trate
pros·tra·tion
prosy
pro·tag·o·nist
prot·a·sis
pro·te·an
pro·tect
pro·tec·tion
pro·tec·tor
pro·tec·tor·ate
pro·té·gé
pro·té·gée
pro·tein
pro tem
pro tem·po·re
pro·test
prot·es·tant
pro·tes·ta·tion
pro·test·er
pro·tes·tor
pro·tho·no·ta·ry
pro·to·col
pro·to·mar·tyr
pro·ton
pro·to·plasm
pro·to·type
pro·to·typ·i·cal
pro·to·zo·an
pro·tract
pro·trac·tion
pro·trac·tor
pro·trude
pro·tru·sion
pro·tru·sive
pro·tu·ber·ance
pro·tu·ber·ant
proud·ful
prov·able

prove
prov·e·nance
prov·en·der
prov·erb
pro·ver·bi·al
pro·vide
prov·i·dence
prov·i·dent
prov·i·den·tial
prov·ince
pro·vin·cial
pro·vi·sion
pro·vi·so
pro·voc·a·teur
prov·o·ca·tion
pro·voc·a·tive
pro·voke
pro·vo·lo·ne
pro·vost
prow
prow·ess
prowl
prox·e·mics
prox·i·mal
prox·i·mate
prox·im·i·ty
proxy
prude
pru·dence
pru·dent
pru·den·tial
prud·ery
prud·ish
prune
pru·ri·ence
prus·sian·ize
psalm
psalm·o·dy
p's and q's
pseud·onym

pseu·do·sci·ence
pshaw
pso·ri·a·sis
psych
psy·che·del·ic
psy·chi·a·trist
psy·chi·a·try
psy·chic
psy·cho
psy·cho·anal·y·sis
psy·cho·an·a·lyt·ic
psy·cho·an·a·lyze
psy·cho·dra·ma
psy·cho·gen·ic
psy·cho·log·i·cal
psy·chol·o·gize
psy·chol·o·gy
psy·cho·met·rics
psy·chom·e·try
psy·cho·path
psy·cho·pa·thol·o·gy
psy·cho·sis
psy·cho·so·mat·ic
psy·cho·ther·a·py
pto·maine
pu·ber·tal
pu·ber·ty
pu·bes·cence
pu·bes·cent
pu·bic
pub·lic
pub·lic-ad·dress sys·tem
pub·li·can
pub·li·ca·tion
pub·li·cist
pub·lic·i·ty

pub·li·cize
pub·lic·ly
pub·lish
puck
puck·ish
pud·ding
pud·dle
pu·den·dum
pudgy
pueb·lo
pu·er·ile
pu·er·il·ism
puff·ery
pu·gi·lism
pu·gi·list
pug·na·cious
pug·nac·i·ty
puis·sance
puke
pul·chri·tude
pul·chri·tu·di·nous
Pu·lit·zer prize
pul·let
pul·ley
pull·over
pul·mo·nary
pul·mo·tor
pulp
pulpy
pul·pit
pul·sate
pul·sa·tion
pulse
pul·ver·ize
pu·ma
pum·ice
pum·mel
pump·er
pum·per·nick·el

pump·kin
punch
punch-drunk
punc·til·io
punc·til·i·ous
punc·tu·al
punc·tu·ate
punc·tu·a·tion
punc·ture
pun·dit
pun·gen·cy
pun·gent
pun·ish
pun·ish·able
pu·ni·tive
pun·ny
pun·ster
punt
pu·ny
pu·pil
pup·pet
pup·pe·teer
pup·pet·ry
pup·py·ish
pur·blind
pur·chase
pur·chas·er
pu·ree
pure·ly
pur·ga·tion
pur·ga·tive
pur·ga·to·ri·al
pur·ga·to·ry
purge
pu·ri·fi·ca·tion
pu·ri·fi·ca·tor
pu·ri·fi·er
pu·ri·fy
Pu·rim
pur·ist

pu·ri·tan
pu·ri·tan·i·cal
pu·ri·tan·ism
pu·ri·ty
purl
pur·lieu
pur·loin
pur·ple
pur·port
pur·pose
pur·pose·ful
pur·pose·ful·ly
pur·pose·ly
pur·po·sive
purr
purse
purs·er
pur·su·ance
pur·su·ant to
pur·sue
pur·suit
pur·vey
pur·vey·ance
pur·vey·or
pur·view
pus
push
push·over
pushy
pu·sil·la·nim·i·ty
pu·sil·lan·i·mous
pus·sy·cat
pus·tule
pu·ta·tive
put-down
put-on
pu·tre·fac·tion
pu·tre·fy
pu·tres·cence
pu·trid

putsch
putt
put·ter
put·ty
put-up
puz·zle
puz·zle·ment
pyg·my
py·ja·mas
py·lon
py·or·rhea
pyr·a·mid
pyre
py·ro·ma·nia
py·ro·tech·nics
Pyr·rhic vic·tory
Py·thag·o·re·an
py·thon
pyx

quack
quack·ery
quad
quad·ran·gle
qua·dran·gu·lar
quad·rant
quad·rate
qua·drat·ic
qua·drat·ics
qua·dren·ni·al
qua·dren·ni·um
quad·ri·cen·ten·
  ni·al
quad·ri·lat·er·al
qua·drille
qua·dril·lion

quad·ri·par·tite
quad·ri·ple·gic
qua·driv·i·um
qua·droon
qua·drum·vir
qua·drum·vi·rate
quad·ru·ped
qua·dru·ple
qua·dru·plet
qua·dru·pli·cate
quad·ru·plic·i·ty
qua·dru·pling
quaff
quag·mire
qua·hog
quail
quaint
quake
quak·er
Quak·er·ism
qual·i·fi·ca·tion
qual·i·fied
qual·i·fi·er
qual·i·fy
qual·i·ta·tive
qual·i·ty
qualm
qualm·ish
quan·da·ry
quan·ti·fi·ca·tion
quan·ti·fi·er
quan·ti·fy
quan·ti·tate
quan·ti·ta·tive
quan·ti·ty
quan·tum
quar·an·tin·able
quar·an·tine
quark
quar·rel

quar·rel·some
quar·ri·er
quar·ry
quar·ry·ing
quart
quar·ter
quar·ter·back
quar·ter·fi·nal
quar·ter horse
quar·ter·ing
quar·ter·ly
quar·ter·mas·ter
quar·tet
quar·tile
quar·to
quartz
quartz·ite
qua·sar
quash
qua·si
qua·si-ju·di·cial
qua·si-leg·is·la·
   tive
qua·si-pub·lic
qua·ter·cen·te·
   na·ry
qua·ter·ni·on
qua·train
qua·tre·foil
qua·ver
quay
quay·side
quean
quea·sy
queen
queen-size
queer
queer·ish
quell
quench

que·ried
quer·u·lous
que·ry
quest
ques·tion
ques·tion·able
ques·tion·naire
queue
quib·ble
quiche
quick
quick·en
quick-freeze
quick·ie
quick-wit·ted
quid
quid·di·ty
quid·nunc
quid pro quo
qui·es·cence
qui·es·cent
qui·et
qui·et·ism
qui·etude
qui·etus
quill
quilt
quince
qui·nie·la
qui·nine
quin·quen·ni·al
quin·quen·ni·um
quin·sy
quin·tain
quin·tes·sence
quin·tet
quin·tile
quin·tu·ple
quin·tu·plet
quin·tu·pli·cate

quip
quip·ster
quire
quirk
quis·ling
quit
quit·claim
quite
quits
quit·tance
quit·ter
quiv·er
qui·xote
quix·ot·ic
quix·ot·i·cal·ly
quiz
quiz·mas·ter
quiz·zi·cal
quoit
quon·dam
quo·rum
quo·ta
quot·able
quo·ta·tion
quote
quo·tid·i·an
quo·tient

R

rab·bet
rab·bi
rab·bin·ate
rab·bin·ic
rab·bit
rabble
rab·ble·ment
rab·ble-rous·er

Ra·be·lai·sian
ra·bid
ra·bies
rac·coon
race
ra·ceme
rac·er
race·track
race·way
ra·chit·ic
ra·chi·tis
ra·cial
rac·ing
rac·ism
rack·et
rack·e·teer
rack·ety
rack rent
ra·clette
ra·con·teur
racy
ra·dar
rad·dle
rad·dled
ra·di·al
ra·di·a·le
ra·di·ance
ra·di·an·cy
ra·di·ant
ra·di·ate
ra·di·a·tion
ra·di·a·tive
ra·di·a·tor
rad·i·cal
rad·i·cal·ism
rad·i·cand
rad·i·cle
ra·dii
ra·dio
ra·dio·ac·tive

ra·dio·ac·tiv·i·ty
ra·dio·broad·cast
ra·dio fre·quen·cy
ra·dio·gram
ra·di·ol·o·gist
ra·di·ol·o·gy
ra·di·ol·y·sis
ra·dio·man
ra·dio·phone
ra·dio·tele·graph
ra·dio·tele·phone
ra·dio·ther·a·py
rad·ish
ra·di·um
ra·di·us
ra·dix
raf·fia
raff·ish
raf·fle
raft
rag·a·muf·fin
rag·bag
rage
rag·ged
rag·gedy
rag·gle-tag·gle
rag·ing
rag·lan
ra·gout
rag·time
rah-rah
raid
rail·ing
rail·lery
rail·road
rail-split·ter
rail·way
rai·ment
rain
rain·bow

rain·coat
rain gauge
rain·wear
rainy
raise
rai·sin
rai·son d'être
raj
ra·ja
rake
rake-off
rak·ish
rak·ish·ness
ral·ly
ral·lye
ram
ram·ble
ram·bunc·tious
ram·e·kin
ram·i·fi·ca·tion
ram·i·fy
ramp
ram·page
ram·pan·cy
ram·pant
ram·part
ram·rod
ram·shack·le
ranch
ran·che·ro
ran·cho
ran·cid
ran·cor
ran·cor·ous
ran·dom
ran·dom·iza·tion
ran·dom·ize
randy
rang
range

rang·i·er
rang·ing
rangy
rank
rank·ing
ran·kle
ran·sack
ran·som
rant
ra·pa·cious
ra·pac·i·ty
rape
rap·id
rap·id-fire
ra·pid·i·ty
ra·pi·er
rap·ine
rap·pa·ree
rap·pel
rap·per
rap·port
rap·proche·ment
rap·scal·lion
rapt
rap·tor
rap·ture
rap·tur·ous·ly
ra·ra avis
rar·efac·tion
rar·efied
rar·efy
rar·ing
rar·i·ty
ras·cal
ras·cal·i·ty
ras·cal·ly
rash
rasp
rasp·ber·ry
raspy

rat-a-tat
ratch·et
rate
rath·er
raths·kel·ler
rat·i·fy
rat·ing
ra·tio
ra·ti·o·ci·nate
ra·ti·o·ci·na·tion
ra·tion
ra·tio·nale
ra·tio·nal·ism
ra·tio·nal·i·ty
ra·tio·nal·ize
rat·tail
rat·tan
rat·ter
rat·tle
rat·tle·brained
rat·tler
rat·tle·snake
rat·tle·trap
rat·tling
rat·ty
rau·cous
raun·chy
rav·age
rave
rav·el
ra·ven
rav·en·ous
ra·vine
rav·ing
rav·i·o·li
rav·ish·ing
raw·hide
rayed
ray·less
ray·on

raze
ra·zor
ra·zor·back
razz
raz·zle-daz·zle
razz·ma·tazz
reach
reach·able
re·act
re·ac·tion
re·ac·tion·ary
re·ac·ti·vate
re·ac·tive
re·ac·tor
read·abil·i·ty
read·able
readi·ly
read·ing
read·out
ready
readi·ness
ready-made
ready-to-wear
re·af·for·es·ta·
  tion
re·agent
re·al
re·alia
re·al·ism
re·al·i·ty
re·al·iza·tion
re·al·ize
re·al·ly
realm
re·al·po·li·tik
re·al·ty
ream
ream·er
reap
re·ap·por·tion

rear
re·arm
re·ar·ma·ment
rear·view mirror
rear·ward
rea·son
rea·son·able
rea·son·ing
re·as·sur·ance
re·as·sure
re·bate
reb·be
reb·el
re·bel·lion
re·bel·lious
re·birth
re·born
re·bound
re·buff
re·buke
re·bus
re·but
re·but·tal
re·but·ter
re·cal·ci·trance
re·cal·ci·trant
re·cal·cu·late
re·call
re·cant
re·cap
re·ca·pit·u·late
re·ca·pit·u·la·
  tion
re·cap·ture
re·cast
re·cede
re·ceipt
re·ceiv·able
re·ceiv·ables
re·ceive

re·cen·cy
re·cent
re·cep·ta·cle
re·cep·tion
re·cep·tion·ist
re·cep·tive
re·cep·tor
re·cess
re·ces·sion
re·ces·sion·al
re·ces·sive
re·charge
re·cher·ché
re·cid·i·vism
re·cid·i·vist
rec·i·pe
re·cip·i·ent
re·cip·ro·cal
re·cip·ro·cate
re·cip·ro·ca·tion
rec·i·proc·i·ty
re·ci·sion
re·cit·al
rec·i·ta·tion
rec·i·ta·tive
re·cite
reck·less
reck·on
re·claim
rec·la·ma·tion
rec·li·nate
re·cline
re·clos·able
re·cluse
re·clu·sion
rec·og·ni·tion
re·cog·ni·zance
rec·og·nize
re·coil
rec·ol·lect

rec·ol·lec·tion
rec·om·mend
rec·om·men·da·
  tion
re·com·mit
rec·om·pense
re·com·pose
rec·on·cil·able
rec·on·cile
rec·on·cil·i·a·tion
re·con·dite
re·con·di·tion
re·con·firm
re·con·nais·sance
re·con·noi·ter
re·con·sid·er
re·con·sti·tute
re·con·struct
re·con·struc·tion
re·con·ver·sion
re·con·vert
re·con·vey
re·cord
re·cord·ing
re·count
re·coup
re·coup·able
re·course
re-cov·er
re·cov·ery
rec·re·ant
rec·re·ate
rec·re·ation
re·crim·i·nate
re·cru·desce
re·cru·des·cence
re·cru·des·cent
re·cruit
re·crys·tal·lize
rec·tal

rect·an·gle
rect·an·gu·lar
rec·ti·fi·able
rec·ti·fi·er
rec·ti·fy
rec·ti·lin·ear
rec·ti·tude
rec·tor
rec·to·ry
rec·tum
re·cum·ben·cy
re·cum·bent
re·cu·per·ate
re·cu·per·a·tive
re·cur
re·curred
re·cur·rent
re·cur·sive
re·cu·san·cy
re·cu·sant
re·cy·cla·ble
re·cy·cle
re·dact
re·dac·tion
re·dac·tor
red-bait·ing
red·breast
red·den
red·dish
re·dec·o·rate
re·dec·o·ra·tion
re·deem
re·de·fine
re·demp·tion
re·demp·tive
re·demp·to·ry
re·de·ploy
re·de·sign
re·de·ter·mine

re·de·vel·op
red-eye
red·in·gote
re·di·rect
re·dis·trib·ute
red-let·ter
red-neck
re·do
red·o·lence
red·o·lent
re·dou·ble
re·doubt
re·doubt·able
re·dound
re·dress
re·duce
re·duc·ibil·i·ty
re·duc·ibly
re·duc·tio ad ab·
  sur·dum
re·duc·tion
re·duc·tion·ism
re·duc·tive
re·dun·dan·cy
re·dun·dant
re·du·pli·cate
re·du·pli·ca·tion
re·echo
reed
re·edit
re·ed·u·cate
reedy
reef·er
reek
reel
re·elect
re·elec·tion
re·em·ploy
re·en·act
re·en·force

re·en·ter
re·en·try
reeve
re·fash·ion
re·fec·tion
re·fec·to·ry
re·fer
re·fer·able
ref·er·ee
ref·er·ence
ref·er·en·dum
ref·er·ent
ref·er·en·tial
re·fer·ral
re·fill
re·fi·nance
re·fine
re·fine·ment
re·fin·ery
re·fin·ish
re·flect
re·flec·tion
re·flec·tive
re·flec·tor
re·flex
re·flexed
re·flex·ive
re·for·est
re·for·es·ta·tion
re·forge
re·form
re·form·able
ref·or·ma·tion
re·for·ma·to·ry
re·form·er
re·fract
re·frac·tion
re·frac·tive
re·frac·tor
re·frac·to·ry

re·frain
re·fresh
re·fresh·en
re·fresh·ment
re·frig·er·ant
re·frig·er·ate
re·frig·er·a·tor
re·fu·el
ref·uge
ref·u·gee
re·ful·gence
re·fund
re·fur·bish
re·fus·al
re·fut·able
ref·u·ta·tion
re·fute
re·gain
re·gal
re·gale
re·ga·lia
re·gard
re·gard·ful
re·gard·less
re·gat·ta
re·gen·cy
re·gen·er·a·cy
re·gen·er·ate
re·gen·er·a·tion
re·gen·er·a·tive
re·gen·er·a·tor
re·gent
reg·i·cide
re·gime
reg·i·men
reg·i·ment
reg·i·men·tal
re·gion
re·gion·al
re·gion·al·ism

re·gis·seur
reg·is·ter
reg·is·trant
reg·is·trar
reg·is·tra·tion
reg·is·try
reg·nant
re·gorge
re·gress
re·gres·sion
re·gres·sive
re·gres·sor
re·gret·ta·ble
re·group
re·grow
reg·u·lar
reg·u·lar·i·ty
reg·u·lar·ize
reg·u·late
reg·u·la·to·ry
reg·u·la·tion
reg·u·la·tor
re·gur·gi·tate
re·gur·gi·ta·tion
re·ha·bil·i·tate
re·ha·bil·i·ta·tion
re·hash
re·hears·al
re·hearse
reichs·mark
re·i·fi·ca·tion
re·i·fy
reign
re·im·burse
re·im·burse·ment
rein
re·in·car·nate
rein·deer
re·in·fec·tion
re·in·force

re·in·force·ment
re·in·forc·er
reins
re·in·state
re·in·sur·ance
re·in·sure
re·in·te·grate
re·in·ter·pret
re·in·vent
re·is·sue
re·it·er·ate
re·ject
re·jec·tion
re·joic·ing
re·join·der
re·ju·ve·nate
re·ju·ve·nes·
   cence
re·kin·dle
re·lapse
re·late
re·la·tion
re·la·tion·ship
rel·a·tive
rel·a·tiv·ism
rel·a·tiv·is·tic
rel·a·tiv·i·ty
re·lax
re·lax·ant
re·lax·ation
re·lay
re·lease
rel·e·gate
rel·e·ga·tion
re·lent·less
rel·e·vance
rel·e·van·cy
rel·e·vant
re·li·abil·i·ty
re·li·able

re·li·ance
re·li·ant
rel·ic
rel·ict
re·lief
re·lieve
re·li·gion
re·li·gion·ist
re·li·gi·ose
re·li·gious
re·line
re·lin·quish
rel·i·quary
rel·ish
re·live
re·lo·cate
re·luc·tance
re·luc·tant
re·main
re·main·der
re·make
re·mand
re·mark
re·mark·able
re·marque
re·match
re·me·di·a·ble
re·me·di·al
re·me·di·a·tion
rem·e·dy
re·mem·ber
re·mem·brance
re·mind·ful
rem·i·nisce
rem·i·nis·cence
rem·i·nis·cent
re·mise
re·miss
re·mis·si·ble
re·mis·sion

re·mit
re·mit·tal
re·mit·tance
re·mit·tent
rem·nant
re·mod·el
re·mon·strance
re·mon·strate
re·morse
re·morse·ful
re·morse·less
re·mote
re·mount
re·mov·able
re·mov·abil·i·ty
re·mov·al
re·move
re·mu·ner·ate
re·mu·ner·a·tion
re·mu·ner·a·tive
re·nais·sance
re·nal
re·na·scence
re·na·scent
ren·con·tre
ren·coun·ter
ren·der
ren·dez·vous
ren·di·tion
ren·e·gade
re·nege
re·ne·go·tia·ble
re·ne·go·ti·ate
re·new
re·new·able
re·new·al
re·nig
re·nom·i·nate
re·nounce
ren·o·vate

re·nown
rent-a-car
rent·al
ren·tier
re·num·ber
re·nun·ci·a·tion
re·of·fer
re·open
re·or·ga·ni·za·
 tion
re·or·ga·nize
re·pair
rep·a·ra·ble
rep·a·ra·tion
rep·ar·tee
re·pa·tri·ate
re·peal
re·peal·er
re·peat
re·peat·er
re·pel
re·pel·lent
re·pent
re·pen·tance
re·pen·tant
re·per·cus·sion
rep·er·toire
rep·er·to·ry
rep·e·ti·tion
rep·e·ti·tious
re·pet·i·tive
re·pine
re·place·ment
re·play
re·plen·ish
re·plete
re·ple·tion
rep·li·ca
rep·li·cate
rep·li·ca·tion

re·ply
re·port
re·port·age
re·port·ed·ly
re·port·er
re·pos·al
re·pose
re·pose·ful
re·po·si·tion
re·pos·i·to·ry
re·pos·sess
rep·re·hend
rep·re·hen·si·ble
rep·re·hen·sion
rep·re·hen·sive
rep·re·sent
re·pre·sen·ta·tion
rep·re·sen·ta·tive
re·press
re·pres·sion
re·pres·sor
re·priev·al
re·prieve
rep·ri·mand
re·print
re·pri·sal
re·prise
re·proach
re·proach·ful·
 ness
rep·ro·bate
rep·ro·ba·tion
re·pro·cess
re·pro·duce
re·pro·duc·tion
re·pro·duc·tive
re·pro·gram
re·proof
re·prove
re·prov·er

rep·tile
rep·til·ian
re·pub·lic
re·pub·li·can
re·pub·li·ca·tion
re·pub·lish
re·pu·di·ate
re·pu·di·a·tion
re·pug·nance
re·pug·nant
re·pulse
re·pul·sion
rep·u·ta·ble
rep·u·ta·tion
re·pute
re·quest
re·quest·or
re·qui·em
re·qui·es·cat
re·quire
re·quire·ment
req·ui·site
req·ui·si·tion
re·quit·al
re·quite
rere·dos
re·run
re·sal·able
re·sale
re·scind
re·scis·sion
res·cue
res·cu·er
re·search
re·seed
re·sem·blance
re·sem·ble
re·sent
re·sent·ment
res·er·va·tion

re·serv·ist
res·er·voir
re·set
re·shape
re·shuf·fle
re·side
res·i·dence
res·i·den·cy
res·i·den·tial
re·sid·u·al
re·sid·u·ary
res·i·due
re·sign
re·sign·ed·ly
res·ig·na·tion
re·sil·ience
re·sil·ien·cy
re·sil·ient
res·in
res·in·ate
res·in·ous
re·sist
re·sis·tance
re·sist·er
re·sist·ible
re·sist·less
re·sis·tor
re·sole
re·sol·u·ble
res·o·lu·tion
re·solve
res·o·nance
res·o·nant
res·o·nate
res·o·na·tor
re·sorp·tion
re·sort
re·sound
re·source
re·source·ful

re·spect
re·spect·abil·i·ty
re·spect·ful
re·spec·tive
re·spec·tive·ly
re·spell
res·pi·ra·tion
res·pi·ra·tor
re·spi·ra·to·ry
re·spite
re·splen·dence
re·splen·dent
re·spond
re·spon·dent
re·spond·er
re·sponse
re·spon·si·bil·i·ty
re·spon·si·ble
re·spon·sive
re·spon·so·ry
re·stage
re·start
re·state
res·tau·rant
res·tau·ra·teur
rest·ful
res·ti·tute
res·ti·tu·tion
res·tive
res·tive·ness
rest·less
re·stor·able
res·to·ra·tion
re·stor·ative
re·store
re·strain
re·straint
re·strict
re·stric·tion
re·stric·tive

re·struc·ture
re·study
re·sult
re·sul·tant
re·sume
ré·su·mé
re·sump·tion
re·sup·ply
re·sur·gence
re·sur·gent
res·ur·rect
res·ur·rec·tion
re·sus·ci·tate
re·sus·ci·ta·tor
re·tail
re·tain
re·tain·er
re·take
re·tal·i·ate
re·tal·i·a·tive
re·tard
re·tar·dant
re·tar·date
re·tar·da·tion
retch
re·tell
re·ten·tion
re·ten·tive
re·ten·tiv·i·ty
re·test
ret·i·cence
ret·i·cent
ret·i·cle
re·tic·u·lar
re·tic·u·late
re·tic·u·la·tion
ret·i·cule
ret·i·na
ret·i·nue
re·tire

re·tir·ee
re·tire·ment
re·tir·ing
re·tool
re·tort
re·touch
re·trace
re·tract
re·trac·tile
re·trac·tion
re·trac·tor
re·train
re·train·ee
re·tread
re·treat
re·treat·ant
re·trench
re·trench·ment
re·tri·al
ret·ri·bu·tion
re·trib·u·tive
re·trib·u·to·ry
re·triev·al
re·trieve
re·triev·er
ret·ro·ac·tive
ret·ro·flex
ret·ro·grade
ret·ro·gress
ret·ro·gres·sion
ret·ro·gres·sive
ret·ro·spect
ret·ro·spec·tion
ret·ro·spec·tive
re·trous·sé
ret·ro·ver·sion
re·try
ret·si·na
re·turn
re·turn·able

re·turn·ee
re·uni·fy
re·union
re·unite
re·us·able
re·use
re·val·i·date
re·val·u·ate
re·val·ue
re·vamp
re·veal
re·veal·ment
rev·eil·le
rev·el
rev·e·la·tion
re·ve·la·to·ry
rev·el·er
rev·el·ry
re·venge
rev·e·nue
re·ver·ber·ant
re·ver·ber·ate
re·ver·ber·a·tion
re·vere
rev·er·ence
rev·er·end
rev·er·ent
rev·er·en·tial
rev·er·ie
re·ver·sal
re·verse
re·vers·ible
re·ver·sion
re·vert
re·vet·ment
re·vict·ual
re·view
re·vile
re·vise
re·vi·sion

re·vis·it
re·vi·so·ry
re·vi·tal·ize
re·viv·al
re·viv·al·ist
re·vive
re·viv·i·fy
re·viv·i·fi·ca·tion
re·vo·ca·ble
re·vo·ca·tion
re·voke
re·volt
rev·o·lu·tion
rev·o·lu·tion·ary
rev·o·lu·tion·ize
re·volve
re·volv·er
re·vue
re·vul·sion
re·wak·en
re·ward
re·wind
re·word
re·work
re·write
re·write man
re·zone
rhap·sod·ic
rhap·so·dist
rhap·so·dize
rhap·so·dy
rheo·stat
rhet·o·ric
rhet·o·ri·cian
rheum
rheu·mat·ic
rheu·ma·tism
rheu·ma·toid
rheu·ma·tol·o·gy
Rh fac·tor

rhine·stone
rhi·ni·tis
rhi·noc·er·os
rhi·zoid
rhi·zome
Rhodes schol·ar
rho·do·mon·tade
rho·do·ra
rhom·boid
rhom·bus
rhu·barb
rhyme
rhym·er
rhyme·ster
rhythm
rhyth·mic
ri·al·to
ri·ant
rib·ald
rib·ald·ry
rib·and
rib·bing
rib·bon
ri·bo·fla·vin
rich·es
rich·ness
Rich·ter scale
rick·ets
rick·ety
rick·sha
ric·o·chet
ri·cot·ta
rid·able
rid·dance
rid·den
rid·dle
rid·dling
rid·er
ridge
rid·i·cule

ri·dic·u·lous
ri·ding
Ries·ling
rife
riff
rif·fle
riff·raff
ri·fle
ri·fle·ry
ri·fling
rift
rig·a·doon
rig·a·ma·role
rig·a·to·ni
rig·ger
rig·ging
right
righ·teous
righ·teous·ness
right·ful
right-hand
right·ly
right-mind·ed
right-of-way
right-to-work law
rig·id
ri·gid·i·ty
rig·ma·role
rig·or
rig·or mor·tis
rig·or·ous
rile
rill
rimmed
ring-around-a-
   rosy
ring·er
ring·let
ring·mas·ter
ring·side

ring·toss
rink
rinse
rins·ing
ri·ot
ri·ot·ous
ri·par·i·an
rip cord
rip·en
rip-off
ri·poste
rip·per
rip·ping
rip·ple
rip-roar·ing
rip·saw
rip·snort·er
Rip van Win·kle
ris·er
ris·i·bil·i·ty
ris·i·ble
risky
ri·sor·gi·men·to
ri·sot·to
ris·qué
rite
rite of pas·sage
rit·u·al
rit·u·al·ize
ritzy
ri·val
ri·val·ry
rive
riv·er·bank
riv·er·bed
riv·er·ine
riv·er·side
riv·et
riv·et·er
ri·vi·era

riv·u·let
roach
road·abil·i·ty
road·bed
road·block
road·house
road show
road·side
road·ster
road·way
roam
roan
roar·er
roast·er
rob·bery
robe
robe de cham·bre
rob·in
Rob·in Hood
Rob·in·son Cru·
  soe
ro·bot
Rob Roy
ro·bust
ro·bus·tious
roch·et
rock and roll
rock-bottom
rock candy
rock·er
rock·et
rock·et·ry
rock garden
rock 'n' roll
rock-ribbed
rock wool
rocky
ro·co·co
ro·dent
ro·deo

ro·do·mon·tade
roe
roe·buck
roent·gen
roent·gen ray
ro·ga·tion
rog·er
rogue
rogu·ery
rogues' gal·lery
roily
rois·ter
role
roll
roll·back
roll·er coast·er
rol·lick
ro·ly-po·ly
ro·maine
ro·man à clef
ro·mance
ro·man·tic
ro·man·ti·cism
ro·man·ti·cize
Ro·meo
romp
ron·deau
rood
roof
roof·ing
roof·top
rook
rook·ery
rook·ie
room·ette
room·ful
room·mate
roomy
roost·er
rope

ropy
Roque·fort
Ror·schach test
ro·sar·i·an
ro·sa·ry
ro·sé
ro·se·ate
rose·bud
rose-col·ored
  glasses
rose·mary
Ro·set·ta stone
ro·sette
Rosh Ha·sha·nah
Ro·si·cru·cian
ros·in
ros·in·ous
ros·ter
ros·trum
rosy
Ro·tar·i·an
ro·ta·ry
ro·tat·able
ro·tate
ro·ta·tion
ro·ta·tor
rote
rot·gut
ro·tis·ser·ie
ro·to·gra·vure
ro·tor
ro·to·till
rot·ten
ro·tund
ro·tun·da
roué
rouge
rough
rough·age
rough-and-ready

rough-and-tum·
 ble
rough-dry
rough·en
rough-hewn
rough·house
rough·ish
rough·ly
rough·neck
rough·rid·er
rough·shod
rou·lette
round
round·about
roun·de·lay
round·er
round ro·bin
round-shoul·
 dered
rouse
roust·about
rout
route
rout·er
rou·tine
rou·tin·ize
ro·ver
row·an
row·di·ly
row·di·ness
row·dy
row·dy·ish
row·dy·ism
row·el
roy·al·ly
roy·al·ist
roy·al·ty
rub-a-dub
rub·ber
rub·ber·neck

rubber-stamp
rub·bery
rub·bing
rub·bish
rub·ble
ru·bel·la
Ru·bi·con
ru·bi·cund
ru·bric
ru·by
ruck·sack
ruck·us
ruc·tion
rud·der
rud·dy
rude·ness
ru·di·ment
ru·di·men·ta·ry
rue
rue·ful
ruff
ruf·fi·an
ruf·fi·an·ly
ruf·fle
ru·fous
rug·by
rug·ged
ru·gose
ru·in
ru·in·ation
ru·in·ous
rul·er
rul·ing
rum·ba
rum·ble
rum·bling
ru·mi·nant
ru·mi·nate
rum·mage
rum·my

ru·mor
ru·mor·mon·ger
rump
rum·ple
rum·ply
rum·pus
run·about
run·around
run·away
run·down
rune
rung
run in
run·nel
run·ner
run·ny
run·off
run-of-the-mill
run-on
runt
run-through
run·way
ru·pee
rup·ture
ru·ral
ruse
rush
rush·ee
rus·set
Rus·sian rou·lette
rust
rus·tic
rus·ti·cate
rus·tic·i·ty
rus·tle
rus·tler
rusty
ru·ta·ba·ga
ruth·ful
ruth·less

rut·tish
rye whis·key

S

Sab·ba·tar·i·an
Sab·bath
sab·bat·i·cal
sa·ber
sa·ble
sa·bot
sab·o·tage
sab·o·teur
sac
sac·cha·rin
sac·cha·rine
sac·cha·rin·i·ty
sac·er·do·tal
sac·er·do·tal·ism
sac fungus
sa·chem
sa·chet
sack
sack·cloth
sack·ing
sa·cral
sac·ra·ment
sac·ra·men·tal
sa·cred
sac·ri·fice
sac·ri·fi·cial
sac·ri·lege
sac·ri·le·gious
sac·ris·tan
sac·ris·ty
sa·cro·il·i·ac
sac·ro·sanct
sa·crum

sad·den
sad·dle
sad·dler
sad·dlery
sa·dism
sa·dist
sa·dis·tic
sa·do·mas·och·
   ism
sad sack
sa·fa·ri
safe-con·duct
safe-deposit box
safe·guard
safe·keep·ing
safe·ty
saf·flow·er
saf·fron
sa·ga
sa·ga·cious
sa·gac·i·ty
sage
sage·brush
sa·go
sa·hib
sail·able
sail·er
sail·or
saint
saint·hood
saint·like
sake
sa·ke
sa·laam
sal·abil·i·ty
sal·able
sa·la·cious
sa·la·cious·ly
sa·la·cious·ness
sal·ad

sal·a·man·der
sa·la·mi
sal am·mo·ni·ac
sal·a·ry
sale
sales check
sales·clerk
sales·girl
sales·la·dy
sales·man
sales·peo·ple
sa·lience
sa·lien·cy
sa·lient
sa·line
sa·lin·i·ty
sa·li·nize
sa·li·va
sal·i·vary
sal·i·vate
sal·low
sal·ly
sal·ma·gun·di
salm·on
sa·lon
sa·loon
sal soda
salt
sal·ta·tion
sal·ta·to·ri·al
sal·ta·to·ry
salt·cel·lar
salt·i·er
sal·tine
salt·pe·ter
salt·shak·er
salty
sa·lu·bri·ous
sa·lu·bri·ty
sa·lu·ki

sal·u·tary
sal·u·ta·tion
sa·lu·ta·to·ri·an
sa·lu·ta·to·ry
sa·lute
sa·lut·ing
salv·able
sal·vage
sal·vage·able
sal·va·tion
salve
sal·ver
sal·via
sal·vif·ic
sal·vo
Sa·mar·i·tan
sam·ba
same
same·ness
sam·o·var
Sam·o·yed
sam·pan
sam·ple
sam·pler
sam·pling
sam·u·rai
san·a·tar·i·um
san·a·tive
san·a·to·ri·um
sanc·ti·fi·ca·tion
sanc·ti·fi·er
sanc·ti·fy
sanc·ti·mo·nious
sanc·ti·mo·ny
sanc·tion
sanc·ti·ty
sanc·tu·ary
sanc·tum
sanc·tum sanc·
  to·rum

san·dal
san·dal·wood
sand·bag
sand·bank
sand·blast
sand·er
sand·er·ling
sand·ling
sand·lot
sand·man
sand·pa·per
sand·pip·er
sand·wich
sandy
sane
sang·froid
san·gui·nary
san·gui·nari·ly
san·guine
san·guin·e·ous
san·i·tar·i·an
san·i·tari·ly
san·i·tar·i·um
san·i·tary
san·i·ta·tion
san·i·tize
san·i·to·ri·um
san·i·ty
san·se·vie·ria
sans ser·if
sap·head
sa·pid·i·ty
sa·pi·ence
sa·pi·ent
sap·ling
sap·o·na·ceous
sa·pon·i·fy
sap·per
sap·phic
sap·phire

sap·pi·ness
sap·py
sap·suck·er
sarape
sar·casm
sar·cas·tic
sar·coph·a·gous
sar·coph·a·gus
sar·dine
sar·don·ic
sard·onyx
sa·ri
sa·rong
sar·sa·pa·ril·la
sar·to·ri·al
sa·shay
sas·sa·fras
sassy
sa·tan·ic
sa·tan·i·cal·ly
sa·tan·ism
satch·el
sat·ed
sa·teen
sat·el·lite
sa·tia·ble
sa·ti·ate
sa·ti·ety
sat·in
sat·iny
sat·ire
sa·tir·ic
sat·i·rist
sat·i·rize
sat·is·fac·tion
sat·is·fac·to·ri·ly
sat·is·fac·to·ry
sat·is·fi·able
sat·is·fy
sat·is·fy·ing·ly

sa·trap
sa·tra·py
sat·u·rate
sat·u·ra·tion
sat·ur·na·lia
sat·ur·nine
sa·tyr
sauce
sauce·pan
sau·cer
sauc·i·ness
saucy
sau·er·bra·ten
sau·er·kraut
sau·na
saun·ter
sau·ri·an
sau·sage
sau·té
sau·téed
sau·té·ing
sau·terne
sav·able
sav·age
sav·age·ry
sa·van·na
sa·vant
sav·ior
sa·voir faire
sa·vor
sa·vory
Sa·voy·ard
sav·vy
saw
saw·dust
sawed
sawed-off
sawn
saw·yer
sax·o·phone

sax·o·phon·ist
say·able
say·ing
say-so
scab·bard
scab·by
sca·bies
sca·brous
scaf·fold
scaf·fold·ing
scal·able
sca·lar
scal·a·wag
scald
scald·ing
scale
sca·lene
scal·lion
scal·lop
scal·lo·pi·ni
scal·ly·wag
scalp
scal·pel
scalp·er
scaly
scamp
scam·per
scam·pi
scan
scan·dal
scan·dal·ize
scan·dal·mon·ger
scan·dal·ous
Scan·di·na·vian
scanned
scan·ner
scan·sion
scant
scant·ies
scant·ling

scanty
scape
scape·goat
scap·u·la
scap·u·lar
scar
scar·ab
scar·a·mouch
scarce·ly
scar·ci·ty
scare
scare·crow
scaredy-cat
scare·mon·ger
scarf
scar·i·fy
scar·la·ti·na
scar·let
scarp
scar·ry
scary
scat
scathe
scath·ing
scat·o·log·i·cal
sca·tol·o·gy
scat·ter
scat·ter·brained
scat·ter·gram
scat·ter·ing
scaup
scav·enge
scav·en·ger
sce·nar·io
sce·nar·ist
scene
scen·ery
sce·nic
scent
scep·ter

scep·tered
scep·tic
scep·ti·cal
scep·ti·cism
sched·ule
Sche·her·a·zade
sche·ma
sche·mat·ic
sche·mat·i·cal·ly
sche·ma·tize
scheme
schem·ing
scher·zo
schip·per·ke
schism
schis·mat·ic
schis·ma·tist
schis·ma·tize
schist
schiz·oid
schizo·phrene
schizo·phre·nia
schizo·phren·ic
schle·miel
schlock
schmaltz
schmo
schmuck
schnapps
schnau·zer
schnit·zel
schnook
schnor·rer
schnoz·zle
schol·ar
schol·ar·ship
scho·las·tic
scho·las·ti·cism
scho·li·ast
scho·li·um

school
school·ing
school·man
school·marm
school·mas·ter
school·mate
school·mis·tress
schoo·ner
schtick
schuss
schwa
sci·at·ic
sci·at·i·ca
sci·ence
sci·en·tif·ic
sci·en·tif·i·cal·ly
sci·en·tism
sci·en·tist
scil·i·cet
scil·la
scim·i·tar
scin·til·la
scin·til·lant
scin·til·late
scin·til·la·tion
sci·o·lism
sci·on
sci·re fa·cias
scis·sile
scis·sion
scis·sor
scis·sors
sclaff
scle·ro·sis
scle·rot·ic
scoff
scoff·law
scold
scol·lop
sconce

scone
scoop
scoot
scoot·er
scope
scorch
score
score·keep·er
scorn
scorn·ful
scorn·ful·ly
scor·pi·on
Scot
scotch
Scotch
sco·ter
scot-free
Scot·land Yard
Scots·man
Scot·tish
scoun·drel
scoun·drel·ly
scour
scourge
scourg·ing
scour·ing
scout
scout·mas·ter
scow
scowl
scrab·ble
scrab·bly
scrag
scrag·gly
scrag·gy
scram
scram·ble
scram·bling
scrap
scrap·book

scrape
scraped
scrap·per
scrap·pi·ness
scrap·ple
scrap·py
scratch
scratchy
scrawl
scraw·ni·ness
scraw·ny
scream
scream·ing·ly
scree
screech
screed
screen
screw
screw·ball
screw·driv·er
screwy
scrib·ble
scrib·bler
scribe
scrim
scrim·mage
scrimp
scrim·shaw
scrip
script
scrip·to·ri·um
scrip·tur·al
scrip·ture
script·writ·er
scriv·en·er
scrod
scrof·u·la
scrof·u·lous
scroll
scrooge

scrounge
scrub
scrub·ber
scrub·by
scruff
scruffy
scrump·tious
scru·ple
scru·pu·los·i·ty
scru·pu·lous
scru·ta·ble
scru·ta·tor
scru·ti·neer
scru·ti·nize
scru·ti·ny
scu·ba
scud
scud·ding
scuff
scuf·fle
scuf·fling
scull
scul·lery
scul·lion
sculpt
sculp·tor
sculp·tress
sculp·tur·al
sculp·ture
sculp·tur·esque
scum
scum·my
scup·per
scup·per·nong
scur·ril·i·ty
scur·ri·lous
scur·ry
scur·vy
scutch·eon
scut·tle

scut·tle·butt
scythe
sea bass
Sea·bee
sea·borne
sea·coast
sea·far·er
sea·far·ing
sea·food
sea·go·ing
sea is·land cot·ton
seal
seal·ant
seal·er
seal point
seal·skin
Sea·ly·ham
   ter·ri·er
seam
sea·man
sea·man·ship
seam·less
seam·ster
seamy
sé·ance
sea·plane
sea·port
sear
search
search·ing·ly
search·light
search war·rant
sea·scape
sea·shell
sea·shore
sea·sick·ness
sea·side
sea·son
sea·son·able
sea·son·al

sea·son·al·ly
sea·son·ing
seat
sea·ward
sea·way
sea·wor·thy
se·ba·ceous
sec
se·cant
se·cede
se·ces·sion
se·ces·sion·ist
se·clude
se·clu·sion
se·clu·sive
se·clu·sive·ness
sec·ond·ari·ly
sec·ond·ary
sec·ond-best
sec·ond-class
sec·ond·er
sec·ond-guess
sec·ond·hand
sec·ond-rate
sec·ond-story
  man
sec·ond-string
se·cre·cy
sec·re·tar·i·at
sec·re·tary
sec·re·tary-
  gen·er·al
se·crete
se·cre·tion
se·cre·tive
se·cret·ly
se·cre·to·ry
sect
sec·tar·i·an

sec·tar·i·an·ism
sec·ta·ry
sec·tion·al
sec·tion·al·ism
sec·tor
sec·u·lar
sec·u·lar·ism
sec·u·lar·ize
se·cure
se·cure·ly
se·cure·ment
se·cu·ri·ty
se·dan
se·date
se·da·tion
sed·a·tive
sed·en·tary
se·der
sedge
sed·i·ment
sed·i·men·ta·ry
sed·i·men·ta·tion
se·di·tion
se·di·tious
se·duce
se·duce·ment
se·duc·tion
se·duc·tive
se·duc·tive·ness
se·duc·tress
sed·u·lous
see·able
seed
seed·i·er
seed·ling
seeds·man
seedy
see·ing
See·ing Eye

seek
seem·ing
seem·ly
seep
seep·age
seer
seer·ess
seer·suck·er
see·saw
seethe
seeth·ing
seg·ment
seg·men·tal
seg·men·ta·tion
seg·ment·ed
seg·re·gate
seg·re·ga·tion
seg·re·ga·tion·ist
se·gue
sei·gneur
sei·gneur·ial
sei·gneury
seine
seis·mic
seis·mo·graph
seis·mol·o·gy
seize
seiz·ing
sei·zure
sel·dom
se·lect
se·lect·ee
se·lec·tion
se·lec·tive
se·lec·tiv·i·ty
se·lect·man
self-abase·ment
self-ab·sorbed
self-ab·sorp·tion

self-ac·tiv·i·ty
self-ad·dressed
self-ad·just·ing
self-ad·vance·ment
self-anal·y·sis
self-as·sured
self-cen·tered
self-clos·ing
self-com·pla·cent
self-com·posed
self-con·ceit
self-con·cept
self-con·cern
self-con·demned
self-con·scious
self-con·tained
self-con·trol
self-crit·i·cal
self-de·ceived
self-de·cep·tion
self-de·feat·ing
self-de·fen·sive
self-de·ni·al
self-de·struc·tion
self-de·ter·mi·na·tion
self-dis·ci·pline
self-dis·cov·ery
self-ed·u·cat·ed
self-ef·fac·ing
self-em·ploy·ment
self-ev·i·dent
self-ex·am·i·na·tion
self-ex·plan·a·to·ry
self-ex·pres·sion

self-for·get·ful
self-ful·fill·ing
self-gov·ern·ing
self-grat·i·fi·ca·tion
self-help
self-hyp·no·sis
self-iden·ti·fi·ca·tion
self-im·age
self-im·por·tance
self-imposed
self-im·prove·ment
self-in·duced
self-in·flict·ed
self-ini·ti·at·ed
self-in·sur·er
self-in·ter·est
self·ish
self-jus·ti·fi·ca·tion
self·less
self-mas·tery
self-op·er·at·ing
self-per·cep·tion
self-per·pet·u·at·ing
self-pity
self-por·trait
self-pos·sessed
self-pos·ses·sion
self-praise
self-pres·er·va·tion
self-pro·claimed
self-pro·pelled
self-pun·ish·ment
self-ques·tion·ing

self-rat·ing
self-re·al·iza·tion
self-re·crim·i·na·tion
self-re·flec·tion
self-re·gard
self-reg·u·lat·ing
self-re·li·ance
self-re·proach
self-re·spect
self-re·straint
self-righ·teous
self-sac·ri·fice
self-sa·cri·fic·ing
self·same
self-sat·is·fy·ing
self-seek·ing
self-ser·vice
self-serv·ing
self-start·er
self-stim·u·la·tion
self-suf·fi·cien·cy
self-suf·fi·cient
self-sup·port
self-sus·tain·ing
self-taught
self-treat·ment
self-wind·ing
sell·er
sell-off
sell·out
selt·zer
sel·vage
se·man·tic
se·man·ti·cist
sema·phore
sem·blance
se·men

se·mes·ter
semi·ab·stract
semi·an·nu·al
semi·au·to·mat·ic
semi·au·ton·o·
  mous
semi·breve
semi·cir·cle
semi·civ·i·lized
semi·co·lon
semi·con·scious
semi·dark·ness
semi·de·tached
semi·fi·nal
semi·for·mal
semi·gloss
semi-in·de·pen·
  dent
semi·lit·er·ate
semi·mo·nas·tic
semi·month·ly
sem·i·nal
sem·i·nar
sem·i·nar·i·an
sem·i·na·rist
sem·i·nary
se·mi·ot·ic
semi·pal·mat·ed
semi·per·ma·
  nent
semi·per·me·able
semi·po·lit·i·cal
semi·pre·cious
semi·pri·vate
semi·pro
semi·pro·fes·sion·
  al
semi·qua·ver
semi·re·tired

semi·skilled
Se·mit·ic
semi·tone
semi·trop·i·cal
semi·week·ly
sem·o·li·na
sem·pi·ter·nal
semp·stress
sen·ate
sen·a·tor
sen·a·to·ri·al
send-off
se·nec·ti·tude
se·nes·cence
sen·e·schal
se·nile
se·nil·i·ty
se·nior
se·nior·i·ty
sen·na
sen·nit
se·nor
se·no·ra
se·no·ri·ta
sen·sate
sen·sa·tion
sen·sa·tion·al·
  ism
sense
sense·less
sen·si·bil·i·ty
sen·si·ble
sen·si·tive
sen·si·tiv·i·ty
sen·si·tize
sen·sor
sen·so·ry
sen·su·al
sen·su·al·is·tic

sen·su·al·ly
sen·su·ous
sen·su·ous·ness
sen·tence
sen·ten·tious
sen·tience
sen·tient
sen·ti·ment
sen·ti·men·tal·i·
  ty
sen·ti·nel
sen·try
se·pal
sep·a·ra·ble
sep·a·ra·bly
sep·a·rate
sep·a·ra·tion
sep·a·rat·ist
sep·a·ra·tor
se·pia
sep·ten·ni·al
sep·tet
sep·tic
sep·tu·a·ge·nar·i·
  an
sep·tum
sep·ul·cher
se·pul·chral
sep·ul·ture
se·quel
se·quence
se·quen·tial
se·ques·ter
se·ques·trate
se·ques·tra·tion
se·quin
se·qui·tur
se·quoia
se·ra·glio

se·ra·pe
ser·aph
sere
ser·e·nade
ser·en·dip·i·tous
ser·en·dip·i·ty
se·rene
se·ren·i·ty
serf
serge
ser·geant
se·ri·al
se·ri·al·iza·tion
se·ri·a·tim
se·ries
ser·if
se·rio·com·ic
se·ri·ous
se·ri·ous·ness
ser·mon
ser·mon·ize
ser·pent
ser·pen·tine
ser·rate
ser·ra·tion
ser·ried
se·rum
ser·vant
serv·er
ser·vice
ser·vice·able
ser·vic·ing
ser·vi·ette
ser·vile
ser·vile·ly
ser·vil·i·ty
ser·vi·tor
ser·vi·tude
ser·vo·mo·tor

ses·a·me
ses·qui·cen·te·na·
  ry
ses·qui·cen·ten·
  ni·al
ses·qui·pe·da·
  lian
ses·sile
ses·sion
ses·tet
se·ta·ceous
set-aside
set·back
set-in
set·screw
set·tee
set·ter
set·ting
set·tle
set·tle·ment
set·tler
set-to
set·up
sev·en·fold
sev·en·teen
sev·enth
sev·en·ty
sev·er·able
sev·er·al
sev·er·ance
se·vere·ly
se·ver·i·ty
Sevres
sew·age
sew·er
sew·er·age
sew·ing
sex·a·ge·nar·i·an
sexed

sex·ism
sex·less
sex·ol·o·gy
sex·tant
sex·tet
sex·ton
sex·tu·ple
sex·tu·plet
sex·tu·pli·cate
sex·u·al
sex·u·al·i·ty
sexy
Shab·bat
shab·bi·ness
shab·by
Sha·bu·oth
shack
shack·le
shad
shade
shad·i·er
shad·i·ness
shad·ing
shad·ow
shad·owy
shady
shaft
shag
shag·bark
shag·gi·er
shag·gy
shah
shak·able
shake
shak·er
Shake·spear·ean
shake-up
sha·ko
shak·i·ly

shak·i·ness
shaky
shale
shal·lot
shal·low
sha·lom
sha·lom alei·
  chem
shalt
sham
sham·ble
sham·bles
shame·faced
shame·ful
sham·poo
sham·poo·er
sham·rock
shang·hai
Shan·gri-la
shank
shan·tung
shan·ty
shap·able
shape
shape·less
shape·ly
shard
share
share·able
share·crop·per
share·hold·er
shark
shark·skin
sharp·en
sharp·er
sharp·shoot·er
sharp-wit·ted
shat·ter
shat·ter·proof
shave

shav·ing
shave·ling
shav·er
shave·tail
Sha·vi·an
shawl
shay
sheaf
shear
sheath
sheathe
sheath·ing
she·bang
she·been
she'd
shed·der
sheep
sheep·fold
sheep·herd·er
sheep·ish
sheep·shank
sheep·skin
sheer
sheer·ness
sheet
sheet·ing
Sheet·rock
sheikh
sheikh·dom
shek·el
shelf
she'll
shel·lac
shel·lacked
shel·lack·ing
shell·fish
shel·ter
shel·ty
shelve
shelv·ing

she·nan·i·gan
shep·herd
shep·herd·ess
shep·herd's pie
Sher·a·ton
sher·bet
sher·iff
sher·lock
sher·ry
she's
shib·bo·leth
shied
shield
shift
shift·less
shifty
Shih Tzu
shik·sa
shill
shil·le·lagh
shil·ling
shilly-shally
shim
shim·mer
shim·mery
shim·my
shin
shin·dig
shine
shin·gle
shin·gles
shin·ing
shin·ny
shiny
ship·board
ship·ment
ship·pa·ble
ship·per
ship·ping
ship·shape

ship·wreck	short	shrew·ish
ship·wright	short·age	shriek
shire	short·cake	shrie·val·ty
shirk	short·change	shrift
shirk·er	short-cir·cuit	shrike
shirr	short·com·ing	shrill
shirt	short·en	shrimp
shirt-sleeve	short·en·ing	shrine
shirt·tail	short·hand	shrink
shish ke·bab	short-lived	shrink·age
shiv·a·ree	short·ly	shrive
shiv·er	short shrift	shriv·en
shoal	short·sight·ed	shriv·el
shoat	short-tem·pered	shroud
shock	short-term	shrub·bery
shod	short·wave	shrug
shod·di·ness	shot·gun	shrunk
shod·dy	should	shtick
shoe	shoul·der	shuck
shoe·horn	shouldn't	shud·der
shoe·lace	shout	shuf·fle
shoe·mak·er	shove	shuf·fle·board
shoe·string	shov·el	shun
sho·far	shov·el·er	shunt
shone	shov·el·ful	shush
shoo	show biz	shut
shoo·fly	show·case	shut-eye
shoo-in	show·down	shut-in
shook-up	show·er	shut·ter
shoot	show·i·er	shut·ter·bug
shoot-the-chutes	show·man	shut·tle
shop·keep·er	show-off	shut·tle·cock
shop·lift	show·piece	shy
shop·per	show·stop·per	shy·ing
shop·worn	showy	shy·lock
shore	shrank	shy·ster
shore·line	shrap·nel	sib·i·lant
shore·ward	shred	sib·i·late
shor·ing	shrew	sib·ling
shorn	shrewd	sick·en

sick·en·ing
sick·le
sick·le-cell
  ane·mia
sick·li·ness
sick·ly
sick·ness
side
side·burns
side-glance
side·kick
side·light
side·line
si·de·re·al
side·slip
side·step
side·swipe
side·wards
side·ways
sid·ing
si·dle
si·dling
siege
si·er·ra
si·es·ta
sieve
sift
sigh
sight
sight·less
sight·less·ness
sight·ly
sight-see·ing
sig·ma
sign
sig·nal
sig·nal·ize
sig·nal·ly
sig·nal·man
sig·na·to·ry

sig·na·ture
sig·net
sig·ni·fi·able
sig·nif·i·cance
sig·nif·i·can·cy
sig·nif·i·cant
sig·ni·fi·ca·tion
sig·ni·fy
si·gnor
si·gno·ra
si·gno·re
si·gno·ri·na
sign·post
si·lage
si·lence
si·lent
si·lents
sil·hou·ette
sil·i·cate
sil·i·con
silk
silk·en
silk·i·er
silk-stock·ing
silky
sill
sil·ly
si·lo
silt
sil·ver
sil·ver·fish
sil·ver·ly
sil·ver·smith
sil·ver·ware
sil·very
sim·i·an
sim·i·lar
sim·i·lar·i·ty
sim·i·le
si·mil·i·tude

sim·mer
si·mo·le·on
si·mo·nize
si·mon-pure
si·mo·ny
sim·pa·ti·co
sim·per
sim·ple
sim·ple·ton
sim·plex
sim·plic·i·ty
sim·pli·fi·ca·tion
sim·pli·fy
sim·plis·tic
sim·plis·ti·cal·ly
sim·ply
sim·u·la·crum
sim·u·late
sim·u·la·tion
si·mul·cast
si·mul·ta·neous
since
sin·cere
sin·cer·i·ty
sine
si·ne·cure
si·ne die
si·ne qua non
sin·ew
sin·ewy
sin·fo·niet·ta
sin·ful
sing-along
singe
singe·ing
sin·gle
sin·gle-hand·ed
sin·gle·ness
sin·glet
sin·gle·ton

sin·gly
sing·song
sin·gu·lar
sin·gu·lar·i·ty
sin·is·ter
si·nis·tral
sink·er
sin·less
sin·ner
si·nol·o·gy
sin·u·os·i·ty
sin·u·ous
si·nus
si·nus·itis
si·phon
sire
si·ren
sir·loin
si·roc·co
si·sal
sis·si·fied
sis·sy
sis·ter
sis·ter·hood
sis·ter-in-law
sis·ter·ly
sit-down
site
sit-in
sit·ter
sit·ting
sit·u·ate
sit·u·at·ed
sit·u·a·tion
sit-up
six-pack
six·pence
six-shoot·er
six·teen
sixth

six·ty
siz·able
size
siz·ing
siz·zle
siz·zler
skate
ske·dad·dle
skeet
skein
skel·e·tal
skel·e·ton
skel·e·ton·ize
skep·tic
skep·ti·cism
sketch
skew
skew·er
skew·ness
ski
skid
skid·der
skid·dy
skid row
skied
skiff
skill
skil·let
skill·ful
skim
skim·mer
skim·ming
skimp
skimp·i·ly
skimpy
skin-deep
skin·flint
skinned
skin·ny
skip

skip·per
skirl
skir·mish
skirr
skirt
skit
skit·ter
skit·tish
skit·tle
skoal
skul·dug·gery
skulk
skull
skull·cap
skunk
sky·cap
sky-high
sky·jack·er
sky·lark
sky·light
sky·line
sky·rock·et
sky·scrap·er
sky·ward
sky·writ·ing
slab
slab·ber
slack
slack·en
slack·er
slag
slain
slake
slak·ing
sla·lom
slam
slam-bang
slam·ming
slan·der
slan·der·ous·ly

slang
slang·i·ness
slangy
slant
slant·wise
slap·dash
slap·hap·py
slap·stick
slash
slash·ing
slat
slate
slat·ing
slat·tern
slaty
slaugh·ter
slaugh·ter·ous
slave
sla·ver
slav·ery
slav·ey
slav·ish
slay
sleave
slea·zy
sled·ding
sledge
sledge·ham·mer
sleek
sleep
sleep-in
sleep·i·ness
sleep·walk·er
sleepy
sleepy·head
sleet
sleety
sleeve
sleigh
sleight

slen·der·ize
sleuth
slew
slice
slice-of-life
slick
slide
slid·ing
slight
sli·ly
slim
slime
slim·i·ly
slim·i·ness
slim·ming
slimy
sling
sling·shot
slink
slink·i·er
slinky
slip·cov·er
slip·knot
slip·page
slipper
slip·pery
slip·shod
slip·stream
slith·er
slith·ery
sliv·er
sliv·o·vitz
slob
slob·ber
slob·bered
sloe-eyed
slog
slo·gan
slo·gan·eer
sloop

slop
slope
slop·pi·ness
slop·py
slosh
slot
sloth
sloth·ful
slouch
slouchy
slough
slov·en
slo·ven·li·ness
slow·ly
slub
sludge
slug
slug·abed
slug·fest
slug·gard
slug·ger
slug·gish
sluice
sluice·way
slum
slum·ber
slum·ber·ous
slum·gul·lion
slum·lord
slum·my
slump
slur
slurred
slur·ring
slurp
slur·ry
slush
slushy
slut
smack

smack·er
small
small-fry
small-scale
small-time
smarmy
smart
smart al·eck
smart·en
smarty-pants
smash
smash·ing
smash·up
smat·ter·ing
smear
smeary
smell
smelly
smelt
smelt·er
smid·gen
smi·lax
smile
smirch
smirk
smite
smith
smith·er·eens
smithy
smock
smog
smog·gy
smok·able
smoke
smoky
smol·der
smooch
smooth
smooth·en
smooth-tongued

smoothy
smor·gas·bord
smote
smoth·er
smudge
smug
smug·gle
smug·gler
smug·ly
smut
snack
snaf·fle
sna·fu
snag
snail
snake
snak·i·ly
snaky
snap
snap·drag·on
snap·per
snap·pish
snap·py
snap·shot
snare
snarl
snatch
snaz·zy
sneak
sneak·er
sneaky
sneer
sneeze
sneezy
snick·er
snide
sniff
snif·fle
snif·fling
snif·ter

snig·ger
snip
snipe
snip·ing
snip·pet
snip·py
snitch
sniv·el
sniv·el·ing
snob
snob·bery
snob·bish
snood
snook·er
snoop
snoop·er
snoopy
snooty
snooze
snore
snor·kel
snort
snot·ty
snout
snow
snow·ball
snow·bank
snow·bird
snow·drift
snow·fall
snow·flake
snow·mo·bile
snow·plow
snow·shoe
snowy
snub
snub·by
snub-nosed
snuff
snuff·er

snuf·fle
snug
snug·gery
snug·gle
snug·gling
soak
so-and-so
soap
soap·box
soap opera
soapy
soar
soar·ing
sob
so·ber
so·ber·ly
so·ber·sides
so·bri·ety
so·bri·quet
so-called
soc·cer
so·cia·bil·i·ty
so·cia·ble
so·cial
so·cial·ism
so·cial·ist
so·cial·is·tic
so·cial·ite
so·cial·ize
so·cial·ly
so·ci·etal
so·ci·ety
so·cio·eco·nom·ic
so·cio·log·i·cal
so·ci·ol·o·gy
so·ci·om·e·try
sock
sock·dol·a·ger
sock·et
sod

so·da
so·da·list
so·da·lite
so·dal·i·ty
sod·den
so·di·um
sod·omy
so·fa
sof·fit
soft
soft·ball
soft-cov·er
soft·en
soft·heart·ed
soft-ped·al
soft-shell clam
soft-shoe
soft-soap
soft-spo·ken
softy
sog·gi·ness
sog·gy
soi·gné
soil·age
soil·ure
soi·ree
so·journ
so·lace
so·lar
so·lar·i·um
solar plexus
sol·der
sol·der·ing iron
sol·dier
sole
so·le·cism
sol·emn
so·lem·ni·fy
so·lem·ni·ty
sol·em·nize

so·le·noid
so·lic·it
so·lic·i·ta·tion
so·lic·i·tor
so·lic·i·tous
so·lic·i·tude
sol·id
sol·i·dar·i·ty
so·lid·i·fi·ca·tion
so·lid·i·fy
so·lid·i·ty
sol·id-state
so·lil·o·quist
so·lil·o·quize
so·lil·o·quy
so·lip·sism
sol·i·taire
sol·i·tary
sol·i·tude
so·lo
so·lo·ist
so·lon
so long
sol·stice
sol·sti·tial
sol·u·bil·i·ty
sol·u·ble
so·lu·tion
solv·able
solve
sol·ven·cy
sol·vent
so·mat·ic
so·ma·tol·o·gy
som·ber
som·bre·ro
some
som·er·sault
som·er·set
some·thing

some·time
some·times
some·where
some·wheres
som·me·lier
som·nam·bu·lant
som·nam·bu·lism
som·no·lence
som·no·lent
so·nant
so·nar
so·na·ta
song·fest
song·ster
son·ic
son·ic boom
son-in-law
son·net
son·ny
so·nor·i·ty
so·no·rous
soon·er
soot
soothe
sooth·say·er
sooth·say·ing
soot·i·ness
sooty
soph·ism
soph·ist
so·phis·tic
so·phis·ti·cate
so·phis·ti·cat·ed
so·phis·ti·ca·tion
soph·ist·ry
soph·o·more
soph·o·mor·ic
so·po·rif·ic
sop·ping
sop·py

so·pra·no
sor·bent
sor·cer·er
sor·cer·ess
sor·cery
sor·did
sore·head
sore·ly
sor·ghum
so·ri·tes
so·ro·ral
so·ror·i·ty
sor·rel
sor·row
sor·row·ful
sor·ry
sor·tie
SOS
so-so
sot·tish
sot·to vo·ce
sou·brette
sou·bri·quet
souf·flé
sough
sought
soul·ful
sound
sound·less
soup
soup·çon
soup du jour
soupy
source
sour·ish
sou·sa·phone
souse
sou·tane
south
south·er·ly

south·ern
south·land
south·paw
sou·ve·nir
sou´·west·er
sov·er·eign
sov·er·eign·ty
so·vi·et
so·vi·et·ism
so·vi·et·ize
soya
soy·bean
spa
space·craft
spac·ing
spa·cious
spack·le
spade
spa·dille
spa·ghet·ti
spal·peen
span
span·gle
span·iel
spank
span·ker
span·ner
spar
spare
spare·ribs
spar·ing
spark
spar·kle
spar·kler
sparky
spar·row
sparse
spar·si·ty
Spar·tan
spasm

spas·mod·ic
spas·tic
spat
spate
spa·tial
spa·tial·ly
spat·ter
spat·u·la
spav·in
spawn
spay·ing
speak·easy
speak·er
spear
spear·head
spear·mint
spe·cial
spe·cial·ist
spe·ci·al·i·ty
spe·cial·iza·tion
spe·cial·ize
spe·cial·ly
spe·cial·ty
spe·cie
spe·cies
spe·cif·ic
spec·i·fi·ca·tion
spec·i·fic·i·ty
spec·i·fy
spec·i·men
spe·cious
speck
speck·le
spec·ta·cle
spec·tac·u·lar
spec·ta·tor
spec·ter
spec·tral
spec·tro·scope
spec·trum

spec·u·late
spec·u·la·tion
spec·u·la·tive
spec·u·la·tor
spec·u·lum
speech
speech·ify
speech·less
speed
speed·ball
speed·om·e·ter
speed·ster
speed·way
speedy
spe·le·ol·o·gist
spe·le·ol·o·gy
spell·bind
spell·bound
spell·down
spell·er
spelt
spe·lunk·er
spe·lunk·ing
spend·able
spend·thrift
spent
sperm
sper·ma·ce·ti
spew
sphag·num
spher·al
sphere
spher·i·cal
spher·oid
sphe·roi·dal
sphinx
spice
spic·i·ness
spick-and-span
spicy

spi·der
spi·dery
spiel
spi·er
spiffy
spig·ot
spike
spiky
spill·age
spill·way
spilth
spin·ach
spi·nal·ly
spin·dle
spin·dly
spin·drift
spine
spine·less
spin·et
spin·na·ker
spin·ner
spin·ning
spin-off
spi·nous
spin·ster
spiny
spi·ral
spire
spi·rea
spir·it
spir·it·ed
spir·it·ism
spir·it·less
spir·i·tu·al
spir·i·tu·al·ism
spir·i·tu·al·i·ty
spir·i·tu·ous
spi·ro·chete
spit·ball
spite

spit·ed
spite·ful
spit·fire
spit·tle
spit·toon
splash
splashy
splat·ter
splay·foot·ed
spleen
splen·did
splen·did·ly
splen·dif·er·ous
splen·dor
sple·net·ic
splice
splint
splin·ter
split
split-level
split·ting
splotch
splurge
splut·ter
spoil
spoil·age
spoil·er
spoil·sport
spoke
spokes·man
spokes·wom·an
spo·li·a·tion
spon·dee
sponge
spongy
spon·sor
spon·ta·ne·ity
spon·ta·ne·ous
spoof
spooky

spool
spoon
spoo·ner·ism
spoon·ful
spoor
spo·rad·ic
spore
spor·ran
sport
sport·ful
sport·ive
sports·cast
sports·man·ship
sporty
spot-check
spot·less
spot·light
spot·ted
spot·ter
spot·ty
spou·sal
spouse
spout
sprain
sprat
sprawl
spray
spread
spread-ea·gle
spread·er
spree
sprig
spright·li·ness
spright·ly
spring
spring·board
spring·er
spring·time
springy
sprin·kle

sprin·kling
sprint
sprite
sprock·et
sprout
spruce
spry
spud
spume
spumy
spu·mo·ni
spunk
spunk·i·ly
spunky
spur
spu·ri·ous
spurn
spurred
spurt
sput·nik
sput·ter
spu·tum
spy·glass
squab
squab·ble
squad
squad·ron
squal·id
squall
squally
squa·lor
squan·der
square
squar·ish
squash
squashy
squat
squat·ter
squat·ty
squaw

squawk
squeak
squeaky
squeal
squea·mish
squee·gee
squeeze
squelch
squib
squid
squig·gle
squill
squint
squire
squirm
squir·rel
squirt
squish
squoosh
stab
sta·bile
sta·bil·i·ty
sta·bi·lize
sta·bi·liz·er
sta·ble
sta·bler
sta·bling
stac·ca·to
stack
stack·able
sta·dia
sta·di·um
staff
stag
stage
stage·craft
stage·struck
stag·ger
stag·ing
stag·nant

stag·nate
stag·na·tion
stagy
staid
stain
stain·er
stain·less
stair·case
stair·way
stair·well
stake
sta·lac·tite
sta·lag
sta·lag·mite
stale
stale·mate
Sta·lin·ism
stalk
stalk·ing-horse
stall
stal·lion
stal·wart
sta·men
stam·i·na
stam·mer
stamp
stam·pede
stamp·er
stance
stan·chion
stand
stan·dard
stan·dard-bear·er
stan·dard
  de·vi·a·tion
stan·dard·ize
stand·by
stand·ee
stand-in
stand·off

stand·off·ish
stand·pat
stand·pat·ter
stand·point
stand·still
stank
stan·za
sta·ple
sta·pler
star·board
starch
star-cham·ber
starchy
star-crossed
star·dom
stare
stark
star·let
star·ling
star·ry
star-span·gled
start
star·tle
star·tling
star·va·tion
starve
starve·ling
stash
sta·sis
state
state·craft
state·hood
state·less
state·ly
state·ment
state·side
states·man
states' rights
stat·ic
sta·tion

sta·tion·ary
sta·tio·ner
sta·tio·nery
stat·ism
sta·tis·tic
sta·tis·ti·cal
stat·is·ti·cian
sta·tis·tics
stat·u·ary
stat·ue
stat·u·esque
stat·u·ette
stat·ure
sta·tus
sta·tus quo
stat·ute
stat·u·to·ry
staunch
stave
stay·sail
stead
stead·fast
stead·ing
steady
steak
steal
stealth
stealth·i·ly
stealthy
steam
steam·er
steam·roll·er
steam·ship
steamy
steed
steel
steely
steel·yard
steep
stee·ple

stee·ple·chase
stee·ple·jack
steer
steer·age
steers·man
stein
stel·lar
stem·less
stemmed
stem·ware
stem-wind·er
stench
sten·cil
ste·nog·ra·pher
ste·nog·ra·phy
steno·type
sten·to·ri·an
step·broth·er
step·child
step·daugh·ter
step·fa·ther
step·lad·der
step·moth·er
steppe
step·per
step·ping-stone
step·sis·ter
step·son
step stool
ste·reo
ste·reo·graph
ste·reo·phon·ic
ste·reo·type
ster·ile
ster·il·iza·tion
ster·il·ize
ster·ling
stern
ster·num
ster·to·rous

stetho·scope
Stet·son
ste·ve·dore
stew
stew·ard
stew·ard·ess
stew·ard·ship
stick
stick-in-the-mud
stick·le
stick·ler
stick·pin
stick·um
stick·up
sticky
stiff
stiff·en
stiff-necked
stiff·ness
sti·fle
stig·ma
stig·mat·ic
stig·ma·tism
stig·ma·tize
stile
sti·let·to
still·birth
still·born
still life
stil·ly
stilt
Stil·ton
stim·u·lant
stim·u·late
stim·u·lus
sting
stin·gi·ness
sting·less
stin·gy
stink

stint
sti·pend
stip·ple
stip·u·late
stip·u·la·tion
stir
stirk
stirps
stir·ring
stir·rup
stitch
stitch·ery
stoat
stock
stock·ade
stock·bro·ker
stock·hold·er
stock·ing
stock-in-trade
stock·keep·er
stock·man
stock mar·ket
stock·pile
stock·pot
stock·room
stock split
stock·tak·ing
stocky
stock·yard
stodgy
sto·gie
sto·ic
sto·i·cal
sto·icism
stok·er
stole
stol·id
stol·len
stom·ach
stom·ach·ache

stomp
stone
Stone Age
stone-broke
stoned
stone·ma·son
stone·wall
stone·ware
stony
stood
stooge
stoop
stop-and-go
stop·cock
stop·gap
stop·light
stop·over
stop·per
stop·watch
stor·age
store
store·house
store·keep·er
store·room
sto·ried
stork
storm
storm·i·ly
stormy
sto·ry
sto·ry·book
sto·ry·tell·er
stoup
stout
stout·heart·ed
stove
stow
stow·age
stow·away
stra·bis·mus

strad·dle
Strad·i·var·i·us
strafe
strag·gle
strag·gly
straight
straight·away
straight·en
strain
strait
strait·en
strait·jack·et
strait·laced
strand
strange
stran·gle
stran·gle·hold
stran·gu·late
stran·gu·la·tion
strap·hang·er
strap·less
strapped
strap·ping
strat·a·gem
stra·te·gic
strat·e·gy
strat·i·fi·ca·tion
strat·i·fy
strato·sphere
strato·spher·ic
stra·tum
straw
straw·ber·ry
stray
streak
streak·ing
streaky
stream
stream·er
stream·line

street
street·walk·er
strength
strength·en
strength·less
stren·u·ous
strep throat
strep·to·coc·cus
strep·to·my·cin
stress
stress·ful
stress·less
stretch
stretch-out
strew
stri·at·ed
stri·a·tion
strick
strick·en
strict
stric·ture
stride
stri·dence
stri·den·cy
stri·dent
strid·u·late
strid·u·lous
strife
strike
strike-bound
strike-out
strik·er
strik·ing
string
strin·gen·cy
strin·gent
string·ing
strip
stripe
strip·er

strip·ing
strip·per
strip·tease
stripy
strive
strobe
stro·bo·scope
strode
stroke
stroll·er
strong·hold
strong-mind·ed
stron·ti·um 90
stro·phe
stro·phic
strove
struck
struc·tur·al
struc·tur·al·ize
struc·ture
stru·del
strug·gle
strum·ming
strum·pet
strung
strut
strych·nine
stub·ble
stub·born
stub·born·ness
stub·by
stuc·co
stud
stud·ding sail
stu·dent
stud·ied
stu·dio
stu·di·ous
study
stuff·ing

stuffy
stul·ti·fi·ca·tion
stul·ti·fy
stum·ble
stum·ble·bum
stump
stumpy
stung
stunk
stun·ner
stun·ning
stun·sail
stunt
stu·pe·fac·tion
stu·pe·fy
stu·pen·dous
stu·pid
stu·pid·i·ty
stu·pid·ly
stu·por
stur·dy
stur·geon
stut·ter
sty·gian
style
styl·ish
sty·lis·tic
styl·ize
sty·lus
sty·mie
styp·tic
Sty·ro·foam
sua·sion
suave
sua·vi·ty
sub·al·tern
sub·arc·tic
sub·con·ti·nent
sub·con·tract
sub·cul·ture

sub·cu·ta·ne·ous
sub·dea·con
sub·de·pot
sub·di·vide
sub·due
sub·dued
sub·en·try
sub·freez·ing
sub·group
sub·head
sub·head·ing
sub·hu·man
sub·ject
sub·jec·tive
sub·jec·tiv·ism
sub·join
sub·ju·gate
sub·ju·ga·tion
sub·junc·tive
sub·lease
sub·let
sub·lev·el
sub·li·mate
sub·lime
sub·lim·i·nal
sub·lim·i·ty
sub·lu·na·ry
sub·ma·chine
  gun
sub·ma·rine
sub·ma·ri·ner
sub·merge
sub·merse
sub·mers·ible
sub·mis·sion
sub·mis·sive
sub·mit
sub·nor·mal
sub·or·di·nate

sub·orn
sub·or·na·tion
sub·poe·na
sub·ro·ga·tion
sub·scribe
sub·script
sub·scrip·tion
sub·sec·tion
sub·se·quence
sub·se·quent
sub·serve
sub·ser·vi·ence
sub·ser·vi·ent
sub·side
sub·sid·iary
sub·si·di·za·tion
sub·si·dize
sub·si·dy
sub·sist
sub·sis·tence
sub·soil
sub·spe·cies
sub·stance
sub·stan·dard
sub·stan·tial
sub·stan·ti·ate
sub·stan·tive
sub·sta·tion
sub·sti·tute
sub·sti·tu·tion
sub·stra·tum
sub·struc·ture
sub·sume
sub·sump·tion
sub·teen
sub·tend
sub·ter·fuge
sub·ter·ra·nean
sub·tile

sub·til·ty
sub·ti·tle
sub·tle
sub·tle·ty
sub·top·ic
sub·to·tal
sub·tract
sub·trac·tion
sub·trac·tive
sub·trop·i·cal
sub·urb
sub·ur·bia
sub·ven·tion
sub·ver·sion
sub·vert
sub·vo·cal
sub·way
suc·ceed
succès d'es·time
suc·cess
suc·cess·ful
suc·ces·sion
suc·ces·sive
suc·ces·sor
suc·cinct
suc·cor
suc·co·tash
suc·cu·lence
suc·cu·lent
suc·cumb
suck·le
suck·ling
su·crose
suc·tion
sud·den
su·do·rif·ic
suds
sudsy
sue

suede
su·et
suf·fer
suf·fer·ance
suf·fer·ing
suf·fice
suf·fi·cien·cy
suf·fi·cient
suf·fix
suf·fo·cate
suf·fo·ca·tion
suf·fra·gan
suf·frage
suf·frag·ette
suf·frag·ist
suf·fuse
sug·ar
sug·ar·coat
sug·ary
sug·gest
sug·gest·ible
sug·ges·tion
sug·ges·tive
sui·cid·al
sui·cide
sui ge·ner·is
suit·able
suite
suit·ing
suit·or
su·ki·ya·ki
Suk·koth
sul·fa drug
sul·fur
sul·fu·ric
sul·fu·rous
sulky
sul·len
sul·ly

sul·tan
sul·tan·ate
sul·try
su·mac
sum·ma
sum·ma cum lau·
de
sum·ma·ri·za·
tion
sum·ma·rize
sum·ma·ry
sum·ma·tion
sum·ma·tive
sum·mer·time
sum·mit
sum·mon
sum·mons
sum·mum bo·
num
sump
sump·tu·ary
sump·tu·ous
sun·baked
sun·bathe
sun·beam
sun·bon·net
sun·burst
sun·dae
sun·di·al
sun·dries
sun·dry
sunk·en
sun·less
sun·light
sun·lit
sun·ny
sun·ny-side up
sun·set
sun·shine

sun·tan
su·per
su·per·abun·dant
su·per·an·nu·ate
su·per·an·nu·a·
tion
su·perb
su·per·car·go
su·per·cil·i·ary
su·per·cil·ious
su·per·fi·cial
su·per·fi·ci·al·i·ty
su·per·flu·ity
su·per·flu·ous
su·per·high·way
su·per·hu·man
su·per·in·tend
su·per·in·ten·
dence
su·per·in·ten·
den·cy
su·per·in·ten·
dent
su·pe·ri·or
su·pe·ri·or·i·ty
su·pe·ri·or·ly
su·per·la·tive
su·per·man
su·per·mar·ket
su·per·nat·u·ral
su·per·nu·mer·
ary
su·per·or·di·nate
su·per·pow·er
su·per·sede
su·per·son·ic
su·per·sti·tion
su·per·sti·tious
su·per·struc·ture

su·per·vise
su·per·vi·sion
su·per·vi·sor
su·pine
sup·per
sup·plant
sup·ple
sup·ple·ment
sup·ple·men·tal
sup·ple·men·ta·ry
sup·pli·ance
sup·pli·ant
sup·pli·cant
sup·pli·cate
sup·pli·ca·tion
sup·pli·ca·to·ry
sup·ply
sup·port
sup·port·able
sup·port·er
sup·port·ive
sup·pos·able
sup·pose
sup·posed
sup·po·si·tion
sup·pos·i·ti·tious
sup·pos·i·tive
sup·pos·i·to·ry
sup·press
sup·press·ible
sup·pres·sion
sup·pres·sive
sup·pres·sor
sup·pu·rate
sup·pu·ra·tion
su·pra·na·tion·al
su·prem·a·cist
su·prem·a·cy
su·preme

sur·cease
sur·charge
sur·cin·gle
surd
sure·foot·ed
sure·ly
sure·ty
surf
sur·face
sur·face-to-air mis·sile
surf·board
surf cast·er
sur·feit
surge
sur·geon
sur·gery
sur·gi·cal
sur·jec·tion
sur·jec·tive
sur·ly
sur·mise
sur·mount
sur·name
sur·pass
sur·plice
sur·plus
sur·plus·age
sur·prise
sur·re·al
sur·re·al·ism
sur·re·al·is·tic
sur·ren·der
sur·rep·ti·tious
sur·rey
sur·ro·gate
sur·ro·ga·tion
sur·round
sur·round·ings
sur·tax

sur·tout
sur·veil·lance
sur·vey
sur·vey·or
sur·viv·able
sur·viv·al
sur·vive
sur·vi·vor·ship
sus·cep·ti·bil·i·ty
sus·cep·ti·ble
sus·cep·tive
sus·pect
sus·pend
sus·pend·er
sus·pense
sus·pen·sion
sus·pi·cion
sus·pi·cious
sus·pire
sus·tain
sus·te·nance
sus·ten·ta·tion
su·sur·ra·tion
su·sur·rus
sut·ler
su·ture
svelte
swab·ber
swad·dle
swag
swag·ger
swain
swale
swal·low
swam
swamp
swamp·i·ness
swampy
swan dive
swank

swank·i·ly

swap

sward

swarm

swar·thy

swash·buck·le

swash·buck·ling

swas·ti·ka

swat

swatch

swath

swathe

swat·ter

sway

sway·back

swear

sweat

sweat·shop

sweaty

swede

sweep

sweep-sec·ond

sweep·stakes

sweet

sweet·en

sweet·en·ing

sweet·heart

sweet·ish

sweet·meat

swell

swell·ing

swel·ter

swept-back

swerve

swift

swift·ly

swift·ness

swig

swill

swim

swim·ming·ly

swim·suit

swin·dle

swine

swine·herd

swing

swing·er

swin·ish

swipe

swirl

swish

swishy

Swiss chard

switch

switch·back

switch·blade

switch·board

switch-hit·ter

swiv·el

swiv·el-hipped

swiz·zle

swol·len

swoon

swoop

swoosh

sword

swords·man

swore

sworn

swum

syc·a·more

sy·co·phan·cy

sy·co·phant

sy·co·phan·tic

sy·co·phant·ish

syl·lab·ic

syl·lab·i·cate

syl·lab·i·ca·tion

syl·lab·i·fi·ca·
   tion

syl·lab·i·fy

syl·la·ble

syl·la·bus

syl·lo·gize

sylph

syl·van

sym·bi·o·sis

sym·bol

sym·bol·ic

sym·bol·ism

sym·bol·ize

sym·met·ri·cal

sym·me·try

sym·pa·thet·ic

sym·pa·thize

sym·pa·thy

sym·phon·ic

sym·pho·nist

sym·pho·ny

sym·po·sium

symp·tom

symp·tom·at·ic

symp·tom·atol·o·
   gy

syn·a·gogue

syn·apse

syn·ap·sis

syn·chron·ic

syn·chro·nism

syn·chro·nize

syn·co·pate

syn·co·pa·tion

syn·co·pe

syn·cre·tism

syn·di·cal·ism

syn·di·cate

syn·drome

syn·ec·do·che

syn·er·get·ic

syn·er·gis·tic

syn·od
syn·od·i·cal
syn·onym
syn·on·y·mous
syn·op·sis
syn·op·size
syn·op·tic
syn·tax
syn·the·sis
syn·the·size
syn·thet·ic
syph·i·lis
sy·ringe
syr·up
sys·tem
sys·tem·at·ic
sys·tem·atize
sys·tem·ic
sys·to·le
syz·y·gy

T

Ta·bas·co
tab·by
tab·er·na·cle
ta·bla
tab·la·ture
ta·ble
tab·leau
ta·ble·cloth
ta·ble d'hôte
ta·ble-hop
ta·ble·spoon·ful
tab·let
ta·bling
tab·loid
ta·boo

tab·o·ret
tab·u·lar
ta·bu·la ra·sa
tab·u·late
tab·u·la·tor
ta·cet
ta·chis·to·scope
ta·chom·e·ter
ta·chym·e·ter
tac·it
tac·i·turn
tac·i·tur·ni·ty
tack·board
tacki·ness
tack·le
tacky
tact
tact·ful
tac·tic
tac·ti·cal
tac·ti·cian
tac·tics
tac·tile
tac·til·i·ty
tact·less
tad·pole
taf·fe·ta
taff·rail
taf·fy
tag sale
tail
tail·back
tail·board
tail·er
tail·gate
tail·light
tai·lor
tai·lor·ing
tai·lor-made
tail·spin

taint
take·down
take-home pay
take·off
take·over
tak·ing
talc
tal·cum pow·der
tale·bear·er
tal·ent
tales·man
tal·is·man
talk·ative
talk·ie
talk·ing-to
talky
tall·boy
tal·lith
tal·low
tal·ly
tal·ly·ho
tal·ly·man
Tal·mud
tal·on
ta·ma·le
tam·a·rack
tam·bour
tam·bou·rine
tame
tame·able
tam-o'-shanter
tamp
tam·per
tam·pon
tan·a·ger
tan·bark
tan·dem
tang
tan·ge·lo
tan·gen·cy

tan·gent
tan·gen·tial
tan·ger·ine
tan·gi·ble
tan·gle
tan·gle·ment
tan·go
tangy
tank·age
tan·kard
tanked
tank·er
tan·ner
tan·nery
tan·nic
tan·ning
tan·ta·lize
tan·ta·mount
tan·ta·ra
tan·trum
tap-dance
tape deck
tape mea·sure
ta·per
tape re·cord·er
tap·es·tried
tap·es·try
tape·worm
tap·i·o·ca
ta·pir
ta·pis
tap·pet
tap·room
tap·root
taps
tap·ster
tar·a·did·dle
tar·an·tel·la
ta·ran·tu·la
tar·di·ly

tar·dy
tare
tar·get
Tar·heel
tar·iff
tar·mac
tarn
tar·nish
ta·ro
tar·ot
tar·pau·lin
tar·pon
tar·ra·gon
tar·ry
tar·sus
tart
tar·tan
tar·tar
Tar·zan
task
task·mas·ter
task·mis·tress
tas·sel
taste
taste·ful
taste·less
tast·er
tasty
ta·ta·mi
tat·ter
tat·ter·de·ma·
  lion
tat·tered
tat·ter·sall
tat·ting
tat·tle
tat·tler
tat·too
tat·too·er
tat·too·ist

tat·ty
taught
taunt
tau·rine
taut
taut·en
tau·to·log·i·cal
tau·tol·o·gous
tau·tol·o·gy
tav·ern
taw·dry
taw·ny
tax·able
tax·a·tion
tax-ex·empt
taxi
taxi·cab
taxi·der·my
tax·ied
taxi·ing
taxi·me·ter
tax·on·o·my
tax·pay·er
T-bone
teach
teach·able
teach·er
teach·ers col·lege
teach-in
tea·cup
teak
tea·ket·tle
teak·wood
teal
team
team·mate
team·ster
team·work
tear·ful
tear·ing

tear·jerk·er
tear-off
teary
tease
tea·spoon·ful
teat
tech·ni·cal
tech·ni·cal·i·ty
tech·ni·cian
tech·nique
tech·noc·ra·cy
tech·no·crat
tech·no·crat·ic
tech·no·log·i·cal
tech·nol·o·gy
tec·ton·ics
Te De·um
te·dious
te·di·um
tee
teed off
teem
teen·age
teen·ag·er
teen·sy
teen·sy-ween·sy
teeny·bop·per
tee·ny-wee·ny
tee shirt
tee·ter
tee·ter-board
tee·ter-tot·ter
teeth
teethe
teeth·ing
tee·to·tal
tee·to·tal·er
Tef·lon
teg·u·ment
tele·cam·era

tele·cast
tele·com·mu·ni·
   ca·tion
tele·ge·nic
tele·gram
tele·graph
tele·graph·ic
te·leg·ra·phy
tele·me·ter
te·le·o·log·i·cal
te·le·ol·o·gy
te·lep·a·thy
tele·phone
tele·phon·ic
te·le·pho·ny
tele·pho·to
tele·print·er
Tele·Promp·Ter
tele·scope
tele·scop·ic
tele·thon
tele·type·writ·er
tele·typ·ist
tele·vise
tele·vi·sion
tele·vi·sor
tel·ex
te·lic
tell·er
tell·tale
tel·lu·ri·an
tel·lu·ric
tem·blor
tem·er·ar·i·ous
tem·per
tem·pera
tem·per·a·ment
tem·per·a·men·
   tal
tem·per·ance

tem·per·ate
tem·per·a·ture
tem·pered
tem·pes·tu·ous
tem·plate
tem·ple
tem·po
tem·po·ral
tem·po·ral·i·ty
tem·po·rar·i·ly
tem·po·rary
tem·po·rize
tempt
temp·ta·tion
tempt·er
tempt·ing
tem·pu·ra
ten·a·ble
te·na·cious
te·nac·i·ty
ten·an·cy
ten·ant
ten·ant farm·er
ten·ant·ry
ten·den·cy
ten·den·tious
ten·der·foot
ten·der·heart·ed
ten·der·ize
ten·der·loin
ten·der·mind·ed
ten·don
ten·dril
ten·e·brous
ten·e·ment
te·net
ten·nis
ten·on
ten·or
ten·pin

tense
ten·sile
ten·sion
ten·si·ty
ten·sor
ten-strike
ten·ta·cle
tent·age
ten·ta·tive
ten·ter·hook
tenth-rate
ten·u·ous
ten·ure
te·pee
tep·id
te·pid·i·ty
te·qui·la
ter·cen·te·na·ry
ter·cen·ten·ni·al
ter·gi·ver·sate
ter·gi·ver·sa·tor
ter·gi·ver·sa·tion
ter·i·ya·ki
term
ter·ma·gant
ter·mi·na·ble
ter·mi·nal
ter·mi·nate
ter·mi·na·tion
ter·mi·nol·o·gy
ter·mi·nus
ter·mite
tern
terp·si·cho·re·an
ter·race
ter·ra-cot·ta
ter·ra fir·ma
ter·rain
ter·ra in·cog·ni·ta

Ter·ra·my·cin
ter·ra·pin
ter·rar·i·um
ter·raz·zo
ter·res·tri·al
ter·ri·ble
ter·ri·er
ter·rif·ic
ter·ri·fy
ter·ri·to·ri·al
ter·ri·to·ri·al·i·ty
ter·ri·to·ry
ter·ror
ter·ror·ism
ter·ror·ize
ter·ry
terse
ter·tia·ry
tes·sel·late
tes·ta·ment
tes·tate
tes·ta·tor
test-drive
tes·ter
test-fly
tes·ti·cle
tes·ti·fy
tes·ti·mo·ni·al
tes·ti·mo·ny
test·ing
tes·ty
tet·a·nus
tetchy
tête-à-tête
teth·er
teth·er·ball
tet·ra·chlo·ride
tet·ra·he·dral
tet·ra·he·dron
te·tral·o·gy

te·tram·e·ter
Teu·ton·ic
tex·as leagu·er
text·book
tex·tile
tex·tu·al
tex·ture
T for·ma·tion
T-group
thane
thank·ful
thank·less
thanks·giv·ing
thatch
thau·ma·tur·gy
thaw
the·ater
the·ater·go·er
the·at·ri·cal
the·at·ri·cal·ly
thé dan·sant
theft
their
the·ism
-theist
the·mat·ic
theme
thence
thence·forth
thence·for·ward
theo·cen·tric
the·oc·ra·cy
theo·crat·ic
the·od·o·lite
theo·lo·gian
theo·log·i·cal
the·ol·o·gize
the·ol·o·gy
the·o·rem
the·o·ret·i·cal

the·o·re·ti·cian
the·o·rist
the·o·rize
the·o·ry
the·os·o·phist
the·os·o·phy
ther·a·peu·tic
ther·a·pist
ther·a·py
there·abouts
there·af·ter
there·at
there·by
there·for
there·fore
there·in
there·in·af·ter
there·of
there·to
there·to·fore
there·un·to
there·upon
there·with·al
ther·mal
ther·mo·dy·nam·ics
ther·mom·e·ter
ther·mo·nu·cle·ar
ther·mos
ther·mo·stat
the·sau·rus
the·sis
thes·pi·an
thew
they'd
they'll
they're
they've
thick
thick·en

thick·et
thick·ness
thick·set
thick-skinned
thief
thieve
thiev·ery
thiev·ish
thigh
thim·ble
thim·ble·ful
thim·ble·rig
thine
thing·am·a·bob
thing·am·a·jig
thing·um·my
think
think·able
think·ing
thin·ly
thin·ner
thin·ness
thin·nish
thin-skinned
third
third-class
third-rate
thirst
thirst·i·ly
thirst·i·ness
thirsty
thir·teen
thir·ty
this·tle
this-world·ly
thith·er
thith·er·to
thole
thong
tho·rac·ic

tho·rax
thorn
thorny
thor·ough
thor·ough·bred
thor·ough·fare
thor·ough·go·ing
though
thought
thought·ful
thought·less
thought·less·ness
thou·sand
thrall
thrall·dom
thrash
thrash·er
thread
thread·bare
threat
threat·en
three-di·men·sion·al
three·fold
three-piece
three-quar·ter
three·some
thren·o·dy
thresh·er
thresh·old
threw
thrice
thrift·i·er
thrift·less
thrifty
thrill
thrips
thrive
throat
throat·i·ness

throaty
throb
throe
throm·bo·sis
throne
throng
throt·tle
throt·tle·hold
through
through·out
throve
throw
throw·away
throw-in
thrum
thrush
thrust
thrust stage
thru·way
thud
thug
thumb
thumb·nail
thumb·tack
thump
thun·der
thun·der·bolt
thun·der·clap
thun·der·head
thun·der·ous
thun·der·show·er
thun·der·storm
thu·ri·ble
thu·ri·fer
thus
thus·ly
thwack
thwart
thyme
thy·roid

thy·self
ti·ara
tib·ia
tic
tick·er
tick·et
tick·ing
tick·le
tick·ler
tick·lish
tick·tack·toe
tid·al
tid·bit
tid·dle·dy·winks
tide
tide·wa·ter
ti·di·ness
tid·ing
ti·dy
tie-in
tiered
tie-rod
tie tack
tie-up
tif·fin
ti·ger
tight
tight·en
tight·fist·ed
tight-lipped
tights
tight·wad
tight·wire
ti·gress
tile
til·ing
till·age
till·er
til·ler·man
tilt

tilth
tim·bal
tim·ber
tim·bered
tim·ber·land
tim·ber·line
tim·bre
tim·brel
time-con·sum·ing
time·keep·er
time·less
time·ly
time-out
tim·er
time-sav·er
time·ta·ble
tim·id
tim·ing
tim·o·rous
tim·o·thy
tim·pa·ni
tim·pa·nist
tinc·to·ri·al
tinc·ture
tin·der
tin·foil
tinge
tin·gle
tin·horn
tin·ker
tin·kle
tin·kly
tin·ni·tus
tin·ny
Tin Pan Al·ley
tin·sel
tin·tin·nab·u·la·
   tion
ti·ny
ti·ni·ness

tip-in
tip-off
tip·pet
tip·ple
tip·si·ly
tip·ster
tip·sy
tip·toe
ti·rade
tire·less
tire·some
tir·ing-house
tis·sue
ti·tan·ic
tit for tat
tith·able
tithe
tith·ing
ti·tian
tit·il·late
tit·il·lat·ing
tit·i·vate
ti·tle
ti·tle·hold·er
ti·tlist
tit·mouse
tit-tat-toe
tit·ter
tit·tle-tat·tle
tit·u·lar
toad
toad·stool
toady
to-and-fro
toast
toast·mas·ter
toast·mis·tress
toasty
to·bac·co
to·bac·co·nist

to·bog·gan
to·by
toc·ca·ta
toc·sin
to·day
tod·dle
tod·dler
tod·dy
to-do
toed
toe·hold
toe-in
toe·nail
tof·fee
to·ga
to·geth·er
tog·gery
tog·gle
toil
toi·let
toi·let·ry
toi·lette
toil·some
toil·worn
to-ing and fro-
ing
to·ken
to·ken·ism
tole
tol·er·a·ble
tol·er·ance
tol·er·ant
tol·er·ate
tol·er·a·tion
toll·booth
toll·gate
tom·a·hawk
to·ma·to
tomb
tom·boy

tomb·stone
tom·cat
Tom Col·lins
tome
tom·fool·ery
tom·my·rot
to·mor·row
tom-tom
ton·al
to·nal·i·ty
tone-deaf
tone·less
tong
tongs
tongue
tongued
tongu·ing
tongue-in-cheek
tongue-lash
tongue-tie
tongue twist·er
ton·ic
to·nic·i·ty
to·night
ton·nage
ton·neau
ton·sil
ton·sil·lec·to·my
ton·sil·li·tis
ton·so·ri·al
ton·sure
tony
To·ny
tool
tool·mak·ing
tooth
tooth·ache
toothed
tooth·less
tooth·paste

tooth·pick
tooth·some
toothy
to·paz
top·coat
top·dress·ing
to·pee
top·er
top-heavy
to·pi·ary
top·i·cal
top·less
top-lev·el
top-notch
to·po·graph·i·cal
to·pog·ra·phy
to·pol·o·gy
top·per
top·ping
top·ple
top·pling
top·sail
top·side
top·sy-tur·vy
top·sy-tur·vi·ly
toque
torch·bear·er
to·re·ador
tor·ment
tor·men·tor
tor·na·do
tor·pe·do
tor·pid
tor·por
torque
tor·rent
tor·ren·tial
tor·rid
tor·rid·i·ty
tor·sion

tor·so
tort
torte
tor·tel·li·ni
tor·ti·lla
tor·toise
tor·to·ni
tor·tu·ous
tor·ture
tor·tur·ous
toss-up
to·tal
to·tal·i·tar·i·an
to·tal·i·tar·i·an·
   ism
to·tal·i·ty
to·tal·iza·tor
to·tal·ize
to·tal·ly
tote
to·tem
to·tem·ism
totem pole
tot·ter
tot·tery
touch
touch·able
touch·down
tou·ché
touch-me-not
touch·stone
touch-type
touch-up
touchy
tough
tough·en
tough·ie
tough-mind·ed
tou·pee
tour

tour de force
tour·ism
tour·ist
tour·na·ment
tour·ne·dos
tour·ney
tour·ni·quet
tou·sle
tout
tow·age
to·ward
tow·el
tow·el·ing
tow·er
tow·head
to wit
town
towns·folk
town·ship
tow·path
tow·rope
tox·ic
tox·i·col·o·gist
tox·i·col·o·gy
tox·in
trace
trac·er
trac·ery
tra·chea
tra·cho·ma
trac·ing
track
track·er
track·ing
tract
trac·ta·ble
trac·tion
trac·tive
trac·tor
trade·mark

trade-off
trades·man
trade union
tra·di·tion
tra·di·tion·al·ism
tra·duce
traf·fic
traf·ficked
traf·fick·ing
tra·ge·di·an
tra·ge·di·enne
trag·e·dy
trag·ic
tragi·com·e·dy
trail
trail·blaz·er
trail·er
train
train·bear·er
train·ee
traipse
trait
trai·tor
trai·tor·ous
trai·tress
tra·ject
tra·jec·to·ry
tram·car
tram·line
tram·mel
tra·mon·tane
tramp
tram·ple
tram·po·line
tram·way
trance
tran·quil
tran·quil·ize
tran·quil·li·ty
trans·act

trans·ac·tion
trans·at·lan·tic
tran·scend
tran·scen·dence
tran·scen·dent
tran·scen·den·tal
tran·scen·den·
    tal·ism
trans·con·ti·nen·
    tal
tran·scribe
tran·script
tran·scrip·tion
tran·sect
tran·sec·tion
tran·sept
trans·fer
trans·fer·al
trans·fer·ee
trans·fer·ence
trans·fig·u·ra·
    tion
trans·fix
trans·form
trans·for·ma·tion
trans·form·er
trans·fuse
trans·fu·sion
trans·gress
trans·gres·sion
tran·sience
tran·sien·cy
tran·sient
tran·sis·tor
tran·sis·tor·ize
tran·sit
tran·si·tion
tran·si·tive
tran·si·to·ry
trans·late

trans·la·tion
trans·lit·er·ate
trans·lo·cate
trans·lu·cent
trans·mis·si·ble
trans·mis·sion
trans·mit
trans·mit·tance
trans·mit·ter
trans·mog·ri·fy
trans·mu·ta·tion
trans·mute
trans·oce·an·ic
tran·som
trans·pa·cif·ic
trans·par·en·cy
trans·par·ent
tran·spire
trans·plant
trans·pon·tine
trans·port
trans·port·able
trans·por·ta·tion
trans·port·er
trans·pose
trans·po·si·tion
trans·ship
tran·sub·stan·ti·
    a·tion
trans·val·u·a·
    tion
trans·val·ue
trans·ver·sal
trans·verse
trans·ves·tite
trap·door
tra·peze
trap·e·zoid
trap·ping
trap·shoot·er

trash
trashy
trat·to·ria
trau·ma
trau·ma·tize
tra·vail
trav·el
trav·eled
trav·el·er
trav·el·ogue
tra·verse
trav·er·tine
trav·es·ty
trawl·er
tray
treach·er·ous
treach·ery
trea·cle
trea·cly
tread
trea·dle
tread·mill
trea·son
trea·son·able
trea·son·ous
trea·sure
trea·sur·er
trea·sury
treat
treat·able
trea·tise
treat·ment
trea·ty
tre·ble
tree·less
tre·foil
trek
trekked
trek·king
trel·lis

trel·lised
trel·lis·work
trem·ble
trem·bly
tre·men·dous
trem·o·lo
trem·or
trem·u·lous
trench
tren·chant
tren·cher
trend
trendy
trep·i·da·tion
tres·pass
tress
tres·tle
trews
trey
tri·able
tri·ad
tri·al
tri·an·gle
tri·an·gu·lar
tri·an·gu·lar·i·ty
tri·an·gu·late
tri·an·gu·la·tion
tri·bal
trib·al·ism
tribe
trib·u·la·tion
tri·bu·nal
tri·bune
trib·u·tary
trib·ute
trice
trich·i·no·sis
trick
trick·ery
trick·le

trick·ster
tricksy
tricky
tri·col·or
tri·cor·nered
tri·cot
tri·cy·cle
tri·dent
trid·u·um
tried
tri·en·ni·al
tri·en·ni·um
tri·er
tri·fle
tri·fling
trig·ger
trig·ger-hap·py
trig·o·no·met·ric
trig·o·nom·e·try
tril·lion
tril·li·um
trim
tri·mes·ter
trim·mer
trim·ming
trim·ness
trin·ket
tri·no·mi·al
trio
tri·o·let
tri·par·tite
tripe
trip-ham·mer
triph·thong
tri·ple
tri·plex
trip·li·cate
tri·pod
trip·per
trip·ping·ly

trip·tych
tri·reme
trist·ful
trite
trite·ness
tri·umph
tri·um·phant
tri·um·vir
tri·um·vi·rate
tri·une
triv·et
triv·ia
triv·i·al
triv·i·al·ize
triv·i·um
tri·week·ly
trod
trodden
troi·ka
troll
trol·ley
trol·lop
trom·bone
trom·bon·ist
trompe l'oeil
troop
trope
tro·phy
trop·ic
tro·po·sphere
trot
troth
Trots·ky·ism
trot·ter
trou·ba·dour
trou·ble
trou·ble·mak·er
trou·ble·shoot·er
trou·ble·some
trou·blous

trough
trounce
trou·sers
trous·seau
trout
trow·el
tru·an·cy
tru·ant
tru·ant·ry
truce
truck·age
truck·er
truck·le
tru·cu·lence
tru·cu·lent
trudge
true
true-blue
true-false test
truf·fle
tru·ism
trull
tru·ly
trump
trum·pery
trum·pet
trum·pet·er
trun·cate
trun·ca·tion
trun·cheon
trun·dle
trunk
truss
trust
trust·bust·er
trust·ee
trust·wor·thy
trusty
truth·ful
try·ing

try·out
tryst
tset·se
T-shirt
T square
tu·ba
tub·by
tube
tu·ber
tu·ber·cle
tu·ber·cu·lar
tu·ber·cu·lo·sis
tu·ber·ous
tub·ing
tu·bu·lar
tuck
tuck·er
tuf·fet
tuft
tug-of-war
tu·ition
tu·lip
tulle
tum·ble
tum·bling
tum·brel
tu·mes·cence
tu·mid
tum·my
tu·mor
tu·mor·ous
tu·mult
tu·mul·tu·ous
tun
tu·na
tun·able
tun·dra
tune·ful
tun·er
tune-up

tung·sten
tu·nic
tun·nel
tun·ny
tur·ban
tur·bid
tur·bid·i·ty
tur·bine
tur·bo·jet
tur·bo·prop
tur·bot
tur·bu·lence
tur·bu·lent
turd
tu·reen
turf
tur·gid
tur·key
tur·key-cock
tur·moil
turn
turn·buck·le
turn·coat
tur·nip
turn·key
turn·pike
turn·stile
turn·ta·ble
turn·ver·ein
tur·pen·tine
tur·pi·tude
turps
tur·quoise
tur·ret
tur·tle
tur·tle·back
tur·tle·neck
tusk
tus·sive
tus·sle

tus·sock
tu·te·lage
tu·te·lary
tu·tor
tu·to·ri·al
tut·ti-frut·ti
tu·tu
tu-whit tu-whoo
tux·e·do
twad·dle
twain
twang
tweak
tweed
Twee·dle·dum
    and Twee·dle·
    dee
tweedy
tweet·er
twee·zers
twelve
twerp
twice
twid·dle
twig
twi·light
twill
twin bed
twine
twinge
twi-night
twin·kle
twin-size
twirl
twirp
twist
twist·er
twit
twitch
twit·ter

twixt
two-by-four
two-cycle
two-faced
two·fer
two·fold
two·some
ty·coon
tyke
tym·pa·num
tyne
type·face
type·set·ter
type·writ·er
ty·phoid
ty·phoon
ty·phus
typ·i·cal
typ·i·fy
typ·ist
ty·po
ty·pog·ra·pher
ty·pog·ra·phy
ty·ran·ni·cal
ty·ran·ni·cide
tyr·an·nize
tyr·an·nous
tyr·an·ny
ty·rant
ty·ro

U

ubiq·ui·tous
ubiq·ui·ty
ud·der
ugh

ug·li·fy
ug·li·ness
ug·ly
ukase
uke
uku·le·le
ul·cer
ul·cer·ate
ul·cer·ation
ul·cer·ous
ul·na
ul·ster
ul·te·ri·or
ul·ti·ma·cy
ul·ti·mate
ul·ti·ma Thu·le
ul·ti·ma·tum
ul·ti·mo
ul·tra
ul·tra·con·ser·va·
  tive
ul·tra·high
  fre·quen·cy
ul·tra·ism
ul·tra·lib·er·al
ul·tra·mil·i·tant
ul·tra·mod·ern
ul·tra·na·tion·al·
  ism
ul·tra·son·ic
ul·tra·vi·o·let
ul·tra vi·res
ul·u·lant
ul·u·late
um·ber
um·bil·i·cal
um·bi·li·cus
um·bra
um·brage
um·bra·geous

um·brel·la
um·laut
um·pire
ump·teenth
un·abat·ed
un·able
un·abridged
un·ac·cept·able
un·ac·com·mo·
  dat·ed
un·ac·com·pa·
  nied
un·ac·count·able
un·ac·count·ed
un·ac·cus·tomed
un·adorned
un·adul·ter·at·ed
un·af·fect·ed
un·alien·able
un·aligned
un·al·loyed
un·al·ter·able
un·am·big·u·ous
un-Amer·i·can
una·nim·i·ty
unan·i·mous
un·an·swer·able
un·an·tic·i·pat·ed
un·ap·peal·ing
un·ap·peas·able
un·ap·pe·tiz·ing
un·ap·proach·
  able
un·ar·gu·able
un·armed
un·ar·tic·u·lat·ed
un·ashamed
un·asked
un·as·sail·able
un·as·ser·tive

un·as·sist·ed
un·as·sum·ing
un·at·tached
un·at·trac·tive
un·avail·able
un·avail·ing
un·avoid·able
un·aware
un·awares
un·bal·anced
un·barred
un·bear·able
un·beat·able
un·beat·en
un·be·com·ing
un·be·known
un·be·lief
un·be·liev·able
un·be·liev·er
un·be·liev·ing
un·bend
un·bend·ing
un·bi·ased
un·bid·den
un·bind
un·blessed
un·blink·ing
un·block
un·blush·ing
un·born
un·bo·som
un·bound
un·bri·dle
un·bri·dled
un·bro·ken
un·buck·le
un·budg·ing
un·bur·dened
un·bur·ied
un·but·toned

un·called-for
un·can·ny
un·ceas·ing
un·ceas·ing·ly
un·cer·e·mo·ni·ous
un·cer·tain
un·cer·tain·ty
un·chal·lenge·able
un·change·able
un·chang·ing
un·char·ac·ter·is·tic
un·char·i·ta·ble
un·chart·ed
un·chiv·al·rous
un·chris·tian
un·cir·cum·cised
un·civ·i·lized
un·clasp
un·clas·si·fied
un·cle
un·clean
un·clench
Uncle Tom·ism
un·climb·able
un·clothed
un·cloud·ed
un·clut·ter
un·coiled
un·com·fort·able
un·com·mer·cial
un·com·mit·ted
un·com·mon
un·com·mu·ni·ca·ble
un·com·mu·ni·ca·tive
un·com·plain·ing

un·com·pli·cat·ed
un·com·pli·men·ta·ry
un·com·pre·hend·ing
un·com·pro·mis·ing
un·con·cerned
un·con·di·tion·al
un·con·for·mi·ty
un·con·ge·nial
un·con·quer·able
un·con·scio·na·ble
un·con·scious
un·con·sid·ered
un·con·sti·tu·tion·al
un·con·trol·la·ble
un·con·ven·tion·al
un·con·vinc·ing
un·cork
un·cou·ple
un·couth
un·cov·er
un·cov·ered
un·crit·i·cal
un·crush·able
unc·tion
unc·tu·ous
un·curl
un·daunt·ed
un·de·bat·able
un·de·fend·ed
un·dem·o·crat·ic
un·de·mon·stra·tive
un·de·ni·able
un·der

un·der·achiev·er
un·der·age
un·der·arm
un·der·bid
un·der·body
un·der·brush
un·der·bud·get·ed
un·der·cap·i·tal·ized
un·der·class·man
un·der·clothes
un·der·cloth·ing
un·der·coat
un·der·cov·er
un·der·cur·rent
un·der·cut
un·der·de·vel·oped
un·der·dog
un·der·ed·u·cat·ed
un·der·em·pha·sis
un·der·em·ployed
un·der·es·ti·mate
un·der·ex·pose
un·der·foot
un·der·gird
un·der·go
un·der·grad·u·ate
un·der·ground
un·der·growth
un·der·hand
un·der·in·sured
un·der·laid
un·der·lie
un·der·line
un·der·ling

un·der·manned
un·der·mine
un·der·neath
un·der·nour·
 ished
un·der·paid
un·der·part
un·der·pass
un·der·pin
un·der·play
un·der·priv·i·
 leged
un·der·pro·duc·
 tion
un·der·rate
un·der·rep·re·
 sen·ta·tion
un·der·rep·re·
 sent·ed
un·der·score
un·der·sea
un·der·sell
un·der·shirt
un·der·side
un·der·signed
un·der·sized
un·der·staffed
un·der·stand
un·der·state
un·der·stood
un·der·strength
un·der·study
un·der·take
un·der·tak·er
und·er-the-coun·
 ter
un·der·tone
un·der·tow
un·der·used
un·der·uti·lize

un·der·val·u·a·
 tion
un·der·val·ue
un·der·wa·ter
un·der·way
un·der·wear
un·der·weight
un·der·world
un·der·write
un·der·writ·er
un·de·sir·able
un·de·vi·at·ing
un·dies
un·dip·lo·mat·ic
un·dis·guised
un·do
un·do·ing
un·dra·mat·ic
un·dreamed
un·dress
un·due
un·du·lant
un·du·late
un·du·la·tion
un·du·ly
un·dy·ing
un·earned
un·earth
un·earth·ly
un·ease
un·eas·i·ly
un·easy
un·eco·nom·ic
un·emo·tion·al
un·em·ploy·able
un·em·ployed
un·end·ing
un·en·dur·able
un·en·thu·si·as·
 tic

un·equal
un·equiv·o·ca·bly
un·equiv·o·cal
un·err·ing
un·es·sen·tial
un·even
un·even·ness
un·event·ful
un·ex·cep·tion·
 able
un·ex·cep·tion·al
un·ex·pect·ed
un·ex·ploit·ed
un·ex·pres·sive
un·fad·ing
un·fail·ing
un·fair
un·faith·ful
un·fal·ter·ing
un·fa·mil·iar
un·fash·ion·able
un·fas·ten
un·fath·om·able
un·fa·vor·able
un·feel·ing
un·feigned
un·fet·tered
un·fin·ished
un·fit
un·fit·ting
un·flag·ging
un·flap·pa·ble
un·flat·ter·ing
un·flinch·ing
un·fo·cused
un·fold
un·for·get·ta·ble
un·for·giv·ing
un·formed
un·for·tu·nate

un·found·ed
un·fre·quent·ed
un·friend·ly
un·frock
un·fruit·ful
un·furl
un·gain·ly
un·gal·lant
un·glue
un·glued
un·god·ly
un·gov·ern·able
un·gra·cious
un·gram·mat·i·cal
un·grate·ful
un·grudg·ing
un·guard·ed
un·guent
un·hal·lowed
un·hand
un·handy
un·hap·pi·ly
un·hap·py
un·healthy
un·heard-of
un·help·ful
un·hes·i·tat·ing
un·hinge
un·ho·ly
un·hook
un·hur·ried
uni·cam·er·al
uni·cel·lu·lar
uni·corn
uni·cy·cle
uni·di·rec·tion·al
uni·fi·ca·tion
uni·form
uni·for·mi·ty

uni·fy
uni·lat·er·al
uni·lin·ear
un·imag·in·able
un·im·pas·sioned
un·im·peach·able
un·im·proved
un·in·for·ma·tive
un·in·hib·it·ed
un·in·tel·li·gent
un·in·tel·li·gi·ble
un·in·ten·tion·al
un·in·ter·rupt·ed
union·ism
union·iza·tion
union·ize
unique
uni·sex
uni·son
uni·tar·i·an
uni·tary
unite
uni·ty
uni·ver·sal
uni·ver·sal·i·ty
uni·verse
uni·ver·si·ty
univ·o·cal
un·just
un·kempt
un·kind
un·know·able
un·know·ing
un·known
un·lace
un·latch
un·law·ful
un·lead·ed
un·leash
un·let·tered

un·like
un·like·li·hood
un·like·ly
un·lim·ber
un·lim·it·ed
un·list·ed
un·load
un·lock
un·loose
un·loos·en
un·made
un·man·ly
un·man·nered
un·man·ner·ly
un·mask
un·meant
un·men·tion·able
un·mer·ci·ful
un·mer·ci·ful·ly
un·mind·ful
un·mis·tak·able
un·mit·i·gat·ed
un·nat·u·ral
un·nec·es·sar·i·ly
un·nec·es·sary
un·nerve
un·num·bered
un·ob·tru·sive
un·oc·cu·pied
un·of·fi·cial
un·or·ga·nized
un·or·tho·dox
un·pack
un·paid
un·pal·at·able
un·par·al·leled
un·pin
un·pleas·ant
un·plug
un·plumbed

un·pop·u·lar
un·prec·e·dent·ed
un·pre·dict·able
un·prej·u·diced
un·pre·tend·ing
un·pre·ten·tious
un·prin·ci·pled
un·print·able
un·pro·fessed
un·prof·it·able
un·prom·is·ing
un·qual·i·fied
un·ques·tion·able
un·rav·el
un·re·al·is·tic
un·re·al·i·ty
un·rea·son·able
un·rea·son·ing
un·re·gen·er·ate
un·re·lent·ing
un·re·mit·ting
un·re·served
un·re·spon·sive
un·re·strained
un·right·eous
un·ripe
un·ri·valed
un·ruf·fled
un·ruly
un·sat·u·rat·ed
un·sa·vory
un·say
un·scathed
un·schooled
un·sci·en·tif·ic
un·scram·ble
un·screw
un·scru·pu·lous
un·sea·son·able
un·seat

un·seem·ly
un·seg·re·gat·ed
un·se·lect·ed
un·self·ish
un·set·tle
un·shack·le
un·sheathe
un·ship
un·shod
un·sight·ly
un·skilled
un·snarl
un·so·cia·ble
un·so·cial
un·so·phis·ti·cat·ed
un·sought
un·sound
un·spar·ing
un·speak·able
un·sports·man·like
un·spot·ted
un·sta·ble
un·stat·ed
un·steady
un·stop·pa·ble
un·stressed
un·struc·tured
un·stud·ied
un·sub·stan·tial
un·suc·cess·ful
un·suit·able
un·sung
un·swerv·ing
un·tan·gle
un·tapped
un·taught
un·ten·a·ble
un·think·able

un·think·ing
un·thought
un·ti·dy
un·tie
un·time·ly
un·ti·tled
un·to
un·told
un·touch·able
un·to·ward
un·tried
un·trod
un·trou·bled
un·true
un·truth·ful
un·tu·tored
un·twine
un·twist
un·used
un·usu·al
un·ut·ter·able
un·var·nished
un·veil
un·voiced
un·war·rant·able
un·wary
un·washed
un·wa·ver·ing
un·wea·ried
un·whole·some
un·wieldy
un·will·ing
un·wind
un·wise
un·wit·ting
un·wont·ed
un·world·ly
un·worn
un·wor·thy
un·wrap

un·writ·ten
un·yield·ing
un·zip
up-and-coming
up-and-down
up·beat
up·braid
up·bring·ing
up·com·ing
up·date
up·draft
up·end
up·field
up·grade
up·heav·al
up·hill
up·hold
up·hol·ster
up·hol·stery
up·keep
up·land
up·lift
up·man·ship
up·per-class
up·per crust
up·per·cut
up·per hand
up·per most
up·pish
up·pi·ty
up·raise
up·right
up·ris·ing
up·roar·i·ous
up·roar·i·ous·ly
up·set
up·side down
up·stage
up·stairs
up·stand·ing

up·start
up·sweep
up·tight
up-to-date
up-to-the-min·ute
up·town
up·ward
up·wind
ura·ni·um
ur·ban
ur·bane
ur·ban·ism
ur·ban·ist
ur·ban·ite
ur·ban·i·ty
ur·ban·iza·tion
ur·ban·ize
ure·mia
urge
ur·gen·cy
ur·gent
uri·nal
uri·nary
uri·nate
urine
us·age
us·ance
use·ful
use·ful·ness
use·less·ness
ush·er
ush·er·ette
usu·al
usu·al·ness
usu·fruct
usu·rer
usu·ri·ous
usurp
usu·ry
uten·sil

uter·us
util·i·tar·i·an
util·i·tar·i·an·
  ism
util·i·ty
uti·lize
ut·most
uto·pia
uto·pi·an
uto·pi·an·ism
ut·ter
ut·ter·ance
ut·ter·most
uvu·la
ux·o·ri·al
ux·o·ri·ous

va·can·cy
va·cant
va·cate
va·ca·tion
va·ca·tion·er
va·ca·tion·ist
vac·ci·nate
vac·ci·na·tion
vac·cine
vac·il·late
va·cu·ity
vac·u·ous
vac·u·um
va·de me·cum
vag·a·bond
vag·a·bond·age
va·gar·i·ous
va·ga·ry
va·gi·na

vag·i·nal
va·gran·cy
va·grant
vague
vague·ness
vagu·er
vagu·est
vain
vain·glo·ri·ous
vain·glo·ry
vain·ness
va·lance
vale
vale·dic·tion
vale·dic·to·ri·an
vale·dic·to·ry
va·lence
val·en·tine
va·let
val·e·tu·di·nar·i·an
val·e·tu·di·nary
val·iant
val·id
val·i·date
val·i·da·tion
va·lid·i·ty
val·ley
val·or
val·or·ous
valu·able
val·u·ate
val·u·a·tion
val·u·a·tor
val·ue
va·lu·ta
valve
val·vu·lar
va·moose
vam·pire

van·dal
van·dal·ism
van·dal·ize
Van·dyke
vane
van·guard
va·nil·la
van·ish
van·i·ty
van·quish
van·tage
va·pid
va·pid·i·ty
va·por
va·por·iza·tion
va·por·iz·er
va·por·ous
va·pory
vari·able
vari·ance
vari·ant
vari·a·tion
vari·col·ored
var·i·cose
var·i·cos·i·ty
var·ied
var·ie·gate
var·ie·ga·tion
va·ri·etal
va·ri·ety
var·io·cou·pler
var·i·o·rum
var·i·ous
var·let
var·let·ry
var·mint
var·nish
var·si·ty
vary
vary·ing

vas·cul·lar
vase
va·sec·to·my
Vas·e·line
vas·sal
vas·sal·age
vast
Vat·i·can
va·tic·i·nate
vaude·ville
vaude·vil·lian
vault
vault·ing
vaunt
veal
vec·tor
veer
veg·e·ta·ble
veg·e·tal
veg·e·tar·i·an
veg·e·tar·i·an·ism
veg·e·tate
veg·e·ta·tion
veg·e·ta·tive
ve·he·mence
ve·he·ment
ve·hi·cle
veil·ing
vein
vein·ing
ve·lar
veld
vel·le·ity
vel·lum
ve·loc·i·pede
ve·loc·i·ty
ve·lum
vel·vet
vel·ve·teen

vel·vety
ve·nal
vend·ee
vend·er
ven·det·ta
ven·dor
ve·neer
ven·e·nate
ven·er·a·ble
ven·er·ate
ven·er·a·tion
ve·ne·re·al
ven·ery
ve·ne·tian blind
ven·geance
venge·ful
ve·nial
ve·ni·re·man
ven·i·son
ven·om·ous
ve·nous
ven·ti·late
ven·ti·la·tion
ven·ti·la·tor
ven·tral
ven·tri·cle
ven·tril·o·quism
ven·tril·o·quist
ven·ture
ven·tur·er
ven·ture·some
ven·ue
ve·ra·cious
ve·rac·i·ty
ve·ran·da
ver·bal
ver·bal·ism
ver·bal·ize
ver·ba·tim
ver·biage

ver·bose
ver·bos·i·ty
ver·bo·ten
ver·dan·cy
ver·dant
ver·dict
ver·di·gris
ver·dure
verge
verg·er
ve·rid·i·cal
ver·i·fi·able
ver·i·fi·ca·tion
ver·i·fy
ver·i·ly
veri·si·mil·i·tude
ver·i·ta·ble
ver·i·ty
ver·mi·cel·li
ver·mic·u·late
ver·mic·u·lite
ver·mil·ion
ver·min
ver·min·ous
ver·mouth
ver·nac·u·lar
ver·nal
ver·ni·er
ver·sa·tile
ver·sa·til·i·ty
verse
ver·si·cle
ver·si·fi·ca·tion
ver·si·fi·er
ver·si·fy
ver·sion
vers li·bre
ver·sus
ver·te·bra
ver·te·brate

ver·tex
ver·ti·cal
ver·tig·i·nous
ver·ti·go
verve
ves·i·cant
ves·per
ves·per·al
ves·sel
vest·ee
ves·ti·ary
ves·ti·bule
ves·tige
vest·ing
vest·ment
ves·try
ves·ture
vet·er·an
vet·er·i·nar·i·an
vet·er·i·nary
ve·to
vex
vex·ing
vex·a·tion
vex·a·tious
vi·a·ble
via·duct
vi·and
vi·at·i·cum
vibes
vi·brant
vi·bra·phone
vi·brate
vi·bra·tion
vi·bra·tor
vi·bur·num
vic·ar·age
vic·ar·ate
vi·car·i·ate
vi·car·i·ous

vice-pres·i·den·cy
vice-pres·i·dent
vice·re·gal
vice·roy
vice ver·sa
vi·chys·soise
vic·i·nage
vi·cin·i·ty
vi·cious
vi·cis·si·tude
vic·tim
vic·tim·ize
vic·tor
Vic·to·ri·an
vic·to·ri·ous
vic·to·ry
vict·ual
vict·ual·ler
vi·cu·ña
vi·de·li·cet
vid·eo
vid·eo·tape
vi·du·ity
vie
vied
vi·er
Viet·cong
Viet·minh
Viet·nam·ese
view·er
view·find·er
view·ing
view·point
vig·il
vig·i·lance
vig·i·lant
vig·i·lan·te
vig·i·lan·tism
vi·gnette
vig·or

vig·or·ous
vile
vil·i·fi·ca·tion
vil·i·fy
vil·la
vil·lage
vil·lain
vil·lain·ous
vil·lainy
vin·ai·grette
vin·ca
vin·ci·ble
vin·cu·lum
vin·di·cate
vin·di·ca·tion
vin·dic·a·tive
vin·di·ca·to·ry
vin·dic·tive
vine
vin·e·gar
vin·e·gary
vin·ery
vine·yard
vi·nous
vin·tage
vint·ner
vi·nyl
vi·ol
vi·o·la
vi·o·la·ble
vi·o·late
vi·o·la·tion
vi·o·lence
vi·o·lent
vi·o·let
vi·o·lin
vi·o·lon·cel·lo
vi·per
vi·per·ish
vi·per·ous

vi·ra·go
vi·ral
vi·res·cence
vi·res·cent
vir·gin
vir·gin·al
vir·gin·i·ty
vir·gule
vir·i·des·cent
vi·rid·i·ty
vir·ile
vi·ril·i·ty
vir·tu·al
vir·tu·al·i·ty
vir·tu·al·ly
vir·tue
vir·tue·less
vir·tu·os·i·ty
vir·tu·o·so
vir·tu·ous
vir·u·lence
vir·u·lent
vi·rus
vi·sa
vi·saed
vis·age
vis-à-vis
vis·cera
vis·cer·al
vis·cid
vis·cose
vis·cos·i·ty
vis·count
vis·cous
vise
vis·i·bil·i·ty
vis·i·ble
vi·sion
vi·sion·ary
vis·it

vis·i·tant
vis·i·ta·tion
vis·i·tor
vi·sor
vis·ta
vis·taed
vi·su·al
vi·su·al·iza·tion
vi·su·al·ize
vi·ta
vi·tal
vi·tal·i·ty
vi·tal·ize
vi·tals
vi·ta·min
vi·ti·ate
vi·ti·a·tion
vit·re·ous
vit·ri·fy
vi·trine
vit·ri·ol
vi·tu·per·ate
vi·tu·per·a·tion
vi·tu·per·a·tive
vi·va
vi·va·cious
vi·vac·i·ty
vi·va vo·ce
viv·id
viv·i·fy
vi·vip·a·rous
vivi·sect
vivi·sec·tion
vix·en
viz·ard
vo·ca·ble
vo·cab·u·lary
vo·cal
vo·cal·ic
vo·cal·ist

vo·cal·ize
vo·ca·tion
vo·ca·tion·al
voc·a·tive
vo·cif·er·ate
vo·cif·er·ous
vod·ka
vogue
vogu·ish
voice
voice·less
voice-over
void·able
void·ance
voile
voir dire
vo·lant
vol·a·tile
vol·a·til·i·ty
vol-au-vent
vol·ca·nic
vol·ca·no
vol·ca·nol·o·gist
vole
vo·li·tion
vol·i·tive
vol·ley
vol·ley·ball
volt·age
vol·ta·ic
vol·ta·me·ter
volte-face
vol·u·ble
vol·ume
vo·lu·mi·nous
vol·un·ta·rism
vol·un·tary
vol·un·tari·ly
vol·un·teer
vol·un·teer·ism

vo·lup·tu·ary
vo·lup·tuous
vo·lute
vom·it
voo·doo
voo·doo·ism
vo·ra·cious
vo·rac·i·ty
vor·la·ge
vor·tex
vor·ti·cal
vor·tic·i·ty
vo·ta·ress
vo·ta·ry
vot·er
vo·tive
vo·tress
vouch
vouch·er
vouch·safe
vow·el
vow·el·ize
vox po·pu·li
voy·age
voya·geur
voy·eur
voy·eur·ism
vroom
vul·ca·ni·za·
  tion
vul·ca·nize
vul·gar
vul·gar·i·an
vul·gar·ism
vul·gar·i·ty
vul·gar·ize
vul·gate
vul·ner·a·ble
vul·pine
vul·ture

wacki·ness
wacky
wad·able
wad·ding
wad·dle
wa·fer
waf·fle
waft
wage
wa·ger
wag·gery
wag·gish
wag·gle
Wag·ne·ri·an
wag·on
wa·gon-lit
wa·hi·ne
wa·hoo
waif
wail
wail·ful
wain·scot·ing
wain·wright
waist
waist·band
waist·coat
waist·line
wait·er
wait·ress
waive
waiv·er
wake
wake·ful
wake·ful·ness
wak·en
wale
walk·er

walk·ie-look·ie
walk-in
walk-up
wall·board
wal·let
wall·flow·er
wal·lop
wal·lop·ing
wal·low
wal·nut
wal·rus
waltz
wam·pum
wand
wan·der
wan·der·ing
wan·der·lust
wane
wan·gle
wan·ly
wan·ton
wan·ton·ness
war·ble
war·bler
war·bling
war·den
ward·er
ward heeler
ward·robe
ward·room
ware·house
war·fare
war-horse
wari·er
war·like
war·lock
war·lord
warm-blood·ed
warmed-over
warm·heart·ed

war·mon·ger
warmth
warm-up
warn·ing
warp
warp and woof
war·path
war·plane
war·rant
war·rant·able
war·ran·tee
war·ran·tor
war·ran·ty
war·ren
war·ring
war·rior
war·ship
wart
war·time
wary
wash·able
wash·bowl
wash·cloth
washed-out
wash·er
wash·ing
wash·out
wash·stand
washy
wasn't
wasp
WASP
wasp·ish
was·sail
wast·age
waste
waste·bas·ket
waste·ful
waste·land
waste·pa·per

wast·er
wast·ing
wast·rel
watch
watch·dog
watch·er
watch·ful
watch·mak·ing
watch·man
watch·word
wa·ter
water ballet
water closet
wa·ter·col·or
wa·ter·course
wa·ter·cress
wa·ter·fall
wa·ter·fowl
wa·ter·front
watering place
wa·ter·line
wa·ter·log
wa·ter·logged
wa·ter·loo
wa·ter·mark
wa·ter·mel·on
water meter
wa·ter·pow·er
wa·ter·proof
wa·ter-re·pel·lent
wa·ter-re·sis·tant
wa·ter·shed
wa·ter·side
wa·ter-ski·er
water snake
water sup·ply
water table
wa·ter·wheel
water wings
wa·ter·works

wa·tery
watt·age
wat·tle
wave·length
wave·let
wa·ver
wav·i·ness
wavy
waxed paper
wax·en
wax·er
wax·like
wax·work
waxy
way·bill
way·far·er
way·lay
way-out
way·side
way·ward
way·worn
weak·en
weak·fish
weak·heart·ed
weak-kneed
weak·ling
weak-mind·ed
weak·ness
weal
weald
wealth
wealth·i·er
wealthy
wean
wean·ling
weap·on
weap·on·ry
wear·able
wea·ri·ful
wea·ri·less

wea·ri·ly
wea·ri·ness
wear·ing
wea·ri·some
wea·ry
wea·sel
weath·er
weath·er-beat·en
weath·er-bound
weath·er bu·reau
weath·er·cock
weath·ered
weath·er·glass
weath·er·man
weather map
weath·er-wise
weath·er·worn
weave
weav·er
web·bing
web·by
web·foot
wed·ding
we·deln
wedge
Wedg·ies
Wedg·wood
wed·lock
weed·er
weed·less
weedy
week·day
week·end
week·end·er
week·ly
week·night
ween
weep·ing
weepy
wee·vil

weigh-in
weight
weight·less
weighty
wei·ma·ra·ner
wei·ner
weir
weird
weird·ie
weirdo
wei·sen·hei·mer
welch
wel·come
wel·com·ing
weld·er
wel·fare
wel·far·ism
wel·kin
well-ad·vised
well-ap·point·ed
well-be·ing
well-be·loved
well·born
well-bred
well-de·fined
well-dis·posed
well-done
well-fixed
well-groomed
well-han·dled
well-heeled
well-in·ten·
  tioned
well-knit
well-mean·ing
well-off
well-read
well-round·ed
well-spo·ken
well·spring

well-tak·en
well-timed
well-to-do
well-wish·er
well-worn
welsh
Welsh rab·bit
Welsh rare·bit
welt
welt·an·schau·
  ung
wel·ter
wel·ter·weight
welt·schmerz
wench
wend
weren't
were·wolf
wes·kit
west·er·ly
west·ern
west·ern·iza·tion
west·ern·ize
west·ing
west·ward
wet-blan·ket
weth·er
wet·land
wet-nurse
wet suit
wet·ta·ble
wet·tish
wet wash
we've
whack
whack·ing
whale·boat
whal·er
wham
wham·my

wharf
wharf·age
wharf·mas·ter
what·ev·er
what·not
what·so·ev·er
wheat
wheat·en
wheat germ
whee
whee·dle
wheel
wheel·bar·row
wheel·chair
wheeled
wheel·er-deal·er
wheels·man
wheel·wright
wheeze
wheezy
whelk
whelp
when·as
whence
when·ev·er
when·so·ev·er
where·abouts
where·as
where·at
where·by
where·fore
where·from
where·in
where·of
where·on
where·so·ev·er
where·to
where·up·on
wher·ev·er
where·with

where·with·al
wher·ry
whet
wheth·er
whet·stone
whew
whey
whey-face
which·ev·er
whiff
whif·fle
whif·fle·tree
while
whilst
whim
whim·per
whim·si·cal
whim·sy
whin
whine
whin·ny
whip·cord
whip·lash
whip·per·snap·per
whip·pet
whip·ping
whip·poor·will
whip·saw
whir
whirl
whirl·i·gig
whirl·pool
whirl·wind
whirly
whisk
whisk broom
whis·ker
whis·key
whis·per

whis·per·er
whis·per·ing
whis·pery
whist
whis·tle
whis·tler
whit
white·cap
white·col·lar
white el·e·phant
white-head·ed
whit·en
white·ness
whit·en·ing
white-tie
white trash
white·wall
white·wash
white·wash·er
white·wash·ing
whit·ey
whith·er
whit·ing
whit·ish
whit·tle
whit·tling
whiz
whiz·bang
whoa
who·dun·it
who·ev·er
whole·heart·ed
whole-hog
whole·sale
whole·sal·er
whole·some
whole-souled
whol·ly
whom·ev·er
whom·so·ev·er

whoop
whoop·ee
whoop·er
whoop·ing cough
whoop·la
whoops
whoosh
whop
whopped
whop·per
whop·ping
whore
whore·house
whore·son
whorl
whor·tle·ber·ry
whose
whose·so·ev·er
who·so·ev·er
who's who
wick·ed
wick·er
wick·er·work
wick·et
wide-an·gle
wide-eyed
wide·ly
wide receiver
wide·spread
wide-spread·ing
wid·get
wid·ish
wid·ow
wid·ow·er
wid·ow·hood
widow's walk
width
wield
wieldy
wie·ner

Wie·ner schnit·
  zel
wie·ner·wurst
wie·nie
wife·ly
wig·gle
wight
wig·wag
wig·wam
wil·co
wild·cat
wil·der·ness
wild-eyed
wild·fowl
wild·ing
wild·life
wild oat
wild·wood
wile
will·able
will·ful
wil·lies
wil·li·waw
will-o'-the-wisp
wil·low
wil·low·ware
wil·lowy
wil·ly-nil·ly
wilt
wily
wim·ple
wince
winch
wind·age
wind·bag
wind·blown
wind·break
wind·chill
wind·fall
wind·ing

wind·jam·mer
wind·lass
wind·mill
win·dow
win·dow-dress
win·dow·pane
win·dow-shop
wind·pipe
wind·row
wind·shield
wind sock
wind·storm
wind·swept
wind·up
wind·ward
windy
wine·glass
win·ery
wing·back
wing·ding
wing-foot·ed
wing·man
wing·span
wing·spread
wink·er
win·kle
win·ner
win·ning
win·now
win·some
win·ter
win·ter·green
win·ter·ize
win·ter-kill
win·ter·ly
win·ter·time
win·try
winy
wip·er
wire·haired

wire·less
wire-pull·er
wire-pull·ing
wire·tap
wir·ing
wiry
wis·dom
wise·acre
wise·crack
wise guy
wi·sen·hei·mer
wish·bone
wish·ful
wish-wash
wishy-washy
wisp
wisp·ish
wist·ful
witch
witch·craft
witch·ery
witch ha·zel
witch-hunt
with·al
with·draw
with·draw·al
with·drawn
withe
with·er
with·er·ing
with·ers
with·hold
with·in
with·in·doors
with-it
with·out
with·stand
wit·less
wit·ness
wit·ted

wit·ti·cism
wit·ti·ness
wit·ty
wive
wiz·ard
wiz·ard·ry
wiz·en
wob·ble
woe·be·gone
woe·ful
woe·ful·ness
woke
woken
wold
wolf·hound
wolf·ish
wol·ver·ine
wom·an
wom·an·hood
wom·an·ish
wom·an·ize
wom·an·kind
wom·an·ly
womb
won·der
won·der·ful
won·der·ment
won·drous
wont
won·ton
wood·bin
wood·box
wood-carv·er
wood·chop·per
wood·chuck
wood·craft
wood·cut
wood·cut·ting
wood·ed
wood·en

wood·en·ware
wood·land
wood·lot
wood·man
wood·pile
wood pulp
wood·shed
woods·man
woodsy
wood·wind
wood·work
wood·work·ing
woody
woof
woof·er
wool·en
wool-gath·er
wool·ly
woolly bear
wool·ly-head·ed
woo·zy
word·age
word·ing
word·less
word-of-mouth
wordy
work·able
work·a·day
work·bas·ket
work·bench
work·book
work·box
work·er
work·ing
work·ing-class
work·ing·man
work·man·like
work·man·ship
work·out
work·ta·ble

work-up
work·week
work·wom·an
world·ling
world·ly
world·ly-wise
world pre·miere
world series
world-shak·ing
world·wide
worm-eat·en
worm gear
worm's-eye view
wormy
worn-out
wor·ri·ment
wor·ri·some
wor·ry
wor·ry·wart
worse
wors·en
wor·ship
wor·ship·ful
worst
wor·sted
wor·thi·er
worth·less
worth·while
wor·thy
would
would-be
wouldn't
wound
wrack
wraith
wran·gle
wran·gler
wrap·per
wrap·ping
wrap up

wrath

wrath·ful

wreak

wreath

wreathe

wreck·age

wreck·er

wreck·er's ball

wrench

wrest

wres·tle

wres·tling

wretch

wretch·ed

wrig·gle

wright

wring·er

wrin·kle

wrist·band

wrist·lock

wrist·watch

writ

writ·able

write

writ·ing

write-in

write-off

writ·er

write-up

writhe

writ·ing

wrong·do·er

wrong·do·ing

wrong·er

wrong·est

wrong·ful

wrong·head·ed

wrought

wrung

wry·neck

wun·der·kind

wurst

xan·tho·chroid

x-ax·is

X chro·mo·some

x-co·or·di·nate

xe·non

xe·no·phile

xe·no·phobe

xe·no·pho·bia

xe·rog·ra·phy

xe·rox

x-ray

xy·lo·graph

xy·log·ra·phy

xy·lo·phone

xy·lo·phon·ist

yacht

yacht·ing

yachts·man

ya·hoo

Yah·weh

yack

yacking

yak

yam

yam·mer

yang

Yan·kee

Yan·kee-Doo·dle

yap·ping

yard·age

yard·arm

yard·bird

yard goods

yard line

yard·stick

yar·mul·ke

yar·row

yaw

yawl

yawn

yawp

yawp·ing

y-ax·is

Y chro·mo·some

y-co·or·di·nate

year·book

year-end

year·ling

year·long

year·ly

yearn

yearn·ing

yeast

yeasty

yegg

yel·low-dog

yel·low·ish

yelp

yelp·er

yen

yeo·man

yeo·man·ry

ye·shi·va

yes-man

yes·ter·day

yes·ter·year

ye·ti

yew
yield·ing
yip·pee
yo·del
yo·del·er
yo·ga
yo·gi
yo·gurt
yoicks
yoke
yo·kel
yolk
yon·der
yoo-hoo
yore
you'll
youn·ger
young·ish
young·ling
young·ster
you're
your·self
your·selves
youth·ful
you've
yowl
yo-yo
yule
Yule log

yule·tide
yum·my
yum-yum

Z

za·ba·glio·ne
za·ny
zap
zapped
zap·ping
z-ax·is
zeal
zeal·ot
zeal·ot·ry
zeal·ous
ze·bra
zeit·geist
ze·nith
zeph·yr
zep·pe·lin
ze·ro
zest
zesty
zig·zag
zig-zagged

zig·zag·ging
zilch
zil·lion
zinc
zin·fan·del
zingy
zin·nia
Zi·on·ism
zip
zip-code
zipped
zip·per
zip·ping
zip·py
zir·con
zith·er
zo·di·ac
zom·bie
zon·al
zoo·log·i·cal
zo·ol·o·gy
zoom
zoy·sia
zuc·chet·to
zuc·chi·ni
zwie·back
zy·gote
zy·mur·gy

OTHER ESSENTIALS

SPELLING RULES

There is a widespread belief that English spelling is illogical and ungoverned by rules. This is not wholly true. Most English words are spelled according to established rules. There are exceptions to each rule, but they are not as numerous as is commonly believed.

These spelling rules are simple and easily learned. If you apply them, you will improve your spelling ability greatly, for you will be able to spell correctly two-thirds or more of all words.

The Basics

1. *IE* or *EI*. Put *i* before *e*. Examples: ach*ie*ve, bel*ie*f, ch*ie*f, fr*ie*nd, misch*ie*f, p*ie*ty, qu*ie*t, rev*ie*w, ser*ie*s, th*ie*very, y*ie*ld.

Exceptions: After *c*, place *e* before *i*:
             c*ei*ling, perc*ei*ve, rec*ei*ve, rec*ei*pt.
        When the sound is *ay*, place *e* before *i*:
             fr*ei*ght, n*ei*ghbor, v*ei*l, w*ei*gh.

Hint: Memorize this little rhyme which has helped generations of spellers.

> Put *i* before *e*
> Except after *c*
> Or when pronounced *ay*
> As in n*ei*ghbor or w*ei*gh;
> And except s*ei*ze and s*ei*zure
> And also l*ei*sure,
> w*ei*rd, h*ei*ght, and *ei*ther, forf*ei*t and n*ei*-
> ther.

2. **CEDE, -CEED, -SEDE.** The ending -*cede* is more common than -*ceed* or -*sede*. Examples: ac*cede*, con*cede*, pre*cede*, re*cede*, se*cede*.

Only three words end in -*ceed*: ex*ceed*, pro*ceed*, suc*ceed*. Notice that they begin with *ex-*, *pro-*, and *suc-*. Here is a little device that will help you remember them. A boxer is a *pro*·fessional. When he retires, he is an *ex*-fighter. Then he has a *suc*·cessor.

Only one word ends in -*sede*: super*sede*.

3. **PREFIXES.** When a prefix is added to a word, the spelling of the original word is not changed. A prefix is one or more syllables attached to the beginning of a word to change its meaning.

Prefix	Meaning	Example
ab-	away, from	abduct (lead away)
anti-	against	antiseptic (against poisoning)
com-, *con-*	with, together	concelebrate (celebrate together)
de-	down	demote (put down)
hyper-	over, above, beyond	hyperactive (overactive)
il-, *im-*, *in-*, *ir-*	not	illogical, immoral, indisposed, irrelevant
inter-	between, among	interview, international
pro-	forward, instead of	provide (look forward)
re-	back, again	retaliate (fight back) repel (hurl back)
sub-	under	subway, subtract
un-	not	unnatural, unoccupied

Note: Many errors occur when a prefix ends with a letter with which the word begins.

$$un + \text{natural} = \text{unnatural (}not\text{ unatural)}$$
$$mis + \text{step} = \text{misstep (}not\text{ mistep)}$$
$$pre + \text{eminent} = \text{preeminent (}not\text{ preminent)}$$

4. SUFFIXES. A suffix is one or more syllables attached to the end of a word.

Examples: *-able, -ible, -ly, -ness, -ous, -ar, -ery, -ary.*

With the exception of *-able* and *-ible,* suffixes cause few spelling difficulties. Learn when to add *-able* and when to add *-ible.*

-able

Nouns ending in *-ation* form adjectives by adding *-able.*

Noun		Adjective
admir*ation*	⟶	admir*able*
applic*ation*	⟶	applic*able*
communic*ation*	⟶	communic*able*
damn*ation*	⟶	damn*able*

Some other words which do not end in *-ation* add *-able* to form adjectives. All of them are common words.

$$comfort + able = comfortable$$
$$eat + able = eatable$$
$$read + able = readable$$
$$talk + able = talkable$$

There is no hard and fast rule covering these words. You will have to learn them individually.

Hint/ The suffix *-able* is more common than *-ible.* If in doubt, use *-able,* and you will have more than a fair chance of being correct.

-ible

Words ending in *-ible* are often preceded by *ss* before *-ible.*

accessible   permissible   transmissible

Words ending in *-ible* often have a noun form ending in *-ion*.

Noun	*Adjective*
combus*tion* ⟶	combust*ible*
destruc*tion* ⟶	destruct*ible*
diges*tion* ⟶	digest*ible*
percep*tion* ⟶	percept*ible*
reprehens*ion* ⟶	reprehens*ible*

Words with stems ending in soft *c* or *g* use *-ible* to retain the soft sound. The word *produce* has the adjective *producible* because an *-able* would change the pronunciation of *c* from its present soft sound to *k*. Other words in this class are:

conduc*ible*	deduc*ible*	eli*gible*
intelli*gible*	iras*cible*	reduc*ible*

-ly

When forming adverbs from adjectives ending in *-al*, simply add *-ly* to the original word.

Adjective	*Adverb*
accident*al* ⟶	accidental*ly*
practic*al* ⟶	practical*ly*
re*al* ⟶	real*ly*

-ous

When adding *-ous* to a noun ending in a consonant, do not change the spelling of the noun.

danger + *ous* = dangerous
hazard + *ous* = hazardous
marvel + *ous* = marvelous
riot + *ous* = riotous
slander + *ous* = slanderous

Exceptions: Nouns ending in *f* change the *f* to *v* when -*ous* is added.

$$grief + ous = grievous$$
$$mischief + ous = mischievous$$

Nouns ending in *y* drop the *y* and add *e* before -*ous*.

$$beauty + ous = beauteous$$
$$pity + ous = piteous$$
$$plenty + ous = plenteous$$

Nouns ending in *e* drop the *e* before -*ous*.

$$adventure + ous = adventurous$$
$$desire + ous = desirous$$
$$trouble + ous = troublous$$

Occasionally the final *e* is retained before -*ous* to keep the soft sound of *g*.

$$courage + ous = courageous$$
$$advantage + ous = advantageous$$
$$outrage + ous = outrageous$$

-ar

Only a small number of words end in -ar. Memorize six of the most common.

begg*ar*	calend*ar*	coll*ar*
doll*ar*	regul*ar*	singul*ar*

-ary and -ery

Only two commonly used words end in -*ery:* statio-n*ery* and cemet*ery*. If you remember that station*ery* means pap*er*, you will not misspell it. (Anything which is station*ary* is *at* a place.)

More than 300 words end in -*ary*.

5. *FINAL Y.* Final *y* preceded by a *vowel* remains *unchanged* when a termination is added.

attorney + *s* = attorneys
portray + *ing* = portraying
annoy + *ed* = annoyed
employ + *er* = employer

Exceptions: lay + *ed* = laid   gay + *ly* = gaily

Final *y* preceded by a *consonant* changes to *i* when a termination is added.

icy + *est* = iciest
mercy + *less* = merciless
tidy + *ness* = tidiness

Exception: Final *y* is retained before *-ing*.

carry + *ing* = carrying
copy + *ing* = copying
tally + *ing* = tallying

6. **FINAL E.** *Drop* final *e* before a suffix beginning with a *vowel*.

large + *est* = largest   ache + *ing* = aching
love + *er* = lover   argue + *ing* = arguing
desire + *ous* = desirous   divine + *ity* = divinity
austere + *ity* = austerity

Exceptions: canoeing, hoeing, shoeing, toeing.

Retain final *e* before a suffix beginning with a *consonant*.

coarse	like	fierce
coarseness	likeness	fierceness

When a word ends in *double e,* the final *e* is not dropped in order to retain the same pronunciation.

agree	agreeable	agreeing
see	seeable	seeing

Exceptions: Due, true, and whole drop final *e* before *-ly:* duly, truly, wholly.
Some words ending in final *e* drop the *e* before *-ment* and *-ful:* argue, argument; awe, awful.

7. ***WORDS ENDING IN -IC.*** Words ending in *-ic* add *k* before a suffix beginning with *e, i,* or *y* used as a vowel.

frolic	frolic*k*ed	frolic*k*ing
picnic	picnic*k*ed	picnic*k*ing

8. ***DOUBLING THE FINAL CONSONANT.*** When a one-syllable word ends in a single vowel and a consonant, the consonant is doubled before a suffix beginning with a vowel.

One-Syllable Words

hit	hi*tt*er	hi*tt*ing
spin	spi*nn*er	spi*nn*ing

A word of more than one syllable ending in a single vowel and consonant and accented on the final syllable, doubles the final consonant before a suffix beginning with a vowel.

Words of More Than One Syllable

occur	compel	commit	omit
occu*rr*ed	compe*ll*ing	commi*tt*ing	omi*tt*ing

Words ending in *-ful* double the *l* when *-ly* is added.

Words Ending in -ful

careful	beautiful	dutiful
carefu*ll*y	beautifu*ll*y	dutifu*ll*y